Tom Stark

This book is sponsored by
the Theological Commission of
the World Evangelical Fellowship

BIBLICAL INTERPRETATION AND THE CHURCH
The Problem of Contextualization

D1259064

BIBLICAL INTERPRETATION AND THE CHURCH

The Problem of Contextualization

edited by
D. A. CARSON

Thomas Nelson Publishers
Nashville • Camden • New York

Copyright © 1984 World Evangelical Fellowship

First published in the United States by Thomas Nelson Publishers, 1985.

First published in Great Britain by The Paternoster Press, 1984.

All rights reserved. Written permission must be secured from the publisher to use or reproduce any part of this book, except for brief quotations in critical reviews or articles.

Published in Nashville, Tennessee by Thomas Nelson, Inc., Publishers, and distributed in Canada by Lawson Falle, Ltd., Cambridge, Ontario.

Printed in the United States of America.

Library of Congress Cataloging in Publication Data

ISBN 0-8407-7501-6

Contents

Preface

The essays in this volume represent the first fruits of the 'Faith and Life' study unit established by the World Evangelical Fellowship. Dr. Ulrich Betz was appointed chairman, and Dr. R. T. France coordinator. The pressure of too many competing commitments conspired to force Dr. France's resignation after he had done some preliminary exploration; and I fell heir to the task. I would like to record my thanks to Dr. France not only for his help in the transfer of correspondence, but also for continuing to work and write within the framework of the study unit.

Our first mandate from the Theological Commission of WEF was to explore some of the hermeneutical issues that bear on the tasks of world-wide missions at the end of the twentieth century. Thus although our studies are hermeneutical, they deal with immediate problems and needs: that is, there is less interest in what might be called theoretical hermeneutics than in applied hermeneutics. Even so, to keep the topic manageable, we narrowed the focus to the church and then selected a variety of hermeneutical problems relevant to understanding the nature, scope and mission of the church in various cultures.

The eight contributors to this volume come from seven countries: Australia, Canada, England, West Germany, Guatemala, the United States and Upper Volta. Though two are citizens of the United States, one of these has spent almost half of his life in an eighth country, Brazil. Each contributor prepared his paper in advance of a consultation, in several instances under difficult circumstances. The consultation itself took place in November, 1982, in Cambridge, England, in the gracious surroundings of Tyndale House. Generous arrangements for room and board were made by families at Eden Baptist Church,

Cambridge. Each paper was discussed at length, and critiques were offered by the other members present (all the contributors save one managed to attend; also the study unit's chairman, Dr. Betz, was prevented from coming by serious illness). These members were joined by a small number of other participants. The papers were subsequently revised, and the task of editing them fell to me.

I cannot speak too highly of the committed Christian integrity that stamped those discussions. Of course, not all members agreed on all points; but a cordial, mutual respect and a sincere desire both to understand and to be understood characterised all the sessions. There was very little trace of one-upmanship. Instead, the participants displayed a profound desire to bring every disagreement back, as honestly and as humbly as possible, to the test of Scripture. I learned a great deal in those few days, and continue to count it a privilege to work with Christian leaders who bring such diverse backgrounds and such transparent faith to the hermeneutical and missiological tasks.

We were painfully aware of the many topics relevant to our central theme that were *not* discussed. Some of the topics chosen reflect the special expertise of the members of our study unit; but at the same time they reflect representative problems. The study by Tite Tiénou, for instance, analyses how one African theologian has attempted to 'contextualise' the New Testament doctrine of the church in African soil and hermeneutically assesses the validity of that contextualisation; but it also serves as a model for many more such analyses. Similarly, the essay by Gerhard Maier hermeneutically addresses the problem of the authenticity of Jesus' 'church-sayings', a problem more typical of European and North American ecclesiastical discussions; but again the essay serves as a paradigm for other debates along similar lines that critically affect how we think of the church.

The study unit has decided to pursue the doctrine of the church in at least one more round of papers and discussion. God willing, a considerably expanded group will meet in Cambridge in November, 1984, to present and discuss papers less concerned with hermeneutical questions *per se* than with a hermeneutically-aware enunciation of the identity, unity, function, nature, limits, ministry and discipline of the church. In short, we would like to make use of what we have learned and seek to construct a biblical theology of the church that reflects the flavour of international Christians joined in reverent submission to the Scriptures, and that rejoices in cultural diversity. It is often said that the church needs 'world Christians'. Perhaps our combined efforts may in some small measure encourage the emergence of such leaders.

Soli Deo gloria.

D. A. CARSON
Trinity Evangelical Divinity School

Abbreviations

(Names of certain journals are shown in full, and are therefore not listed below.)

Bib	*Biblica*
BZ	*Biblische Zeitschrift*
CBQ	*Catholic Biblical Quarterly*
ERT	*Evangelical Review of Theology*
HSCP	*Harvard Studies in Classical Philology*
IBMR	*International Bulletin of Missionary Research*
Int	*Interpretation*
IRM	*International Review of Missions*
JBL	*Journal of Biblical Literature*
JTS	*Journal of Theological Studies*
NIDNTT	*New International Dictionary of New Testament Theology*
NTS	*New Testament Studies*
RB	*Revue Biblique*
RHPR	*Revue d'histoire et de philosophie religieuses*
RTR	*Reformed Theological Review*
SJT	*Scottish Journal of Theology*
ST	*Studia Theologica*
TB1	*Theologische Blätter*
TD	*Theology Digest*
TDNT	*Theological Dictionary of the New Testament*
TFB	*Theological Fraternity Bulletin*
ThB	*Theologische Beiträge*
TrinJ	*Trinity Journal*
TWF	*Trinity World Forum*
WTJ	*Westminster Theological Journal*
ZNW	*Zeitschrift für die neutestamentliche Wissenschaft*

1

A Sketch of the Factors Determining Current Hermeneutical Debate in Cross-Cultural Contexts

D. A. CARSON

A few years ago I wrote an article with a somewhat similar title, viz.: 'Hermeneutics: A brief assessment of some recent trends'.[1] In this new essay I do not intend to repeat the earlier material, but rather to proceed along a line that simultaneously probes a little more deeply and yet skips rather superficially over certain difficult questions in order to deal more immediately with the bearing of hermeneutics on the theology of the international Christian church. One danger of the current hermeneutical debate is that hermeneutics may mire itself in introspection: it begins to overlook the fact that, from the perspective of Christian theology, hermeneutics, however defined, is not an end in itself, but a means to the end. To press beyond the confines of the discipline in order to discover what makes it tick and what impact it has on theology is therefore to escape the introspection and to probe more deeply; but it is also to deal rather superficially with narrowly hermeneutical questions of enormous complexity. In an international consultation like that represented by the papers in this volume, the risk must be taken.

I shall eliminate from the discussion the concerns of classical hermeneutics (for instance, all consideration of the principles of how to interpret various figures of speech and the like), and likewise I shall eliminate discussion of structuralism *per se*. The latter is becoming extraordinarily important in academic discussion in the West; but it is not yet a burning issue in the church elsewhere. It is worth mentioning in this paper only as a

11

symptom of a greater issue. What I propose to do is list five
critical problems with substantial hermeneutical implications,
and offer some reflection on how the manner in which we treat
these problems will to a substantial extent determine our exegesis.

A. THE PROBLEM OF PRE-UNDERSTANDING

We have rightly abandoned the positivism of nineteenth century
historical study: competent historians do not today follow von
Ranke. Not only because we are sinful, but also because we are
finite, we cannot have an exhaustive understanding of any
historical event (or of anything else for that matter). Bultmann
and his successors have done us a great service by reminding us
that whenever we approach the sacred text we carry with us an
already established understanding of many issues to which the
text speaks; and therefore we do not arrive as impartial observers
ready to sop up neutral data and integrate it exactly into a
coherent and true understanding. This recognition leads to the
problem of the new hermeneutic (see below); but it deserves
separate reflection. Most who read these pages will already have
come to the position that problems related to one's pre-
understanding do not exclude the possibility of true understanding. They will have seen that finite human beings who cannot
understand anything exhaustively may nevertheless come to
know certain things truly. They will recognize that an individual's pre-understanding is not necessarily immovable: for the
reflective person, such pre-understanding is a 'functional non-
negotiable'[2] which, given enough pressure, can be amended into
a stance with increased proximity to the text.[3]
    But a problem arises in that the term 'pre-understanding'
seems to cover a variety of different epistemological phenomena.
If 'pre-understanding' refers to the mental baggage, the 'functional non-negotiables' that one brings to the text, Christians will
happily recognize the problem and learn a little humility in their
exegesis. They will insist that their 'non-negotiables' *function* this
way only until further insight into the teaching of Scripture
forces them to change. In this way the Scripture can retain
meaningful authority in the believer's life. But if 'pre-

understanding' comes to mean something like 'immutable non-negotiables', a function of an entire world view at odds with Scripture, then Scripture can never enjoy the right to call such 'pre-understanding' into question. Bultmann seems to use *Vorverständnis* in this way from time to time; and certainly this attitude stands behind his famous 1941 essay[4] where he argues that the modern man, familiar with electricity, bombs, trains, metal processes, and the whole array of modern scientific discoveries, cannot possibly believe in a world inhabited by demons, angels, miracles—and even a transcendent-personal God who becomes incarnate.

The problem, however, cannot be dismissed as a merely semantic one: some people use 'pre-understanding' for one thing, and some for another. Rather, when 'pre-understanding' slips into this second range, it becomes *impossible* for the Scriptures to exercise corrective authority over our thoughts and lives in those matters where our 'pre-understanding' is immutably non-negotiable. The epistemologically controlling factors which govern our direction and beliefs are in this case no longer controlled or deeply corrected by Scripture, but by our presuppositions established on quite other grounds. To confuse these two uses of 'pre-understanding' is to devastate both theology and epistemology. The one use helps us to be more careful, encourages us to follow the 'hermeneutical spiral' to bring our horizon of understanding into line with the horizon of understanding of the original author, and ultimately brings our mind into increasing proximity with what the text actually says; but the second becomes a reason for transmuting the text into something else. The arguments in favour of a sympathetic treatment of 'pre-understanding' are *formally* the same in the two cases; but in the first case they lead to improved hermeneutical self-criticism, whereas in the latter they lead to epistemological solipsism and a complete inability to hear any word from God with which we cannot agree. It becomes a way of denying, through the back door as it were, the authority of the Scriptures over our lives.

The paper by Gerhard Maier[5] in this collection charts an example of this phenomenon in the common dismissal of the authenticity of the ἐκκλησία-sayings in Matthew (viz. 16:18; 18:17). The heart of this dismissal is content-criticism, a procedure more intensely shaped by unacknowledged 'pre-understanding' than any other.

The line between these two approaches to 'pre-understanding' is theoretically sharp and clear; but in practice it may be rather hazy. Several essays in this volume deal with this problem. For instance, Peter O'Brien[6] traces the principal steps in the semantic shift of 'principalities and powers' from the spiritual realm to the structures and dynamic forces of society. Some contributors to this development doubtless adopted the kind of naturalistic world view that Bultmann ably defended, and felt either that Paul's categories *had* to be changed, or that at very least Paul would have recognized that his spiritual powers stand behind structures and forces in a contemporary society. Once the position became increasingly entrenched, and a new awareness arose regarding international injustice that seemed to confirm this analysis, all kinds of people whose general treatment of 'pre-understanding' belongs in the first camp nonetheless came to adopt some form of this semantic change — without, of course, denying that spirit-beings do exist and may be involved. Precisely at this juncture it is important to return to the primary sources again, and track down as dispassionately as possible exactly what Paul's phrase meant to him. We may agree or disagree with his results, we may like them or not, but both sound scholarship and the desire to be faithful to Scripture demand that we make the attempt.

Another fine example of the difficulties that may arise in treating pre-understanding dispassionately is found in the paper by Tite Tiénou.[7] Tiénou points out that Sawyerr asks some important questions about church models in Africa that have largely been imposed by the West. It is scarcely surprising that Baptists on the whole develop baptistic ecclesiology among their converts, complete with Roberts' *Rules of Order*; and the same or similar things could be said about virtually every other group. Sawyerr points out how important the family is both in African society and as a unit of the church in the New Testament, and then goes on to make some valuable suggestions regarding the restructuring of African church life. So far so good: Sawyerr has exposed some of the unwitting 'pre-understandings' of the West and is creatively trying to think through what implications might follow. But Tiénou rightly points out that before long Sawyerr is introducing some 'pre-understandings' of his own, making the New Testament text seem to justify things which are nowhere near its focal concerns, and which are in some cases antithetical to them. What started off as a valid critique of western pre-understandings has degenerated into the adoption, witting or unwitting, of African pre-understandings, both sets rather distortive of Scripture, and neither side sufficiently self-critical to introduce the necessary changes to bring church life into greater conformity with the Scriptures. The problem becomes more difficult when a denomination, deeply entrenched in long held patterns, simply refuses to think these things through afresh; or when an African (for instance) is so deeply concerned with African independence from the West that the authority of the Scriptures no longer really matters. In both cases, consciously or unconsciously, unacknowledged pre-understandings of the first type, when exposed by the opposite group, are in great danger of becoming pre-understandings of the second type: that is, the Scriptures are no longer heeded. The same sad result ensues when people hope and work and pray for capitalistic or Marxist salvation and then read such schemes into the Scriptures, without thoughtfully assessing whether 'salvation' (for instance) means the same thing on the lips of Jesus as it means on the lips of (say) Jerry Falwell or José Miranda. The papers by Emilio Nuñez and Russell Shedd touch on this kind of question.[8]

What is needed is a self-conscious dependency upon the Word of God and an equally self-conscious brokenness and contrition that hungers for the illumination of the Holy Spirit as that Word is studied. Only then will the inevitable auxiliary influences on our theology—such as long-standing tradition, denominational affiliations, our cultural and theological heritage—provide creative energies and ask probing questions, instead of usurping the place of control. Only then will the Word have the power to reform our traditions as well as our lives. Only then will Bible students from vastly different cultural and theological backgrounds entertain any real hope of so learning from one another that it becomes possible to be corrected by one another; for only then will there be an agreed revelation more important and more dominant than our unreconstructed cultural preference.

B. THE PROBLEM OF THE NEW HERMENEUTIC

This problem is of course related to the last one. One begins with the epistemological limitations imposed by 'pre-understanding', and recognizes that as one approaches the text the kinds of answers the text will give will in some measure be determined by the pre-understanding brought by the interpreter. However, the answers will to some degree affect the understanding of the questioner, so as he approaches the text for further reflection and study his new 'pre-understanding' inevitably elicits fresh answers from the text. Thus a hermeneutical circle is set up. In more conservative thought, this is seen rather as a hermeneutical spiral than a circle: it is argued that it is possible in substantial measure to fuse the horizon of understanding of the interpreter with the horizon of understanding of the text so that true communication across the ages or from text to interpreter is possible. More radical interpretations of the problem argue that as the horizons of understanding are progressively shared, the interpreter is interpreting the text while the text is interpreting him. An *Einverständnis* (Fuchs's term, usually rendered either by 'common understanding' or by 'empathy') develops, making the text capable of grabbing the interpreter, as it were, and radically changing his thinking. Thus the language of the text becomes a 'language-event' (*Sprachereignis*) by challenging the interpreter toward 'authentic human existence'. The goal is not so much for the interpreter to comprehend the text, since the text is considered no more 'objective' than the interpreter, as for a 'language-event' to take place. 'The goal is that moment of encounter between text and interpreter in which the "meaning" *occurs* or *takes place*: that is, it is the encounter between text and interpreter in which the interpreter hears and responds to some claim upon his person.'[9] There is no *assured* 'meaning' since the encounter might produce different things in different people, or different experiences in the same person at different times.

The subject is too complex to be treated here. Related to this question are complex philosophical issues and profound questions about the very nature of language. The notes provide some resources for pursuing this matter further, and for formulating credible ways of escape from a vicious form of hermeneutical circle.[10] Suffice it to say that if the circle is as strong as a few of its defendants proclaim, I cannot possibly know it; for I would be unable to understand their own work as they want to be understood. Most scholars of course are aware of this danger; and partly for this reason, some now insist that the hermeneutical spiral is a far better model than the hermeneutical circle.

My purpose here is more modest: to draw attention to recent developments in evangelical missiological literature that relate to this question, one development helpful and insightful, and another fundamentally mistaken. The first points out that the missionary (or for that matter any Christian who witnesses cross-culturally) must concern himself not only with *two* horizons, but with *three*.[11] He must attempt to fuse his own horizon of understanding with the horizon of understanding of the text; and having done that, he must attempt to bridge the gap between his own horizon of understanding, as it has been informed and instructed by the text, and the horizon of understanding of the person or people to whom he ministers. Strictly speaking, of course, this third horizon comes into play every time a person attempts to pass on to another person what he has learned from an original source: it is not necessary to envisage a cross-cultural target. But the problem is particularly acute when the second horizon must cross linguistic and cultural barriers to the third.

This model has two implications, both rather obvious. First, unless one admits that the bridge from the second to the third is impossible, it is difficult to see why anyone would want to argue that the bridge from the first to the second is impossible. Doubtless Fuchs and Ebeling do not expect their readers to possess *perfect* and *exhaustive* knowledge of what they say; but they do expect to be understood, and they seem to be interested in winning disciples to their positions. Scholars are certainly right to point out how difficult the transition from horizon of understanding to horizon of understanding may be; but the best of them recognize that to reduce all communication to a mere fusion of horizons resulting in a 'language-event' brings with it the entailment that they themselves have nothing objective to transmit. Regardless of the theoretical models, no one acts in this way in practice, unless he suffers from severe autism.

These observations have an obvious bearing on problems of contextualization. There is a sense in which every theology will inevitably be shaped by the culture in which it springs up; but this does not necessarily mean that each contextualization of biblical theology remains true to the Bible. To appeal to the demands of the interpreter's cultural context is legitimate, provided the intent is to facilitate the understanding and proclamation of the Bible within that context, not to transfer the authority of the Bible to conceptions and mandates not demonstrably emerging from the horizon of understanding of the biblical writers themselves. Ideally, the diversity of culturally sensitive theologies should not only remain fundamentally faithful to Scripture, but should have the potential to bring about mutual enrichment as exposure to different theological formulations results in self-criticism and broader integration. But the ideal is seldom real. In harsh reality, different cultures may so stress Christ the liberator, or Christ the king, or Christ the Saviour, or Christ the peace-giver, or Christ the eschatological judge, to the exclusion of balancing truth, that complementary biblical presentations are not only unseen but self-consciously excluded. Worse, some appeals to contextualization are wittingly or otherwise dependent on the more radical formulations of the new hermeneutic. The resulting contextualization not only tolerates theological structure substantially removed from biblical theology, but openly mandates control of such structures by the receptor culture, not by the Scriptures. What begins as legitimate insight into biblical truth degenerates into the arbitrary imposition of conceptual structures, whose genius and control spring from authoritative voices alien to the Bible, onto the Bible itself. This can be true, of course, both in the missions-sending society and in the missions-receiving society. What is indisputable is that in this way, essentially *hermeneutical* questions become largely *missiological* questions. The problem has been discussed rather widely;[12] but the links between recent hermeneutical study and recent studies in cross-cultural communication have not always been clearly perceived or delineated. Several essays in this volume aim to make such links at least a little clearer.

The second implication is that the missionary task is far more complex than is often recognized. The problem is doubtless multiplied in the case of short term missionaries who never really grasp the language, let alone the thought processes, of the people to whom they minister. A tremendous number of barriers can doubtless be overcome by a profoundly Christian, loving empathy for the people to whom we minister, and a growing self-critical awareness of the baggage we bring with us; but there are no easy, formulaic solutions. Modern cultural and anthropological awareness is helping to meet some of the needs in new students; but fresh areas keep opening up in front of us, and long-accepted theories are being challenged. For instance, there is a rising interest in the need for distinctively cross-cultural training in counseling;[13] and although the subject is open to abuse, it clearly has some strong merits.

The second development, and in my judgment a fundamentally dangerous one, is the appeal in some recent literature to establish what is *supracultural* in the Scriptures or in one's personal religion, and communicate that. Everything depends on what is meant by 'supracultural'. I am not referring, for instance, to 'universals' of human thought as discovered and formulated by anthropologists. Such 'universals' exist—though doubtless certain formulations demand more testing. For instance, the so-called 'Parry-Lord' theory, [14] which seeks to establish universal, formal distinctions between oral literature and written literature, with the introduction of the latter in any society automatically halting the former, has been shown by Finnegan's careful African field studies[15] to need considerable qualification and revision. Yet Christians will cheerfully concede that 'universals' exist—indeed, they will insist on it, believing as they do that every man reflects the *imago Dei*, however much the image be distorted. In any event, the term 'supracultural' in the context of this paper refers not to purely anthropological commonalities but to content revealed by God. Even so, the term is ambiguous. If it simply refers to the fact that God has revealed certain truth that is objectively true in every culture, it is not offensive; but if there is an attempt to distinguish among parts of the Bible, for instance, according to whether this snippet or that is supracultural or culture-bound, then the attempt is fundamentally misguided and the pursuit of the supracultural an impossible undertaking. The point I am making is that every truth from God comes to us in cultural guise: even the language used[16] and the symbols adopted are cultural expressions. No human being living in time and speaking any language can ever be entirely culture-free about anything. A statement such as 'God is holy' resonates with cultural questions: what does 'God' mean (compare, for instance, 'God' in Dutch reformed thought and in secular Japan!), what does 'holy' mean (compare Isa. 40ff. and the thought world of animistic tribes), and what does 'is' mean (does the verb here indicate symbol, analogy or ontology)? The aim of those who make frank appeal to the supracultural in the

Scripture is in most cases a laudable one: they point out that much of the message of the Bible is clothed in ancient Semitic dress which has to be removed before the message is easily preached in Montreal or Nairobi. But it is doubtful if 'supra-cultural' is the happiest rubric for what is desired. It might be closer to the *desideratum* if we were to say that what we must do is so fuse our horizon of understanding with that of the text, that we sympathetically and reflectively grasp the principles and arguments and coherence of the subject matter, and do our best to apply such matter in our own lives and cultural contexts. And even then, how we apply some particular passage from Scripture is going to depend on other considerations: the way such material can be integrated with other Scriptures, the pastoral function of such material in its own context, and more besides.[17] This brings us close to the next problem; but my point at this juncture is that appeal to the *supracultural* in Scripture is fundamentally danger-ous and may lead to whimsical subjectivity.

C. THE PROBLEM OF THE CANON WITHIN THE CANON

Long recognized by biblical scholars, the problem of 'the canon within the canon' is that although the church officially recognizes a written 'canon', viz. the Bible (whether the sixty-six books of Protestantism, the inclusion also of the Apocrypha in Roman Catholicism, or some other refinement), it invariable shapes its theology by greater reliance on some parts of this canon that on others. This creates a shorter 'canon within the canon' that will almost certainly be at variance with some other 'canon within the canon' utilized by some parallel ecclesiastical grouping. In other words, two churches or two Christians may share a common canon, but disagree implicitly or explicitly over their respective 'canons within the canon'. In such a case it is not surprising that their respective theologies differ substantially from each other. Whether this difference is the *result* or the *cause* of the disparate 'canons within the canon' cannot always be determined; and it is easy to suspect that with the passage of time result and cause intermingle.

What is not always perceived, however, is that there are at least three different ways in which the problem of the canon within the canon may develop. *First*, an ecclesiastical tradition may unwittingly overemphasize certain biblical truths at the expense of others, subordinating or even explaining away passages that do not easily 'fit' the slightly distorted structure that results. Galatians, say, may define a church's grasp of justification and grace in such a way that 1 Corinthians or the Pastoral Epistles are somewhat muted. *Second*, an ecclesiastical tradition may self-consciously adopt a certain structure by which to integrate all the books of the canon, and earnestly believe that the structure is not only sanctioned by Scripture but mandated by it; and as a result, some passages and themes may *automatically* be classified and explained in a particular fashion such that other believers find the tradition in question sub-biblical or too narrow or artificial. Dispensationalists and covenant theologians, for instance, are on the whole equally convinced that their opposing numbers have imposed a grid on Scripture in such a way that the canon cannot enjoy its free and reforming power: some other, lesser canon has intervened. *Third*, many others reject parts of the canon as unworthy, historically inaccurate, mutually contradictory or the like, and adopt only certain *parts* of the Scripture. The parts they accept constitute their 'canon within the canon'. Of course, this third alternative is the most serious, and reduces in one way or another to the question of the truthfulness and authority of Scripture.[18] Even some who lie more or less within the evangelical camp have now defended the position that the New Testament documents, for instance, do not provide us with any unified theology, but with a range of acceptable (yet at places mutually contradictory) theo*logies*.[19]

I have treated this question at some length elsewhere;[20] and to avoid mere repetition, I shall restrict myself here to less severe forms of the problem. But before I do so, it is necessary to emphasize that this third type of 'canon within the canon' problem is *qualitatively* different from the other two. Although the expression 'the canon within the canon' is most frequently applied to this third alternative, the application of the rubric to this approach to Scripture is in one sense deeply regrettable; for strictly speaking, this third procedure no longer has an 'outer' canon, a Scripture that truly serves as 'canon' in any regulatory sense, within which the narrower canon might be found. The 'outer' canon, the Bible, is simply the raw stuff from which the 'inner' canon may be drawn. Yet ironically, this 'inner' canon, the 'canon within the canon', is equally misnamed, for it does not truly enjoy any regulatory status or function either. It is drawn from the 'outer' canon on the basis of (usually unstated) principles not derivable from Scripture; and it is these principles that are truly 'canonical' in that they exercise the real regulatory power.

Thus it ill becomes someone who has arrived at his 'canon within the canon' on the basis of this third procedure to dismiss criticisms of his position by pointing out that *all* Christians fall victim to *some* sort of 'canon within the canon'. The other two procedures for arriving at a 'canon within the canon' are either inadvertent or else honest (if mistaken) interpretation of the structure of the entire canon (i.e. the Bible). The canon stands with its regulatory status and function still intact; and therefore provided the participants in the debate display humility and grace, there is at least the possibility of reform *by* the Scriptures into greater conformity *to* the Scriptures. Problems of hermeneutics and of authority may overlap; but they are distinguishable, and should not be confused.

If we turn to a moment's reflection on the type of 'canon within the canon' established by the first procedure, we restrict ourselves to theological argumentation advanced by many Bible believers in all parts of the world when that argumentation is based on a prejudicial selection of the biblical data.

Suppose, for instance, that a pastor wishes to encourage people to accept his authority and to follow his leadership almost without question. This might arise because he is a demagogue; or it might arise because in his cultural setting people naturally reverence leaders and eschew iconoclasm. He can foster what he regards as a healthy spirituality in this respect by citing passages such as Heb. 13:17 *ad nauseam*; but he will probably be less inclined to cite 1 Pet. 5:11ff. or Matt. 20:24–28. Such a leader may have a theoretically unified canon; but he operates with a canon within the canon when it comes to certain preferred doctrines. The resulting aberration may be entirely unwitting, or it may be perverse; but either way it distorts the Scriptures and has important ramifications in the life of the church.

Many western Christians, for instance, simply do not hear the Scriptures when they speak about the poor; their own experience has been limited to segments of society which from a world perspective are immensely privileged. Their counterparts in the third world may feel very deeply the passages in Scripture which treat poverty; but by the same token they may focus primarily on a subset of those passages—viz. those which insist the rich be far more generous and which warn against hoarding. This situation is somewhat paralleled, at the microcosm, by the pastor of a small church who is very concerned to get across to his congregation the responsibility for the church to pay good teachers with 'double honour' and a respectable stipend, while the church leaders themselves may be very exercised about those passages which insist that spiritual leaders must be free from greed and covetousness and love of material goods. Not only is each side focusing a disproportionate amount of attention on passages which most tellingly apply to others rather than to themselves, each side is also developing, wittingly or not, a canon within the canon.

Two things will help us to escape from these traps. First, we badly need to listen to one another, especially when we least like what we hear; and second, we need to embark, personally and ecclesiastically, on systematic studies of Scripture that force us to confront the entire spectrum of biblical truth, what Paul calls 'the whole counsel of God'.

The name of the game is reductionism. It occurs in many different ways, and needs to be recognized for what it is. And sometimes the first way of proceeding toward a 'canon within the canon' metamorphizes into the third. For instance, G. Ernest Wright argued forcefully some years ago that God's revelation is focused in saving events, in mighty acts, and not in propositional discourse.[21] If he had argued for his positive point without proceeding to the disjunctive negative, he would have been correct; but his disjunction involved him in a reductionistic denial of part of the truth,[22] and unfortunately he has not been alone in his opinion. From time to time it has been argued that the Semitic concept of truth involves integrity in personal relationships and general reliability, but not propositional truth; but again, more comprehensive analysis has demonstrated that the reductionism is false,[23] and results in another form of the truncated canon. The tragedy of all these procedures is that by some route we may avoid hearing the Word of God precisely where we most need to hear it. In this way, an issue at first hermeneutical is in danger of overturning the reforming authority of the Word of God.

D. THE PROBLEM OF SALVATION-HISTORICAL DEVELOPMENT

Broadly speaking, this is another way of referring to the second procedure for developing a 'canon within the canon', discussed above; but it can be divided into two sub-types. In the first, the interpreter adopts a theological framework for interpreting the Bible which he deems true to Scripture (whether or not it be so in fact); in the second, the interpreter adopts a procedure for *using* the Scriptures, and especially certain parts of them, without worrying very much about how the Scriptures fit together. This procedure is usually some form of *paradigmatic* approach: i.e. it fixes on some biblical narrative and seeks to use it as a *paradigm* for current belief or action, without considering very deeply how that narrative fits into the broad stream of salvation-historical development. In the worst case, this way of developing a 'canon within the canon' becomes difficult to distinguish from the third procedure (discussed in the last section).

Perhaps it is easiest to get at this problem by an example. Gustavo Gutiérrez writes:

> The exodus experience is paradigmatic. It remains vital and contemporary due to similar historical experiences which the people of God undergo. As Neher writes, it is characterized 'by the twofold sign of overriding will of God and the free and conscious consent of men.' And its structures are faith in the gift of the Father's love. In Christ and through the Spirit, men are becoming one in the very heart of history, as they confront and struggle against all that divides and opposes them. But the true agents of this quest for unity are those who today are oppressed (economically, politically, culturally) and struggle to become free. Salvation—totally and freely given by God, the communion of men with God and among themselves—is the inner force and the fullness of this movement of man's self-generation which was initiated by the work of creation.[24]

Gutiérrez is aware of the charge to which he leaves himself open, viz. that he is taking an event of the Old Testament and turning it into a paradigm which ignores how the New Testament treats it. Gutiérrez himself responds to his critics by arguing that the temporal/spiritual disjunction is a false one:

> But is this really a true dilemma: either spiritual redemption or temporal redemption? Is not there in all this an 'excessive spiritualization' which Congar advises us to distrust? All indications seem to point in this direction. But there is, perhaps, something deeper and more difficult to overcome. The impression does indeed exist that in this statement of the problem there is an assumption which should be brought to the surface, namely a certain idea of the spiritual characterized by a kind of western dualistic thought (matter-spirit) foreign to the Biblical mentality. And it is becoming more foreign also to the contemporary mentality. This is a disincarnate 'spiritual', scornfully superior to all earthly realities. The proper way to pose the question does not seem to us to be in terms of 'temporal promise or spiritual promise.' Rather, as we have mentioned above, it is a matter of partial fulfillments through liberating historical events, which are in turn new promises marking the road towards total fulfillment. Christ does not 'spiritualize' the eschatological promises; he gives them meaning and fulfillment today (cf. Luke 4:21); but at the same time he opens new perspectives by catapulting history forward, forward towards total reconciliation. The hidden sense is not the 'spiritual' one, which devalues and even eliminates temporal and earthly realities as obstacles; rather it is the sense of a fullness which takes on and transforms historical reality. Moreover, it is only *in* the temporal, earthly, historical event that we can open up to the future of complete fulfillment.[25]

There is insight here, of course; but it does not get to the heart of the issue. The New Testament treats the Passover as a paradigm of Christ and his sacrificial death (1 Corinthians 10), and the exodus as a kind of typological anticipation of the great release which Christ's people come to know when they are freed from their sins. This is not a question of the temporal versus the spiritual: the Bible promises a physical resurrection and a new heaven and a new earth. If Christ 'catapults history forward' in anticipation of the ultimate reconciliation, that ultimate hope is dependent upon Christ's return at the end of the age, not on social revolution; and failure to recognize this point reflects a substantial misunderstanding of the 'already/not yet' tension in New Testament eschatology. Moreover, even the exodus event itself, far from serving as a paradigm of social revolution within a society to transform that society, pictures a people *escaping* that society and forming a new community—and that by the powerful and intervening hand of God. To argue that the miraculous events surrounding the exodus are fulfilled in modern revolution by the oppressed is something like arguing that the proper application of the feeding of the five thousand is the distribution of one's lunch to the poor. There may be in this some remote application somewhere that is not entirely illegitimate; but it rather misses the point. This is not to say there are *no* political implications to the exodus event, but that even from within the framework of an appeal to paradigmatic relationships the 'fit' is not very good. Competent scholarship that appeals to biblical paradigms must be as forthcoming with the discontinuities between a biblical event and the present circumstance, as with the continuities.[26] Moreover, one wonders *on what basis* the exodus event is selected as a paradigm for oppressed peoples today. Why not choose, say, the prophetic insistence that the oppressed people of God do not rebel against Nebuchadnezzar? To ask such a question is to expose the methodological bankruptcy of an appeal to mere paradigms, as long as there is not rigorous and even-handed rationale for the choice of paradigm and for the parallels drawn; and this bankruptcy invites us to pay more attention to intra-canonical relationships and to salvation-historical development. We are forced to ask, for instance, what biblical ground, if any, supports the identification of 'church' and 'kingdom of God', or 'social justice' and 'kingdom of God', upon which various theologies depend.[27] Again, we are forced to ask *why* some particular metaphor for the church should arbitrarily be given controlling authority.[28] I hasten to add that this is not a surreptitious plea to avoid the many passages in Scripture which deal with the oppressed; it is simply an insistence that the salvation-historical lines of thought within the canon must not be overthrown or distorted.

The problem of developing a theology based on a canon with organic growth is not an easy one. The organic model is as good as any. The acorn grows into an oak tree. The botanist who formulates 'the doctrine of the oak tree'—i.e. who writes the definitive tome on oaks—cannot say about acorns everything that he says about oaks; but on the other hand he cannot make the acorns so central in his account that the oaks are displaced; and certainly he cannot in his account turn the acorns into poplars or machine guns. Canon criticism, if it has been wrong in placing the locus of authority in the *changes* in the tradition rather than in the tradition itself, is right at least in forcing upon us a canonical perspective which forbids the *ad hoc* alignment of some canonical event or discourse with something else that bears no relation to canonical development of revelation.

We urgently need some more creative thought on the relationships between the Testaments; but such thought must be principially submissive to the canon as we have it.

E. THE PROBLEM OF TOO LITTLE SELF-CRITICISM

Writing now as a lecturer in an evangelical seminary, I am only too aware of how often students who propound some thesis become very adept at criticizing the alternative positions but rather weak in the matter of finding awkward spots in their own proposals. Good theses depend on criticism and self-criticism of the most even-handed variety.

The same can be said for good theology. There is no doubt that Western missionaries and theologians have exercised a disproportionate and sometimes thoughtless influence in 'third world' churches; and a great deal more needs to be done to rectify the errors and wrongs. But one also senses in the current climate that rising theologians in some third world situations now wish to turn the tables and make Western churches a whipping boy. Ironically, precisely because of the sensed guilt over previous wrongs, an increasing number of Western theologians not only accept this criticism, but do so without evaluation and in a flood of self-abuse. Little of this is helpful to the cause of Christ, the strengthening of his church or the glory of his name. The more communication develops on a basis of frank and equal partnership between church groups from diverse cultures, the more it is important that criticism and self-criticism be even-handed.

Many other hermeneutical foci could be profitably discussed; but if we manage to make some headway on the points introduced thus far, the gain will already have proved substantial.

NOTES

1. D. A. Carson, 'Hermeneutics: A brief assessment of some recent trends', *Themelios* 5/2 (Jan. 1980) 12-20; reprinted in *ERT* 5 (1981) 8–25.
2. cf idem, 'Historical Tradition in the Fourth Gospel—After Dodd, What?' *Gospel Perspectives II*, ed. R. T. France and David Wenham (Sheffield 1981) 83–145, (esp. pp. 100–104).
3. Among many useful discussions, see *inter alia* Anthony C. Thiselton, *The Two Horizons: New Testament Hermeneutics and Philosophical Description* (Exeter 1980); Graham N. Stanton, 'Presuppositions in New Testament Criticism', *New Testament Interpretation*, ed. I. Howard Marshall (Exeter 1977) 60–71; Robert C. Roberts, *Rudolf Bultmann's Theology: A Critical Interpretation* (Grand Rapids 1976) esp. pp. 201–215.
4. Rudolf Bultmann, 'New Testament and Mythology', ET in H.-W. Bartsch, ed., *Kerygma and Myth: A Theological Debate* (London 1972) 1–44.
5. 'The Church in the Gospel of Matthew: Hermeneutical Analysis of the Current Debate', pp. 45–63.
6. 'Principalities and Powers: Opponents of the Church', pp. 110–150.
7. 'The Church in African Theology: Description and Hermeneutical Analysis', pp. 151–165.
8. Respectively, 'The Church in the Liberation Theology of Gutiérrez: Description and Hermeneutical Analysis', pp. 166–194, and 'The Church and Social Justice: Underlying Hermeneutical Issues', pp. 195–233.
9. Carson, 'Hermeneutics', 15.
10. cf *inter alia* Thiselton, *Two Horizons*; idem, 'The New Hermeneutic', *New Testament Interpretation*, ed. I. Howard Marshall (Exeter 1977) 308–333; NIDNTT vol. 1, pp. 573–584; J. I. Packer, 'Infallible Scripture and the Role of Hermeneutics', *Scripture and Truth*, ed. D. A. Carson and John D. Woodbridge (Leicester 1983) 325–356, 412–419; and the bibliography cited in these works.
11. Some writers are now introducing 'fourth horizon' terminology; but this refinement need not detain us here.
12. One of the better treatments is that of Bruce J. Nicholls, *Contextualization: A Theology of Gospel and Culture* (Exeter 1979).
13. David J. Hesselgrave, 'Missionary Psychology and Counseling—A Timely Birth?' *TrinJ* 4 (1983) 72–81.
14. cf esp. M. Parry, 'Studies in the epic technique of oral verse-making. 1. Homer and Homeric style. 2. The Homeric language as the language of an oral poetry', *HSCP* 41 (1930) 73–147; 43 (1932) 1–50; M. Parry and A. B. Lord, *Serbocroatian heroic songs, I. Novi Pazar: English* translations (Cambridge, MA and Belgrade 1954); A. B. Lord, *The singer of tales* (New York 1968); idem, 'Homer as an oral poet', *HSCP* 72 (1968) 1–46.
15. cf Ruth Finnegan, 'Literacy and literature', *Universals of Human Thought: Some African Evidence*, ed. Barbara Lloyd and John Fay (Cambridge 1981) 234–253, and the literature she cites.
16. I am not saying that human language cannot be used to speak of a transcendent God, nor am I suggesting that human language is entirely adequate for talking about God. One of the better brief treatments of this

difficult subject is that of John M. Frame, 'God and Biblical Language: Transcendence and Immanence', *God's Inerrant Word*, ed. John Warwick Montgomery (Minneapolis 1974) 159–177.

17. cf D. A. Carson, 'Unity and Diversity in the New Testament: On the Possibility of Systematic Theology', *Scripture and Truth*, ed. D. A. Carson and John D. Woodbridge (Grand Rapids and Leicester 1983) 65–95, 368–375.

18. see esp. E. Käsemann, ed., *Das Neue Testament als Kanon* (Göttingen 1970), not least his own essay in that volume, 'Bergrundet der neutestamentliche Kanon die Einheit der Kirche?' (pp. 124–133).

19. see esp. James D. G. Dunn, *Unity and Diversity in the New Testament* (London 1977); and his more recent essay, 'The Authority of Scripture According to Scripture, *Churchman* 96 (1982) 104–122, 201–225.

20. 'Unity and Diversity'.

21. esp. *God Who Acts: Biblical Theology as Recital* (London 1952).

22. cf esp. Wayne Grudem, 'Scripture's Self-Attestation and the Problem of Formulating a Doctrine of Scripture', *Scripture and Truth*, ed. D. A. Carson and John D. Woodbridge (Grand Rapids 1983) 19–59, 359–368.

23. cf NIDNTT vol. 3, pp. 874–902; Roger Nicole, 'The Biblical Concept of Truth', *Scripture and Truth*, op. cit. 287–298, 410–411.

24. Gustavo Gutiérrez, *A Theology of Liberation: History, Politics and Salvation*, tr. and ed. by Sister Caridad Inda and John Eagleson (Maryknoll 1973) 159.

25. ibid. 166–167.

26. cf esp. the closing pages of the paper by Nuñez in this collection, pp. 166–194.

27. cf the essay by R. T. France in this volume, 'The Church and the Kingdom of God: Some Hermeneutical Issues', 30–44.

28. cf the paper by Edmund P. Clowney in this collection, 'Interpreting the Biblical Models of the Church: A Hermeneutical Deepening of Ecclesiology, 64–109.

2

The Church and the Kingdom of God
Some Hermeneutical Issues

R. T. FRANCE

A. 'THE KINGDOM OF GOD' AS A THEOLOGICAL SLOGAN

In much modern discussion of the role of the church, particularly in evangelical circles, the phrase 'the kingdom (of God)' has become increasingly prominent and has attracted to itself a whole complex of associations which make it the watchword of those who wish to see evangelicals take a more active role in relation to the political and social issues of the day. 'Indeed, the current danger in some quarters is that a few mentions of the word "kingdom" in any theological document will be enough to guarantee that it be received with uncritical enthusiasm.'[1] It has become within these circles what philosophers might call a 'hurray-word', an epithet to indicate approval, a stamp of authenticity for that which carries the right politico-theological reverberations. Thus we find references to 'kingdom theology', 'kingdom ethics', 'working for the kingdom', etc. I even came across a book with the title *Kingdom Healing*; I am not sure how this differs from other healing except that the term 'kingdom' presumably confers on it some sort of theological imprimatur.

The object of this essay is to examine the relationship between this 'kingdom-language' of current evangelicalism and the biblical phrase 'the kingdom of God'. Undoubtedly all who use this terminology would see it as based on the N.T., but how far does exegesis of the biblical terminology control the way this language

is used today? And if there is any gap between the biblical and
the modern use of such language, does this matter? Are there
dangers here for current evangelical theology?

We may conveniently start from the frequently discussed
question of the relationship between the church and the kingdom
of God,[2] or as it is sometimes formulated, 'Is the church the
kingdom of God?' The evangelical answer to this question is
generally a clear 'No', an answer which may sometimes be
intended to express our disapproval of various aspects of the
empirical church as we know it, but more often indicates a desire
to widen the horizons of Christian people beyond the supposedly
'spiritual' confines of 'the church' to embrace the whole scope of
social and political involvement in the struggles of the non-
Christian world which we take to be our Christian duty.

But what seldom seems to be realized is that it is in fact a
meaningless question, because it rests on a category mistake. 'Is
the church the kingdom of God?' is roughly on a par with such
questions as 'Is an egg happiness?' or 'Is Margaret Thatcher
patriotism?' For the church is a definable empirical entity, but
the kingdom of God is not. That is a bold claim, and I must spend
some time in justifying it.

If you ask the ordinary 'non-theological' Christian what he
understands by 'the kingdom of God' you will probably get no
answer at all! If you do get an answer, it is likely to be in terms of
'heaven' or 'life after death'; or it may be something to do with
the church. If he is more aware of current debate, he may define
it as something to do with social justice, the creation of a new
social order. If he has been influenced by liberation theology he
may go further and see it as a political slogan for the overthrow of
oppressive regimes. If he has a smattering of (old-fashioned)
theological knowledge, he may think with Harnack of the brave
new world where all men will be brothers and the sermon on the
mount their ethical standard, or with Schweitzer of the cataclysmic inbreaking of God's new order which formed the apocalyptic
hope of Jesus and his first followers. All this and more is waiting
to be triggered off by the phrase 'the kingdom of God',
depending on who hears it; and yet people go on using it as if it
had a clear, universally agreed meaning, as if there were
'something' to which it obviously refers, so that there is no need
to discuss what sort of phrase it is.

B. THE MEANING OF THE PHRASE

If there is one thing on which N.T. scholars agree in relation to the kingdom of God, it is that the English word 'kingdom' is now an unfortunate attempt to render the Greek βασιλεία in this context (even if it was more appropriate in the sixteenth century); a better translation would be 'reign' or 'sovereignty'. (The OED gives this as the first meaning of 'kingdom', but correctly describes it as 'obsolete'!) 'Kingdom' today ordinarily suggests a territorial area or political unit ('the United Kingdom')[3], a regime or dynastic period ('the Middle Kingdom' in relation to ancient Egypt), or perhaps an identifiable group of related people or things ('the animal kingdom'). In each case there is a 'thing' which may be pointed to as 'the kingdom'. But 'the kingdom of God' (both in the Hebrew and Aramaic origins of the phrase and therefore also in the derived Greek expression) is not a 'thing'. It is the abstract idea of God being king, his sovereignty, his control of his world and its affairs. That is why the question 'Is the church the kingdom of God?' is meaningless, and the same applies to much current use of the phrase. If you were to substitute 'the reign of God' for every modern use of 'the kingdom (of God)' it would soon become apparent that in many cases it would not work. And yet that is what the biblical phrase means, and the failure of modern usage to observe this original meaning is a cause of some concern.

The tendency to turn the abstract noun into a concrete 'thing' is particularly clear in the very common omission of the words 'of God'. But the biblical phrase is 'the kingdom *of God*',[4] and the first noun has meaning only in relation to the second. 'The kingdom' is as meaningless as 'the sovereignty', or 'the power', or 'the will', which might perhaps serve to identify an impersonal force (cf. *Star Wars*: 'May the Force be with you'!), but completely loses the essential biblical idea of the personal sovereignty of God.[5]

So the phrase 'the kingdom of God' is telling us something about *God* (the fact that he reigns), not describing something called 'the kingdom'. If you want to boil the phrase down to one of its constituent parts, it ought to be 'God' rather than 'the kingdom'. Indeed 'the kingdom (of God)' was used in some Jewish writing as a periphrasis for 'God'.[6] '"The reign of God" signifies "God" and signifies God precisely as Jesus knows him.'[7]

The modern use of 'the kingdom' is therefore questionable not only because it in fact departs from biblical usage, but primarily because it betrays a basic misunderstanding which takes 'the kingdom of God' as a description not of God in his sovereignty but of an identifiable 'thing'. Perhaps it would do us all good if the word 'kingdom' were banned as a translation of βασιλεία, and we had to use always the more correct version 'the reign of God'.

C. NEW TESTAMENT USAGE[8]

If ἡ βασιλεία τοῦ θεοῦ does not denote an identifiable 'kingdom', what sort of phrase is it? Part of the answer has already begun to emerge, but it may be helpful to set out five observations (which require fuller demonstration than we can include here) about the background and use of the phrase in the gospels, before attempting a fuller answer.

1. Jewish Background

The idea that God is king was not new in the teaching of Jesus. Both in the O.T. and in later Jewish literature the idea is developed in two directions. On the one hand God the Creator is king of all the earth, and especially of his people Israel. The world is God's world, and he rules in its affairs. This eternal kingship of God is a basic assumption in all O.T. and Jewish thought. But on the other hand there is also an eschatological dimension; God's sovereignty is not yet universally acknowledged, but the day will come when every knee will bow, and God will be king over all the earth (Isa.45:23; Zech.14:9; etc.).

The actual phrase 'the kingdom of God' (or 'of heaven') is not common, but it occurs in relation to both aspects of the theme. Dan.4:34 speaks of God's kingdom which endures from generation to generation, while Dan.2:44 looks forward to the day when the God of heaven will set up a kingdom which shall never be destroyed. The eternal 'kingdom of our God' is referred to e.g. in Ps. Sol.17:4; Wisd.6:4; 10:10, while a coming apocalyptic kingdom of God is proclaimed in e.g. Test. Mos.10:1; 1QM 6:6, and especially in the regular synagogue prayer which goes back to pre-Christian times, the Kaddish:[9] 'May he let his kingdom rule . . . speedily and soon.' In all these references, while the apocalyptic vision no doubt includes certain specific hopes of political and/or spiritual changes, the noun *malkût* (or its equivalent) is an abstract noun for the rule, reign or sovereignty of God, not in itself the designation of a realm or a specific state of earthly affairs. The content in terms of earthly realities which would be read into this abstract idea would no doubt vary according to the background of the writer, and it is unlikely that what was in the mind of the author of Wisdom was the same as the apocalyptic vision of the Qumran writer, still less the ideal of God's kingship which motivated Judas of Galilee and his Zealot followers.[10]

The kingship of God in Jewish thought, then, is an accepted aspect both of eternal reality and of future hope, but does not correspond to a universally recognizable empirical state of affairs.

2. *Its Place in Jesus' Teaching*

If the phrase 'kingdom of God/heaven' is not common in Jewish literature, in the teaching of Jesus it comes centre stage. Modern scholarship is agreed in finding in this phrase the focus of Jesus' proclamation, the indubitably authentic voice of the master, however much the growing church may have overlaid his teaching in other respects. The fact that it occurs relatively seldom in the rest of the N.T. but some 60 times (not including parallels) in the teaching of Jesus in the Synoptic Gospels points clearly this way. This is the heart of his mission; this what he came for.

But what is it? The next section will begin to show how difficult it is to tie down the answer to this question. Here I simply want to suggest that at least part of the reason why it is so elusive is precisely because of its centrality in Jesus' understanding of his mission. It is a phrase so all-embracing that it can be used of many different aspects of what Jesus has come to do. He has come to reassert the sovereignty of God in all the many ways in which it impinges on human life, and this is far too broad a scope to be tied down into a simple definition. 'The kingdom of God' points to the whole mission of Jesus, in all its richness and diversity of application.

3. The Variety of Associated Linguistic Forms

J. Jeremias[11] lists eighteen verbal connections in which the phrase ἡ βασιλεία τοῦ θεοῦ is found in Jesus' sayings and to which there is no known parallel in the language of Jesus' contemporaries. They are as follows: the kingdom of God is taken by force, suffers violence, has come near, one can enter it, be the least in it, it is in the midst of you, it comes, it is prepared for you, men have made themselves eunuchs for its sake, it is to be sought, it has keys, can be locked against men, a scribe is not far from it, one can be great (or greater or smaller) in it, its mystery is revealed, it is compared to various situations, some will precede others into it, and it has come upon you (lit. 'taken by surprise'?).[12] And these are only the *unique* uses; there are many other verbal associations, such as its being taken away from some people, being preached, coming in power, being prayed for (in the Lord's Prayer), belonging to children and the childlike, to the poor in spirit and the persecuted, while the uncommitted are unfit for it. One could go on, but it is not my purpose here to discuss such usages in detail, only to illustrate the variety of types of language which may appropriately be applied to 'the kingdom of God' as Jesus uses the phrase. In the light of such a list, there is little hope of being able to define the kingdom of God as a single identifiable 'thing'!

4. The Variety of Areas of Reference

The last section has already indicated some of the different contexts in which kingdom of God language may be used. Sometimes it occurs in parallel with some other phrase or idea, which might seem to point towards a definition, but again the variety is more impressive than any uniformity. It is apparently parallel to the righteousness of God (Matt.6:33) and to the will of God (Matt.6:10); sometimes it is equivalent to discipleship (Lk.9:61–62), particularly to the situation of Jesus' followers over against traditional Judaism (Matt.5:19–20; Mk.12:34); sometimes it points beyond the present situation to the future state of God's people (Matt.7:21–23; 8:11–12; 13:43). Notoriously, it refers both to what is already true in Jesus' earthly ministry (Mk.1:15; Matt.12:28; Lk.17:20–21) and to something still to be awaited (Mk.9:1; Matt.6:10; Lk.19:11). It is characteristically described in parables: 'the kingdom of heaven is like . . . '; but these parables refer sometimes to the preaching and penetration of the gospel (Mk.4:26ff,30ff; Matt.13:33), sometimes to the present experience of the convert (Matt.13:44–46) or his obligations as a disciple (Matt.18:23ff), and sometimes to men's ultimate destiny (Matt.13:24ff, 47ff; 20:1ff; 25:1ff).

Again, the list could be extended, but the point is surely already clear: whatever 'the kingdom of God' may have meant to Jesus' contemporaries (and that, as we have seen, is not a matter of a simple definition), in Jesus' teaching it is applied so widely and diversely that the search for a specific situation or event which *is* the kingdom of God becomes ludicrously inappropriate. One might perhaps attempt a definition along the lines of that state of affairs which was intended to result from Jesus' ministry, but such a definition only pushes the question one stage further back: what *was* the aim of Jesus' ministry? Can it be tied down to a single definable concept or situation? If it cannot, then neither can the meaning of the phrase 'the kingdom of God'.

5. *The Originality of Jesus' Usage*

'The phrase, of itself quite intelligible though hardly commonplace in the religious language of first-century Palestine, was subtly and richly laden with mystery by Jesus' use of it.'[13] The old Jewish idea that God is king and that the day will come when his kingship will be universally acknowledged inevitably underlies all Jesus' use of kingdom of God language, but this is no more than the launching-pad from which Jesus' usage has taken off to explore new ideas and connections which his Jewish contemporaries would not have thought of, and to which indeed their traditional understanding of the phrase might present some resistance. Indeed, as G. B. Caird points out, 'Jesus would scarcely have devoted so many of his parables to explaining what he meant by the kingdom of God if he understood by it exactly what everybody else did.'[14]

In passing it may be noted that this is a hermeneutical point of major importance in relation to much of N.T. thought and language. Much of current study in these areas consists of the enthusiastic search for non-Christian 'parallels' and 'background', whether Jewish or pagan, to the ideas of the N.T. In itself this is a necessary and fruitful pursuit, but unfortunately it often carries with it, even if not explicitly, the assumption that these parallels are in some way determinative of the range of meaning available to the relevant N.T. language. At its worst, this approach can tie the N.T. writers so firmly to their presumed 'background' that they are allowed to say nothing original, that is, nothing distinctively *Christian*. The danger was pointed out long ago in Samuel Sandmel's famous article, 'Parallelomania',[15] but it is still with us. Surely a study of the Jewish background of the phrase 'the kingdom of God' followed by a study of the range of its usage in Jesus' teaching is sufficient to explode once and for all any notion that N.T. usage can be confined to, or even determined by, what may be discerned from extant literary sources of its previous and contemporary usage.

John Riches sums up the point: 'Putting it simply, Jesus had to use terms which were understood by his contemporaries or they could not have understood him at all; but he had to use them differently, if he was to say something new.'[16] And Jesus had a lot to say that was new; nothing illustrates this more clearly than the new diversity into which he has stretched the usage of this particular term.

D. THE KINGDOM OF GOD AS A SYMBOL

So we return to our question: what sort of phrase is 'the kingdom of God' as Jesus uses it? If it does not denote a specific situation, event, community or other 'thing', and if it is not even a concept which can be restricted to a limited subject-area, then how does it function?

The most helpful answer I have found is in Norman Perrin's study, *Jesus and the Language of the Kingdom*,[17] where, taking up the terminology of Philip Wheelwright, he affirms that the kingdom of God is not a concept or an idea, but a *symbol*, and more specifically a 'tensive symbol'. The terminology is not immediately clear to anyone not versed in linguistics, and it could be slippery; but Perrin is using it to make the point that there is no one-to-one correspondence between the phrase 'the kingdom of God' and an identifiable situation to which it always refers; its function is rather to evoke a whole complex of ideas, even of emotions, relating to the deeply rooted belief that God is king. So 'its meaning could never be exhausted, nor adequately expressed, by any one referent'. The phrase serves then not so much to define the subject-area of the statement in which it occurs as to establish the conceptual framework within which that statement is to be understood.

Perhaps this is an unnecessarily complicated way of making my point. If so, forget about Perrin and his tensive symbols, and let me simply reiterate crudely that Jesus uses 'the kingdom of God' in such a variety of linguistic connections and in relation to such varied subject-areas that it is impossible to identify any specific situation, event or 'thing' which *is* the kingdom of God.

Thus when in the Lord's Prayer the clause 'Thy kingdom come' is followed by 'Thy will be done', these are not two separate petitions but two ways of saying the same thing—'May your sovereign purpose be achieved.' If it is possible to define 'the will of God' so as to restrict it to a specific event or state of affairs, then, and only then, is it legitimate to restrict 'the kingdom of God' in the same way.

It is in this light that we may understand the long and inconclusive debate about whether Jesus saw the kingdom of God as something already present or something essentially future, the debate between 'realized' and 'consistent' eschatology. Inevitably, since both sides are clearly right, the debate reached a stalemate, and all now agree that in the teaching of Jesus the kingdom of God is both present and future; and since much depends on being able to give an acceptable label to the resultant formula, we have been introduced to 'inaugurated eschatology', 'eschatology in the process of realization', 'fulfilment without consummation', etc. But there was never any need for disagreement here, if only it had been recognized that the phrase 'the kingdom of God' does not function as a direct reference to a specific situation, but indicates a context of meaning which can comfortably embrace the fulfilment of God's sovereign purpose in many different ways and situations, past, present, and future.[18] The Pharisees who tried in Lk.17:20 to tie down the kingdom of God to a specific form and time have had many descendants in the ranks of N.T. scholarship!

E.   CURRENT USAGE COMPARED WITH BIBLICAL

If what I have argued above is correct, it has important implications for present-day use of 'the kingdom of God' in theological discussion. If the phrase does not relate to any single referent, then the phrase by itself cannot be determinative of the reference of the saying within which it occurs. If 'kingdom of God' is not the specific subject-area, but rather denotes the overall conceptual framework of the saying, it must be other elements in the saying, whether in its wording or its context, that indicate what it is all about. To say that it is concerned with the fulfilment of God's sovereign purpose, or that it relates to the aims of Jesus' ministry, does not take us far in determining whether a given saying is about economic reform, ecclesiastical discipline, a restored relationship with God, the apocalyptic denouement, or heavenly rewards. Any of these, and many more subject-areas, may be included within the scope of the purpose of Jesus and the sovereignty of God, and that is all that the phrase 'the kingdom of God' in itself demands. It will not do therefore to use 'kingdom' language in the N.T. as an indicator of, e.g., an apocalyptic orientation, or a socio-political reference, or 'pie in the sky when we die'. We need more specific evidence of which area in the overall context of Jesus' mission is here at issue.

And if this is so in relation to N.T. exegesis, it has implications also for the use of the N.T. term in current theological discussion to which we referred at the outset, at least in so far as that use claims to be biblically based. To refer to any theological stance or programme of action as 'kingdom'-related does not, if the term is used in its N.T. sense, define it any more closely than to say that it is related to the fulfilment of God's will as it is revealed in Jesus. It in no way defines to what aspect of that purpose it is related.

The tendency has been to short-circuit this question by restricting the term 'kingdom' to indicate that which is concerned with social justice, and to use it as a convenient pointer to the need for Christian concern to extend beyond the merely 'spiritual'. If everyone agreed on this new convention, it would not in itself be misleading, but clearly this must restrict meaningful communication to those who have learned this esoteric use of the term, and who will not be influenced by its much broader biblical significance. But the real danger occurs when this conventional restriction of the term is reimported into the N.T., and sayings of Jesus which refer to the kingdom of God are assumed, on the basis of this redefinition, to be about social justice. They may well be so, but equally they may not, and it is not the phrase 'kingdom of God' which is going to help us to see which is the case. Biblical terminology redefined by conventional usage can thus be a very dangerous tool when applied to the exegesis of those passages from which it was originally derived.

If then 'the kingdom of God' in the gospels is a sort of umbrella-term for all that Jesus came to achieve, its content is to be discerned not by a study of any supposedly political or other implications of the word βασιλεία but by an overall study of what, according to the gospels, were 'the aims of Jesus'.[19] This will necessarily involve not only his concern with social issues and values, but his whole understanding of the need of Israel, and his vision of what was God's purpose for his people. It will include an awareness of the radical division of mankind which Jesus increasingly presented as the inevitable outcome of the formation of his own new community of the restored people of God. It will have to take into account the way Jesus (and his followers who wrote the N.T. books) systematically reinterpreted the nationalistic hopes of the O.T. and later Jewish literature in terms of a spiritual liberation which was to be independent of, and even set over against, Israel's national future. It requires, in other words, a study in depth of the whole dynamic of Jesus' words and deeds in their historical context.

Such a study might appropriately focus not only on the 'kingdom of God' sayings, but also on the large number of passages where Jesus explicitly sets out some aspect of his mission in terms such as 'I came to . . .'. Such passages as Mk.2:17; 10:45; Matt.5:17; 10:34f; Lk.12:49; 19:10; Jn.9:39; 10:10; 12:27,46f; 18:37 will reveal a range of concerns which is far wider than much popular writing about 'the kingdom' allows, and which focuses primarily on men's relation with God, even at the expense of the disruption of their relations with one another.

We cannot here undertake such a study, but my point is that it is only against this wider background that the phrase 'the kingdom of God' can be understood in its *biblical* (i.e. N.T.) sense. If, as in some current writing, it is restricted to only a small part of this area, it not only loses the richness of its biblical meaning, but also runs the risk of distorting it by allowing the major emphases of Jesus' mission to be forgotten.

So when people speak of 'the kingdom' and expect us to understand it in terms of the socio-political implications of the gospel, what is happening? It is a case of a perfectly correct emphasis being expressed in inappropriate language. I do not for a moment wish to suggest that the gospel has no socio-political implications or that such concerns had no place in the ministry of Jesus. I regard Jesus as providing in his teaching and example the basis for a radical restructuring of society and its values, which no consistent disciple is entitled to ignore. But I do not regard this as the only or even the primary aspect of Jesus' mission, and if 'the kingdom of God' is applied only to this restricted part of the whole, it is not the right term to use. It is as wrong to *identify* the kingdom of God with social reform as it is to identify it with the church or with heaven, and for the same reason: it is a category mistake.

And it carries with it the insidious danger of losing sight of what is in fact the main focus of the phrase, viz. 'God'. It is remarkable how often in Jesus' teaching 'the kingdom of God' is the subject of an active verb—it is in itself a dynamic agent, not the result of someone else's action. We may seek it, pray for it, preach it, enter it, but men do not create or achieve it. And this is necessarily so by definition, for 'kingdom of God' *means* God in control, God's initiative, God's purpose accomplished. To talk of men, even Christian men, bringing about God's kingdom on earth is to usurp God's sovereignty. Yet this sort of language is increasingly heard in evangelical circles. It is strangely and disquietingly reminiscent of the language of nineteenth-century liberalism, which called on men to create a just and caring society which was called 'the kingdom of God'.[20]

This is the danger of misappropriating a biblical phrase. The ideal it expresses remains a biblical ideal, but the whole theological undergirding of this ideal in Jesus' teaching is in danger of being lost, and the sovereign work of God turned into a human reform programme.

F. CONCLUSION

I do not want to labour the point any further, but let me just
conclude by drawing out the hermeneutical moral from this
case-study in linguistic misappropriation. That moral is surely
the priority in biblical interpretation of what has come to be
called 'the first horizon', i.e. of understanding biblical language
within its own context before we start exploring its relevance to
our own concerns, and of keeping the essential biblical context in
view as a control on the way we apply biblical language to current
issues. As long as we claim, as evangelicals do, to be thinking and
speaking within a biblical framework, we cannot escape this
obligation to take 'the first horizon' seriously.

Of course it is open to anyone to take a biblical term like 'the
kingdom of God' and to treat it in accordance with Humpty
Dumpty's famous dictum: 'When I use a word it means just what
I choose it to mean—neither more nor less.' At least your
meaning will then be clear to anyone who knows and accepts
your definition. What you must not then do, however, is to read
back your own definition into the texts from which you derived
the term, and expect them to answer to the meaning you have
given to it. If you do, here is the perfect recipe for misinterpretation and for the misuse of an important biblical phrase which in
its biblical context takes us to the heart of Jesus' mission. If we
allow such a term to be thus diverted from its intended meaning,
the implications for our whole theological system are likely to be
serious.

1.   S. H. Travis, *I Believe in the Second Coming of Jesus* (London 1982) 51.
2.   On this subject see the careful discussion in G. E. Ladd, *A Theology of the
     New Testament* (Grand Rapids 1974) chap.5, esp. pp.111–119.
3.   The irresistible pull of this usage is illustrated by the fact that when the
     island of Lundy in the Bristol Channel was the personal property of the
     Rev. Hudson Heaven it was dubbed 'the Kingdom of Heaven'!
4.   I trust there is now no need to demonstrate that the phrase 'the kingdom of
     heaven' is Matthew's personal preference for a more idiomatically Jewish
     phrase, which is entirely parallel in usage to the phrase 'the kingdom of
     God' in the other Synoptic Gospels. A few minutes with a synopsis of the
     Gospels is enough to establish this point beyond question.
5.   Matthew does in fact use 'the kingdom' without a genitive six times, but all
     are in the compound phrases 'the gospel of the kingdom' (4:23; 9:35;
     24:14), 'the word of the kingdom' (13:19), and 'the sons of the kingdom'
     (8:12; 13:38), where the context has made clear what βασιλεία is being

referred to. (See J. D. Kingsbury, *Matthew: Structure, Christology, Kingdom* [Philadelphia 1975] 128–137 for the background to the phrase 'the gospel of the kingdom'.) The *only* absolute use in the N.T. of βασιλεία referring to the kingdom of God is in Acts 20:25, perhaps the first step towards today's short-hand phrase; and even there the addition of 'of Jesus' in D and 'of God' in the Byzantine text indicates that early readers were conscious of a 'bareness' in the unqualified 'the kingdom' which would never have been noticed by those accustomed to modern usage.

6. J. Jeremias, *New Testament Theology I: The Proclamation of Jesus* (ET London 1971) 102 n.4; B. F. Meyer, *The Aims of Jesus* (London 1979) 136.

7. B. F. Meyer, ibid. 137. Cf. B. D. Chilton, *God in Strength: Jesus' Announcement of the Kingdom* (SNTU 1; Freistadt 1979) 283–284, where he defines 'the kingdom', following the usage of the Isaiah Targum, as 'the saving revelation of God Himself', and goes on to speak of 'God as kingdom'. The title of his book, 'God in Strength', represents his understanding of what 'the coming of the kingdom' means in the sayings of Jesus.

8. This paper concentrates on the teaching of Jesus as recorded in the Synoptic Gospels. To extend the study to other N.T. uses would show some minor extensions from Jesus' usage, such as the use of 'the kingdom of God' as a term for the subject of Christian preaching in Acts (8:12; 19:8; 20:25; 28:23,31), and Paul's language about 'inheriting the kingdom of God' (1 Cor.6:9–10; 15:50; Gal.5:21) where Jesus had spoken only of 'inheriting the kingdom prepared for you' (Matt. 25:34). But the phrase is not a marked characteristic of any of the N.T. writers in the way that it is of Jesus' teaching; their usage derives from his, and it is therefore in his usage that we may expect to find the peculiarly Christian connotation of the phrase.

9. See e.g. J. Jeremias, *New Testament Theology* 198–199.

10. For the motivation of Judas's revolt see J. K. Riches, *Jesus and the Transformation of Judaism* (London 1980) 93–94.

11. *New Testament Theology* 32–34; cf. B. F. Meyer, *Aims* 131, for a similar list of linguistic connections.

12. For references for all the above see Jeremias, *New Testament Theology*, loc. cit.

13. B. F. Meyer, *Aims* 136.

14. G. B. Caird, *The Language and Imagery of the Bible* (London 1980) 12.

15. *JBL* 81 (1962) 1–13.

16. *Jesus and the Transformation of Judaism* 100. Chapter 5 of Riches's book as a whole sets out this point clearly.

17. (Philadelphia 1976) esp. pp.29–34.

18. Cf. the discussion by B. D. Chilton, *God in Strength* 283–285.

19. The use of this phrase as the title of Ben Meyer's important book indicates the sort of approach required. Meyer provides us with a fine, well-balanced study of Jesus' mission in the social and religious context of his time, and particularly of his Jewish heritage. The book includes a study of the meaning for Jesus of 'the reign of God' (pp.129–137), which avoids the normal danger of over-restricting the phrase precisely by setting it within

an overall study of the dynamics of Jesus' mission, of which 'the reign of God' is properly seen as an inclusive summary or 'slogan'.
20. B. D. Chilton, *God in Strength* 287, concludes as follows: 'At every point, Jesus' announcement directs our attention to God; the effects of the kingdom cannot be worked up into an entity separable from Him. . . . Attempts to see the Kingdom as an apocalyptic regime, as a political movement, as a program for social improvement, i.e., as anything other than the revelation of God also run the risk of putting ideology in the place of faith.'

3

The Church in the Gospel of Matthew
Hermeneutical Analysis of the Current Debate*

GERHARD MAIER

A. INTRODUCTION

1. General Remarks

In order to understand what 'the church' is and how to relate it to, for instance, hermeneutics, theologians of earlier centuries were accustomed to turn to the Bible. They found there the reliable and guiding word of Jesus and his apostles. The sixteenth century Confessions make quite clear how, as a matter of course, they regarded the unchangeable word of the Bible as the basis for their decisions. Thus the epitome of the Formula of Concord—the last great Lutheran Confession of 1577—begins with this statement: 'We believe, teach, and confess that the prophetic and apostolic writings of the Old and New Testaments are the only rule and norm according to which all doctrines and teachers alike must be appraised and judged. . . .'[1] Furthermore, the sixth of the 39 Articles of the Anglican Church (1571) reads: 'Holy Scripture containeth all things necessary to salvation: so that whatsoever is not read therein, nor may be proved thereby, is not to be required of any man, that it should be believed as an article of the Faith, or be thought requisite or necessary to salvation.'[2]

* Translated from German by Harold H. P. Dressler.

45

Historico-critical exegesis, however, as it has arisen since the eighteenth century, has made it much more difficult to establish what 'the church' is. This is so mainly for two reasons: a) because the unity of Scripture has been forcefully challenged; b) because doubts have been raised over the authenticity of the words of Jesus (particularly concerning the church!). The result has been a variety of reconstructed and eventually contradictory theologies and concepts within the New Testament. It comes as no surprise that this divided and partly contradictory variety of positions has also resulted in an unharmonious variety of concepts about the 'church', a variety which ultimately justifies almost any kind of church. One reads statements such as these: that the New Testament Canon not only gives grounds for the 'variety of denominations' but also legitimates 'as churches more or less all cults and heresies, too';[3] in the New Testament 'Christ and Antichrist, faith and superstition, church and counter-church' are to be found simultaneously.

However, this splintering of the New Testament message has led in recent years to reflection. Critical theologians, too, speak of the 'diagnosis of a profound deficiency in modern exegesis' and even of the 'bankruptcy of biblical criticism'.[4]

Should we succeed, in the following pages, in dispersing the arguments against the authenticity of Jesus' words in the Gospel of Matthew, then a biblical basis common to all churches that want to be 'churches of Jesus Christ' would come into view. To be sure, that does not mean that different denominations could not also legitimately emphasize different accents. But it does mean that the limits become recognizable within which the valid historical varieties can still be called biblical and within which we must search for the unity which Eph.4:3ff. assigns to us as our spiritual task.

2.   *Delineation of the Topic*

Our topic, 'the church', appears in many passages in Matthew's gospel. One could list e.g. the calling and sending out of the Twelve in Matthew 10; the parable of the wheat and tares and its interpretation in Matthew 13; the parable of the fish net (ibid.); the so-called 'Church Order' in Matthew 18; the replacement of the old people of God by the new in the parables of Matt.21:33–22:14; the prediction in Matt.23:34; the parables of the parousia in Matthew 24 and 25; in fact, Jesus' entire eschatological discourse in Matthew 24 and 25; and, finally, the great commission in Matt.28:18–20. But the subject matter is brought into sharpest focus in the word of Jesus to Peter in 16:17–19. As in past centuries, so also in recent decades: there continues to be a violent clash of opinions concerning this saying. It is the interpretation of Matt.16:17–19 which is crucial for the understanding of the 'church' in the context of Matthew's Gospel.

Accordingly, we shall focus in this essay on the hermeneutical analysis of the discussion of Matt.16:17ff. It should be made clear from the beginning that we cannot treat this topic exhaustively: rather, we can touch on a selection only which is, naturally, drawn mostly from the German literature. Yet we hope that despite this limitation what follows will be truly representative.

B.   SUBJECTIVE FACTORS

Rarely do exegetes speak more openly of their biases than when they expound Matt.16:17ff. This holds true particularly in the case of their denominational biases but also for other subjective factors.

Both Roman Catholic and Protestant expositors remarkably clearly set forth their confessional stance. O. Kuss reminded his hearers and readers in 1963 'that the faith of the exegete has a decisive significance in the evaluation of exegetical facts in a range of central questions'.[5] And similarly, from the Roman Catholic side, H. Frankemölle observed in 1973, 'The relation of interpretation to the statement of a problem is conditioned by history, indeed often encumbered by it; the interpretation of Matthew's Gospel, in particular, could provide some enlightening examples for this dialectic'; and he adds, 'At this juncture denominational viewpoints shine through clearly.'[6] Protestant exegetes are possibly even more candid. K. L. Schmidt, in 1938, spoke about the 'Protestant' efforts 'to excise the *locus classicus* for the Papal primacy'.[7] And already at an earlier date O. Linton admitted, 'One cannot deny that the debate about the "primacy-passage" in Protestant scholarship was conditioned by the fact that this passage was the very cornerstone of Catholic theology in support of the papal primacy.[8] Such motivation also betrayed itself indirectly where e.g. Matthew's Gospel was seen to be 'the favourite book of Catholicism on the march'.[9] 'Catholic—', as H. J. Holtzmann wrote, '—that is the decisive hallmark which our work (Matthew's Gospel) always displays most clearly.'[10] Even though 'catholic' was defined objectively and not denominationally, viz. as a 'living together of different spirits', nevertheless one cannot miss the association with the present-day Roman Catholic church.

In 1932, O. Linton pointed out a second prejudice apart from the denominational one. He said that Protestant interpretation is also conditioned by 'the course of the critical study of the Bible'. This statement, however, can be understood in two different ways: (a) first in the sense that the widely recognized results of scholarship *in other departments* predetermine the understanding of Matt.16:17ff. Linton himself provides an example of this when he writes, 'A critical attitude against Matt.16:17–19 was already bound up with the penetration of the two-source theory, for in that case the primacy-passage appears as an addition by Matthew.'[11] But (b) 'the course of the critical study of the Bible' could also be taken to mean a change in the focal points of debate (*Weichenstellung*) in the sense that ruling opinions regarding *our passage* have become fixed in such a way that nobody dares to question them seriously anymore. Thus, A. Oepke, in 1948, spoke of an 'axiom' 'within historico-critical theology' at the beginning of our century according to which Matt.16:17ff. could have been created only by the early church.[12] But it is not only the beginning of this century which furnishes documentation of such an attitude.[13] In 1941, Bultmann, among others, asserted that the post-Easter origin of Matt.16:17ff. had been accepted 'as a reliable result of historical criticism for two to three generations'.[14] Indeed, some went so far as to reverse the burden of proof. The *first* question one must ask with regard to historicity ought to be 'whether the reasons now claimed for authenticity can really undermine the doubt about its authenticity'.[15]

Beyond the compulsion of the ruling opinion, a philosophical or dogmatic bias emerges. As O. Kuss (a Roman Catholic) writes: 'The assertion, which occurs in important passages of interpretation, that "this Jesus could not possibly have said this; such and such an idea lay outside his horizon of thought" or something similar, is often just as "dogmatic" a statement as the alternative that he could have said this or that.'[16] Kuss does not seem to be incorrect when one reads in Holtzmann that it is 'impossible to discover Jesus as a founder of a church'.[17] Holtzmann also finds it questionable 'whether Jesus' view of the future could have encompassed a natural development of anything through a long period of time or, even less likely, through the centuries of world history'.[18] The question of whether such inspired prophecy is possible is actually determined by philosophical or dogmatic, rather than strictly exegetical, premises. But what kind of premises are we dealing with? K. L. Schmidt put the blame on 'modernist' trends.[19] A. Oepke went one step further in his discussion with R. Bultmann in 1948. Bultmann has very firm preconceptions about what Jesus was able to do (e.g., with regard to his self-consciousness as Son of Man: 'He could only have done that in the sense that he expected to be exalted at some future date into the position of the Son of Man.'[20]) and he shares in the scepticism with regard to a genuine prophecy of Jesus;[21] what is more, however, he let it be known that he had fundamental reservations about any expectation on Jesus' part of an 'existence organized in church-like fashion'.[22] This is the point raised by Oepke. In his judgment, Bultmann's 'own personal attitude must have played a larger part than he himself realized. He was influenced by Martin Heidegger . . . and had himself observed the close relationship between this philosophy and German idealism. Idealism, however, finds it difficult to come to terms with the church, but is much more at home in a religion of personality.'[23] It is worth noting that the context of this statement is not a generalizing judgment of the theologians in question but a discussion which is strictly related to the Matthean church, in fact even more specifically to Matt.16:17ff.

We state our result: in the interpretation of Matt.16:17ff. subjective factors clearly emerge and, in the form of philosophical or dogmatic decisions taken in advance, influence this interpretation at essential points.[24]

C.   THE QUESTION OF AUTHENTICITY

In recent decades the question of the authenticity of Matt.16:17ff. has been discussed at least as vigorously as the range of statements it contains. Certainly one of the reasons why the question of authenticity gained such significance is the bias just mentioned above. It is striking, however, that recently even Roman Catholic scholars no longer defend its authenticity as a *rocher de bronce*; they either leave the question open (e.g. Schnackenburg[25]) or even respond to it in the negative (e.g. Gnilka[26]).

Up until the end of the 19th century even in the German-speaking world the conviction predominated that Matt.16:17ff. was a genuine and authentic word of Jesus; but matters changed with the work of H. J. Holtzmann, J. Weiss and J. Wellhausen. Since then, the defenders of its authenticity have been in the minority. Theologians as well known as G. Bornkamm, R. Bultmann, M. Dibelius, E. Hirsch, E. Klostermann, W. G. Kümmel, E. Schweizer and H. Strathmann combat the authenticity of Matt.16:17ff. and explain it as an utterance of the 'Risen One' or as a 'formulation of the early church'.[27] In fact, F. W. Beare's recently published (1981) and voluminous commentary shows that similar convictions are now also firmly established in English-speaking areas. One may note as a sort of curiosity that the renowned classical scholar, W. Schadewaldt, wishes to maintain in a lecture (just published posthumously) that Matt.16:17ff. is 'historically genuine'.[28]

The discussion takes place on five levels:

1.   *On the Text-critical Level*

Although there were earlier attempts, by Harnack and others, to omit or modify Matt.16:17ff. on text-critical grounds, such attempts are now generally discredited.[29] K. L. Schmidt put an end to all these with his verdict (in 1938) that 'on textual grounds there are no objections to . . . 16:18'.[30] It is striking that the latest edition of the text by Nestle-Aland does not note any variants for Matt.16:18 and that there are no omissions among the variants for Matt.16:17 and 16:19.

2. On the Literary-critical Level

If one proceeds from the two-source theory, Matt.16:17ff. appears to be an addition which has been inserted into the Markan tradition by the author of Matthew's Gospel or by someone earlier.[31] Yet such a conclusion is not even compelling on the basis of the two-source theory. For even if one regards Matt.16:17ff. as an 'interpolation', that is no judgment about its age and authenticity. Indeed, it may have been the 'interpolation' of genuine logia of Jesus which Mark, for some reason or another, omitted.[32] Even the observation that the content of Matt.16:17–19 is found only in Matthew gives us, as Cullmann points out, no grounds for 'even posing the question of genuineness in this context'.[33] For rigorous critics, too, would not think of declaring the parable of the Good Samaritan or the parable of the Prodigal Son as not genuine simply because they appear only in Luke.[34] K. L. Schmidt's judgment remains sound: 'Literary criticism is in any case so uncertain that the cautious critic must direct his attention to material [content] criticism.'[35]

3. On the Level of Statistic Usage

The focus is here specifically on the term ἐκκλησία. Bultmann writes, 'Doubts are raised already (regarding the genuineness of Matt.16:18) by the fact that the word ἐκκλησία occurs only in Matt.16:18 and 18:17 in words of the Lord.'[36] The remarkable rarity of this term is, of course, one fact which must occupy theological scholarship. Yet it is questionable whether the assumption of inauthenticity is the only obvious explanation of this fact: (a) A *hapax legomenon* can be authentic, too—even if we can no longer recognize the reasons for this particular choice of words. (b) A number of interpreters have found synonyms or at least the subject-matter described as ἐκκλησία in other passages of the gospels, e.g. in the structure of the circle of the Twelve, the body of disciples, or the 'little flock'.[37] From there the discussion leads quickly on to content criticism (cf D below). In any case, vocabulary statistics cannot decide the question.

In this context it is interesting to note an observation made by V. Taylor in 1945 (and earlier). If the words of Matt.16:17–19

really emerged from the early church and must not be attributed
to Jesus, 'how easy it would have been to multiply them in this
relatively late Gospel!'[38] Taylor, then, concludes from the very
uniqueness of the words in Matt.16:17ff. that they are original
and genuine.

4. On the Linguistic Level

In certain cases where a Semitic colouring shines through, that
colouring is taken as an indication of the age of the saying in
question and thus, perhaps, as an aid in support of authenticity.
At this point in the interpretation we now find a paradoxical
situation in the discussion. Both those who defend and those who
deny the authenticity of Matt.16:17ff. have reached an increasing
consensus according to which Matt.16:17–19 demonstrates a
great antiquity within its history of tradition. Younger Roman
Catholic interpreters, even those who want to leave the question
of genuineness open, stress the 'early Palestinian origin' of
Matt.16:18f. or even speak of an 'assured assumption of its great
antiquity (and the very probable assumption of the Semitic
basis)'.[39] On the Protestant side, one finds a corresponding
assumption of the 'thoroughly Semitic flavour' of Matt.16:17ff.[40]
Scholars like O. Cullmann or K. L. Schmidt deduce 'the great
antiquity and Palestinian origin' from, among other things, the
beatitude formulated in an Old Testament style, the Semitic
address using the father's name Bar Jona, the play on words in
Cephas = rock, the Jewish expressions 'flesh and blood' as well
as 'bind' and 'loose', the O.T. and Jewish picture of 'rock' and
the Semitic rhythm of the language.[41] Remarkably, even those
critics who dispute its authenticity share this point of view.
Bultmann, too, believes in the 'Semitic origin' of Matt.16:18f.
and arrives at his judgment that Matt.16:17–19 can be traced
back to 'ancient Aramaic transmission'.[42] Bornkamm's position
is particularly revealing because he shows how much the linguistic analysis causes problems for the hypothesis of inauthenticity:
'I also maintain that this saying is post-Easter . . . despite the
linguistic and historical proofs which witness to its great
antiquity'[43] (1960 against Cullmann and Oepke). Beare readily
admits in 1981, 'The language of these verses is entirely Semitic
in tone; it can not be doubted that it has been drawn by Matthew

from an Aramaic source.' But they consider its place of origin to be the Palestinian church and not Jesus.[44]

Language and antiquity, therefore, provide strong arguments *for* the genuineness of Matt.16:17ff.; but they cannot resolve the question on their own. Thus, ultimately the discussion takes place on the final and fifth level, content criticism. Because of its significance we shall devote a whole section to it.

D.   CONTENT CRITICISM

K. L. Schmidt's observation is still valid today: 'Basically all objections to the ἐκκλησία sayings in Matt. lead to the discussion of material [content] criticism.'[45]

One usually divides content criticism into two problems: 1. Jesus and the church, 2. Peter and his role in the church.[46] However, it seems better to pursue a more accurate differentiation:

1.   The Traditio-historical Argument

For Bornkamm (1960) a 'decisive factor' against its authenticity is 'the fact that the ἐκκλησία sayings in Matt.16:18 cannot be simply grasped in terms of the traditional Jewish idea of the people of God.'[47] In reply one may well ask whether Jesus must always 'simply' repeat traditional Jewish ideas or whether the new situation which he brought about could not also allow new developments in teaching and fellowship. After all, Cullmann in one place regards it as significant that Matt.16:18 bears Jewish and not pagan characteristics, and Schnackenburg refers to Qumran-parallels for the ἐκκλησία-term in Matt 16:18.[48]

2.   The Eschatological Argument

Again and again, the critics point out that Jesus, although he spoke of the coming kingdom of God, did not speak of the coming church. Thus, H. J. Holtzmann quotes with approval P. Batiffol's saying: 'The kingdom of God was promised by Jesus; what came was the church.'[49] In Bultmann's view the congregation of believers loses 'its radical eschatological character' if one maintains that Matt.16:18f. is an authentic word of Jesus.[50] However, one could also suppose that Jesus reckoned with an interim period before the visible arrival of God's rule and that he preached both the church for the interim and the perfected kingdom. Cullmann, for example, argues along these lines. He points out that it is just such a view of the course of salvation history that gives a place for missions.[51] One reaches a similar conclusion if one agrees with Taylor in his emphasis on the idea of the church as the new Israel.[52] It is, however, questionable whether such responses really meet the critics' argument. For them what is at stake is not eschatology in the chronological or salvation historical sense but in the qualitative sense. For interpreters like Holtzmann or Bultmann, the very idea of an organized church already represents a defection from the pure teaching of Jesus. They do not understand how a church as a body with offices and doctrinal decision-making has any resemblance to Jesus' teaching. Hence Holtzmann regards Matthew's 'teaching on the church' as itself a catholisizing deformation.[53] Hence Bultmann asks, 'Is this promise (Matt.16:18f.) really pointing to a time of ecclesiastically organized existence?' and, in the middle of his argument, raises the question, 'How could he (Jesus) have envisaged the future development of an organized congregation of followers and appointed for them Peter as possessor of the power to teach and to discipline?'[54] It is therefore 'quite impossible to regard Matt.16:18–19 as an authentic word of Jesus',[55] and consequently the church stands in contradiction to the proclamation of the imminent in-breaking of God's rule.[56] Was Oepke right, perhaps, when he saw that the deepest root of the eschatological content criticism lay in idealism's religion of personality which distances itself from the church but wants to find its identity in Jesus?[57] In any case, in the final analysis this 'eschatological' argument derives from a given philosophical and dogmatic horizon of understanding.

3. *The Ecclesiological Argument*

This is closely related to the eschatological argument. The chief points in its argumentation follow this line: Jesus addressed himself to all of Israel; the founding of his own congregation, however, would have meant abandoning the whole people and would have led his disciples on the way to becoming a cult (or sect). One can trace this line of argument from Holtzmann (1911)[58] through Bultmann (1941)[59] right down to Beare (1981),[60] who maintains that this would lead us 'into the untenable position that Jesus set out to form a sect of his own, within but separated from Israel, the people of God. "My" church could only mean a sect, like the Qumran community.'[61] Nevertheless, such a view contradicts those statements in the gospel which speak of a special circle of disciples or even explicitly of a new people of God. Those who defend the authenticity refer in particular to the 'constituting of the circle of Twelve', the sending out of the disciples and the announcement of the 'new Israel' (e.g. in Matt.21:33ff.; 22:1ff.) as the 'remnant' or the new, true people of God. Bultmann refutes these references along two lines: (a) the Twelve were called 'only to be preachers' not to gather a holy remnant; (b) all the sayings of Jesus about his followers as a 'select circle' are secondary 'formulations of the church or of the evangelists'.[63] Those sayings of Jesus which concern the delay of the immediate *parousia* are also secondary formations.[64] Without question we are caught here in circular argumentation. In fact, the argument can leave this circle only if it concentrates specifically on the person of Jesus. Hence the ecclesiological debate is constantly switching over into the realm of Christology. O. Linton already wrote in 1932: 'The question of the messiahship of Jesus . . . will be decisive.'[65] On the basis of Daniel 7 he observed that 'the Messiah is no private individual. To him belongs a congregation. To the shepherd belongs the flock.'[66] K. L. Schmidt gave a similar verdict: 'The question of the founding of the Church by Jesus Himself is really the question of His Messiahship.'[67] Relying heavily on F. Kattenbusch, he sees in Jesus the Son of Man of Daniel 7 who represents the 'people of the saints of the Most High' and wants to make his disciples into a 'church'.[68] A. Oepke agrees with Linton and Schmidt: 'The messiah without a church . . . —such a concept is absurd.' He also argues from Daniel 7.[69] Cullmann (1952), Flew (1956) and Kuss (1963) continue the same approach.[70] This could also easily explain the idiom 'my church' (Matt.16:18): this is the congregation of the Messiah—of all those who accept with faith God's activity in Jesus, the Messiah and Son of God.[71]

Bultmann finds none of these considerations convincing. The interpreter who tries to explain the Gospel of John in terms of Mandaic texts considers the derivation of this idea from Daniel 7 to be a 'fanciful construction'.[72] If Jesus had spoken of himself at all as Son of Man, 'he could only have done that in the sense that one day he would be exalted into the position of Son of Man'.[73] Jesus did not want to be a present Messiah or a present Son of Man, let alone a heavenly Son of Man. 'In his historical existence he was a man like every other man.'[74] Only Matthew 'escalates . . . , by appropriate idioms, the figure of Jesus into the divine'.[75] Thereby, of course, the prerequisites for the founding of a church are denied insofar as they are associated with the people of the Messiah.

Once again it is obvious in discussing the ecclesiological argument that we are not dealing with strict exegesis alone. Rather, there are in evidence hermeneutical decisions taken in advance of all detailed exegesis.

4. *The Prophetic Argument*

For exegetes like H. J. Holtzmann, M. Dibelius and R. Bultmann it is questionable 'whether Jesus' view of the future could have encompassed a natural development of anything through a long period of time or, even less likely, through the centuries of world history'.[76] For them the gift of prophecy is a strange phenomenon. Hence, for Bultmann Jesus' prediction of his suffering, dying and resurrection are purely *vaticinia ex eventu*.[77] Logically, then, the *eventus* must have been generally provable. As regards the position of Peter, however, this is not immediately the case, as K. L. Schmidt states: 'The theory of a *vaticinium ex eventu* is shattered by the fact that the *eventus* for Peter has a very different aspect from that which would have to be assumed on the basis of Matt.16:18.'[78] Once again, and especially here, it becomes quite clear in this prophetic argument that the exegesis of a particular passage is controlled by questionable and unstated hermeneutical principles—as, e.g., whether prophetic predictions are possible or impossible.

5. *The Petrine Argument*

Two points need to be considered: (a) Peter with his unstable character was no 'rock' (argument from psychology); (b) Peter

did not play the central role in the early church which
Matt.16:17ff. holds in prospect for him (argument from church
history).[79] The first part may be true psychologically. But one
should ask whether Matt.16:17ff. really describes a particular
psyche or has rather more to do with the power of promise. K. L.
Schmidt draws a parallel with the election of Israel and suggests
that 'we neither can nor should answer the question why God
chose the people of Israel as His people.'[80] Consequently, in the
ensuing period the psychological argument was dropped. Yet the
argument from church history continues to the present time.
Beare wrote in 1981: 'Even more formidable is the objection that
Peter never in fact enjoyed any such primacy in the administra-
tion of the early church as is here assigned to him.' Here Beare
refers to Acts 11:2; 15:1–29; Gal.2:1ff.[81] Does this argument
succeed? O. Linton gives us reason to think that even the critics
have to grant Peter an important rank since otherwise, in their
view, this primacy passage would not have 'formed'.[82] K. L.
Schmidt and R. N. Flew, too, point out that Protestant critics
have occasionally underestimated Peter's role.[83] Moreover, Flew
uses the idea of 'moral authority'[84] to show that the fulfilment of
this promise cannot simply be deduced from external factors: it
involves moral or spiritual dimensions which are difficult to
evaluate externally.

If we look back from this point, we may conclude that
especially in the area of so-called content criticism dogmatic and
philosophical premises act as hermeneutical predeterminants.
Here the 'subjective factors' (cf above) operate in the strongest
way. To phrase it paradoxically: so-called content criticism is the
area of historical criticism which is least of all determined by
content in an objective sense ('*die sog. "Sachkritik" ist der am
wenigsten von Sachlichkeit in einem objectiven Sinne bestimmte
Bereich der historischen Kritik*').

E.   THE CONTENT

During the last decades exegetes have brought much helpful
light to bear on the contents of Matt.16:17ff. It is noteworthy
that Protestant and Catholic interpretations have moved closer
together on a number of points. What now divides Protestant

and Catholic exegetes is not so much the clarification of the saying of Jesus as their application.

According to Augustine, Luther, Calvin and Zwingli the promise in Matt.16:18 did not apply to Peter's person. Augustine took it to refer to Jesus himself; the Reformers, to Peter's faith.[85] Nowadays a broad consensus has emerged which—in accordance with the words of the text—applies the promise to Peter as a person. On this point liberal (H. J. Holtzmann, E. Schweizer)[86] and conservative (Cullmann, Flew)[87] theologians agree, as well as representatives of Roman Catholic exegesis.

The image of a 'rock' together with the Semitic characteristics of the language point to an O.T. and Jewish background. Abraham, for example, is considered in Judaism a 'rock'. The rock of Daniel 2 is considered another parallel (whether correctly or not remains questionable).[89]

Matt.16:18 ought not to be interpreted in terms of a local church—although that is what is meant in Matt.18:17. The ἐκκλσία in Matt.16:18 is a universal entity, namely the people of God belonging to the Messiah.[90]

Its Semitic equivalent, however, is still disputed. K. L. Schmidt strongly supports the Aramaic $k^e ništá$[91] while O. Cullmann prefers the Hebrew $qāhāl$.[92] Considering the evidence of the Qumran literature, R. Schnackenburg suggests the equivalents $sōd$ and '$ēdâh$.[93]

As for the power of the keys and the terms 'bind' and 'loose', Lutheran exegetes continue to plead for a more or less spiritual interpretation. Flew, in his particularly well-balanced presentation, adopts such a view, considering that the keys of God's rule were not 'in its essence governmental authority', but the transmission of γνῶσις ('knowledge') on the basis of the revelation.[94] However, there is an increasing consensus now that this verse is talking about the authority to teach and to discipline, including even to absolve from sins.[95] On the other hand, the tendency prevails among younger Roman Catholic authors like Frankemölle, Gnilka and Pesch to understand the church in Matthew also as a 'brotherhood' and, in any case, to apply Matthew 18 not only to the leaders of the church but to all members of the congregation.[96]

The difficult concept of the 'gates of Hades' remains a real enigma. Of course, the general idea is clear 'that this is a promise that this ἐκκλησία will be invincible before the powers of Hades' or endure until the second coming.[97]

F. CONCLUSION

1. Subjective factors involved in interpretation just cannot be ignored. In view of the hermeneutical strength of philosophical or dogmatic Christian premises, it would be completely wrong to want to return to the illusion of an 'unbiased exegesis'. Nobody can interpret without bias. But the interpreter does have one duty: to recognize his own premises as honestly as he can and to acknowledge them openly wherever that is necessary.

2. That leads us once more to the task of drawing up a biblical hermeneutic—one that is, as far as possible, true to the Bible. No doubt this task is not in any way new and in the course of history has been accomplished in exemplary ways again and again. We must learn from these past achievements. But this is a task that requires constant and fresh reflection which must be done in the light of the experiences of previous interpretation. It is not sufficient just to teach 'exegetical method' in a seminary. Rather, we must think through and describe the basic principles and foundational values of interpretation.

3. In particular there must be some basic thinking on the rights and limits of content criticism for the interpretation of the Old and New Testaments. As far as we know, there is no modern monograph or investigation which deals with this subject in a fundamental way and treats it in the light of the history of interpretation. This is particularly astonishing when one considers that content criticism has a key role to play, not only in questions of authenticity but in other questions of interpretation as well. In view of the discussion outlined above, the interpreter who is loyal to the Bible is well advised to keep his distance from such radical content criticism.

4. Specifically on our topic, one should note that the assumption of the genuineness of Matt.16:17ff. has gained increasing acceptance. Even though Cullmann wrote in 1952 that 'one can no longer talk in terms of a consensus',[98] nevertheless the defenders of its authenticity appear to be no longer a forlorn minority, as in the days of Holtzmann, Weiss and Wellhausen,

but a party just about as strong as the critics. With good reasons, interpretation which is loyal to the Bible can now proceed from the authenticity of Matt.16:17ff.

5. With all due respect to the Reformers, we must admit that the promise in Matt.16:18f. is directed to Peter, and not to a Peter-like faith. The argument about the primacy of the Pope must be pursued from the right basis, not from the wrong basis. The point at which this argument should focus is that of *vicarius Petri* or *vicarius Christi*. That is, the real question is whether the unique historical commission of Peter demands or even allows the idea of successors to Peter.

6. As evangelical theologians, especially, we ought to look at ourselves dispassionately and acknowledge that we often tend unjustifiably toward an individualistic conception of faith. To recognize the authenticity of Matt.16:17ff. demands that we develop a biblically-based ecclesiology. We certainly do not need to fall into the opposite extreme of anti-individualism or liturgical mysticism, but rather to give Matt.16:17ff. its proper place within the whole teaching about the church in Matthew's Gospel and, ultimately, within the whole range of the New Testament.

7. When we speak about the 'church in Matthew's Gospel' we do not mean a church which is fundamentally different from a 'church in John's Gospel' and so on. Rather, it has become clear that Jesus established 'the church' very much in the sense of the New Testament covenant community and with common characteristics in its various local manifestations. Moreover, it is clear that all the different churches—whether within the New Testament or throughout church history—represent manifestations of this one church only insofar as they rightfully claim a New Testament basis. Our concern is unity in diversity and not diversity in contradiction.

NOTES

1. Part I.1 of the *Formula of Concord*, in Theodore G. Tappert, trans. and ed., *The Book of Concord* (Philadelphia 1959) 464.
2. Taken from *The Book of Common Prayer*.
3. cf E. Käsemann, *Das Neue Testament als Kanon* (Göttingen 1970) 371, 402, 407–408.
4. P. Stuhlmacher, 'Hauptprobleme und Chancen kirchlicher Schriftauslegung', *ThB* 9 (1978) 53–59. Cf W. Wink, *Bibelauslegung als Interaktion*

(Stuttgart 1976) 7ff. Cf also my book *The End of the Historical-Critical Method* (ET St. Louis 1977) and D. A. Carson, 'Hermeneutics—A Brief Assessment of Some Recent Trends', *ERT* 5 (1981) 8–25.

5. O. Kuss, *Jesus und die Kirche im Neuen Testament* (Regensburg 1963) 32.
6. H. Frankemölle, 'Amtskritik im Matthäus-Evangelium?' *Bib* 54 (1973) 247, 249.
7. K. L. Schmidt, 'ἐκκλησία', *TDNT* 3 (1965) 519.
8. O. Linton, *Das Problem der Urkirche in der neueren Forschung* (Uppsala 1932) 158.
9. So H. J. Holtzmann, *Lehrbuch der neutestamentlichen Theologie*, 2 vols. (Tübingen 1911) 515k; cf also pp.270, 512ff.; similarly E. von Dobschütz, 'Matthäus als Rabbi und Katechet', *ZNW* 27 (1928) 338–348; and so also A. Jülicher and J. Weiss (cf R. Bultmann, 'Die Frage nach der Echtheit von Matt.16,17–19', *TBl* 20 [1941] col.266; von Dobschütz, 'Matthäus als Rabbi', 347; Holtzmann, *Lehrbuch* 515, 512).
10. Holtzmann, *Lehrbuch* 512.
11. Linton, *Problem* 158.
12. A. Oepke, 'Der Herrnspruch über die Kirche, Matt.16,17–19 in der neuesten Forschung', *ST* 2 (1948) 110.
13. e.g. Holtzmann, *Lehrbuch* 268: 'Today it is established among almost all theologians who are to be taken seriously (ΕΚΚΛΗΣΙΑ) that it is impossible to find a Jesus who founded a church.'
14. Bultmann, 'Frage', col.265.
15. ibid. col.267.
16. Kuss, *Jesus und die Kirche* 32–33.
17. Holtzmann, *Lehrbuch* 268, 263.
18. ibid. p. 272.
19. Schmidt, 'ἐκκλησία', p. 519.
20. Bultmann, 'Frage', col. 277.
21. ibid. col. 278: all statements Jesus utters about his suffering, dying and resurrection are merely *vaticinia ex eventu*.
22. ibid. col. 273.
23. Oepke, 'Herrnspruch', p. 116.
24. cf also O. Cullmann, *Petrus, Jünger—Apostel—Märtyrer* (Zürich 1952) 176.
25. R. Schnackenburg, *Die Kirche im Neuen Testament* (Freiburg 1961) 56.
26. J. Gnilka, 'Die Kirche des Matthäus und die Gemeinde von Qumran', *BZ* 7 (1963) 45, 63. Cf also W. Pesch, 'Die sogenannte Gemeindeordnung Matt.18', *BZ* 7 (1963) 227–228; and H. Frankemölle, 'Amtskritik', p. 250 (regarding Matt.18:15ff.).
27. cf the surveys provided by Bultmann, 'Frage', col.266, and Cullmann, *Petrus* 183ff.
28. W. Schadewaldt, 'Die Zuverlässigkeit der synoptischen Tradition', *TBl* 13 (1982) 216.
29. Linton, *Problem* 169.
30. Schmidt, 'ἐκκλησία', p. 519.
31. Linton, *Problem* 158.
32. Schmidt, 'ἐκκλησία', p. 519.
33. Cullmann, *Petrus* 190.

34. cf R. Bultmann, *Die Geschichte der synoptischen Tradition* (Göttingen 1964) 190, 192, 212.
35. Schmidt, 'ἐκκλησία', p. 520.
36. Bultmann, 'Frage', col. 267. Cf Holtzmann, *Lehrbuch* 268; Linton, *Problem* 175; R. N. Flew, *Jesus and his Church* (London 1965) 90; F. W. Beare, *The Gospel according to Matthew* (Oxford 1981) 353.
37. e.g. Flew, *Jesus* 90; Linton, *Problem* 175; Schmidt, 'ἐκκλησία', p. 520.
38. V. Taylor, *The Gospels* (London 1945) 81.
39. cf Schnackenburg, *Kirche* 56; W. Trilling, *Das wahre Israel* (München 1964) 156–157.
40. Schmidt, 'ἐκκλησία', p. 520; K. L. Schmidt, *Die Kirche des Urchristentums* (Tübingen 1932) 285; Flew, *Jesus* 90; Linton, *Problem* 167.
41. Cullmann, *Petrus* 207; Schmidt, *Kirche* 285.
42. Bultmann, *Geschichte* 149, 277.
43. G. Bornkamm, G. Barth and H. J. Held, *Überlieferung and Auslegung im Matthäus-Evangelium* (Neukirchen 1960) 41–42.
44. cf Beare, *Gospel* 354.
45. Schmidt, 'ἐκκλησία', p. 520.
46. So e.g. Flew, *Jesus* 89; Linton, *Problem* 175; Schmidt, 'ἐκκλησία', p. 520; Beare, *Gospel* 353.
47. Bornkamm, *Überlieferung* 42.
48. Cullmann, *Petrus* 210–211; Schnackenburg, *Kirche* 54–55.
49. Holtzmann, *Lehrbuch* 288.
50. Bultmann, *Geschichte* 150.
51. Cullmann, *Petrus* 224ff., 217.
52. Taylor, *Gospels* 81; cf Trilling, *Das wahre Israel* 162; and Linton, *Problem* 179–180.
53. Holtzmann, *Lehrbuch* 512.
54. Bultmann, 'Frage', col. 273.
55. Bultmann, *Geschichte* 150.
56. Bultmann, 'Frage', col. 273. Cf Linton, *Problem* 159, 175; Flew, *Jesus* 90.
57. Oepke, 'Herrnspruch', p. 116. His remarks could also be applied to Bornkamm, *Überlieferung* 42.
58. Holtzmann, *Lehrbuch* 269.
59. Bultmann, 'Frage', col. 265, quotes this passage from Holtzmann and agrees with him.
60. Beare, *Gospel* 353. Cf also Linton, *Problem* 159.
61. ibid.
62. cf Cullmann, *Petrus* 219; Kuss, *Jesus* 37; Trilling, *Das wahre Israel* 162; Schmidt, 'ἐκκλησία', pp. 521, 525–526.
63. Bultmann, 'Frage', cols. 275 and 274.
64. ibid. col. 274. Cf Kuss, *Jesus* 38.
65. Linton, *Problem* 177.
66. ibid. pp. 148, 177.
67. Schmidt, 'ἐκκλησία', pp. 521–522.
68. ibid.; idem, *Kirche* 293.
69. Oepke, 'Herrnspruch', pp. 140 and 137ff.
70. Cullmann, *Petrus* 213; Flew, *Jesus* 88ff.; Kuss, *Jesus* 38ff.

71. Cullmann, *Petrus* 213; Trilling, *Das wahre Israel* 161. Differently, Bultmann, 'Frage', col. 270.
72. ibid. col. 276.
73. ibid. col. 277.
74. ibid.
75. Bultmann, *Geschichte* 383.
76. Thus Holtzmann, *Lehrbuch* 272. Cf Bultmann, 'Frage', cols. 266, 270.
77. ibid. col. 278.
78. Schmidt, 'ἐκκλησία', p. 523.
79. cf Linton, *Problem* 161, 175; Schmidt, 'ἐκκλησία', p. 523; Flew, *Jesus* 89ff.
80. Schmidt, 'ἐκκλησία', p. 523. Similarly Linton, *Problem* 182–183, and Flew, *Jesus* 92.
81. Beare, *Gospel* 354.
82. Linton, *Problem* 180; also Schmidt, 'ἐκκλησία', p. 523.
83. Schmidt, ibid. p. 523; Flew, *Jesus* 91.
84. Flew, ibid.
85. cf Cullmann, *Petrus* 180–181.
86. Holtzmann, *Lehrbuch* 270, 272; E. Schweizer, *Matthäus and seine Gemeinde* (Stuttgart 1974) 43.
87. Cullman, *Petrus* 231ff.; Flew, *Jesus* 93.
88. cf Kuss, *Jesus* 40–41.
89. cf Cullman, *Petrus* 214ff.
90. cf Flew, *Jesus* 97; Frankemölle, 'Amtskritik', p. 252; Gnilka, 'Kirche', pp. 44–45; Kuss, *Jesus* 40–41; Pesch, 'Gemeindeordnung', p. 227; Trilling, *Das wahre Israel* 162.
91. Schmidt, 'ἐκκλησία', pp. 524-525.
92. Cullmann, *Petrus* 210–211.
93. Schnackenburg, *Kirche* 54–55.
94. Flew, *Jesus* 95.
95. So e.g. Cullmann, *Petrus* 230; Kuss, *Jesus* 40–41; Pesch, 'Gemeindeordnung', p. 238; Schweizer, *Matthäus* 43.
96. Frankemölle, 'Amtsritik', pp. 248, 242; Gnilka, 'Kirche', p. 51; Pesch, 'Gemeindeordnung', p. 234.
97. Kuss, *Jesus* 41.

4

Interpreting the Biblical Models of the Church
A Hermeneutical Deepening of Ecclesiology

EDMUND P. CLOWNEY

Habbakuk, a prize-winning multi-media production by the Inter-Varsity Christian Fellowship in the United States, uses images projected on five screens to dramatise the text of the prophet. In the midst of wrap-around symbols and sounds the viewer may at times experience disorientation. Perhaps his vertigo may be shared by the theologian who seeks to interpret the teaching of Scripture concerning the church of God. On the screens of Holy Writ an overwhelming variety of symbols, images, and metaphors crowd upon one another. The church appears as a flock of sheep, a marching host, a temple and a field, a vine and a pillar. More than eighty of these figures for the church have been catalogued and examined by Paul Minear.[1] Nor is the profusion queued up for cataloguing. Figure blends with figure; the building grows (Eph.2:21; 1Pet.2:5); the city comes from heaven dressed as a bride (Rev.2:2). The buzzing, blooming garden of figures may delight the preacher seeking vivid word-pictures, but what is the theologian to make of them?

The question has become particularly urgent in Roman Catholic theology since Vatican II. 'The Dogmatic Constitution on the Church', *Lumen Gentium*, much revised from the initial draft, departs from an exclusive focus on the 'body of Christ' figure to speak of 'the people of God' (chap.2).[2] It also provides a section on the variety of images used in the O.T. and the N.T.: 'Taken either from the life of the shepherd or from cultivation of the land, from the art of building or from family life and marriage, these images have their preparation in the books of the prophets.'[3]

Following Vatican II, Catholic theologians have been divided on the question as to whether the 'people of God' image has replaced the body of Christ as the central model in *Lumen Gentium*, whether the two images are now to be combined, or whether the body of Christ remains the working model for Roman Catholic ecclesiology. Since the Pope declared in *Mystici Corporis*: 'If we would define and describe this true church of Jesus Christ—which is the One, Holy, Catholic, Apostolic, Roman Church—we shall find no expression more noble, more sublime or more divine than the phrase which calls it "the Mystical Body of Jesus Christ"',[4] it should cause no surprise to find its pre-eminence stoutly defended.

Yet the discussions that *Lumen Gentium* has occasioned raise an even more fundamental issue for biblical hermeneutics. How are we to understand the wealth of metaphorical language in Scripture? Figurative statements about the church are, of course, only selected by that topic from a vast range of figurative language in the Bible. By focusing on the church, however, we may raise general questions as they apply to one group of figures. Since we need a better understanding of the biblical doctrine of the church as well as of biblical hermeneutics, we may profitably consider the two subjects in relation to each other.

A.   UNDERSTANDING METAPHORICAL LANGUAGE

Herwi Rikhof has done this from within Roman Catholic theology in *The Concept of Church*, a book that carries the descriptive subtitle, *A Methodological Inquiry into the Use of Metaphors in Ecclesiology*.[5] He analyzes the theological discussions of the figures used in *Lumen Gentium*, provides a careful examination of contemporary writing about metaphor (as it applies to his purpose), and defends his conclusion as to the mechanism and function of metaphor in theology. He maintains the meaning of metaphorical expressions in religious language but argues that it is the task of theology to paraphrase metaphorical language in theoretical statements that unpack the cognitive content of the metaphorical descriptions.[6] The church, says

Rikhof, may be formally defined as 'the *communio* of the faithful'.[7]

As Rikhof's work demonstrates by its methodical scholarship, a host of issues must be faced to come to conclusions about the interpretation of biblical metaphors.

1. EXTREME POSITIONS

At one extreme we find rhetoricians who view metaphors simply as stylistic adornments. This view finds the metaphor in the word rather than in the expression as a whole. The *Oxford Dictionary* defines metaphor as 'the figure of speech in which a name or descriptive term is transferred to some object different from, but analogous to, that to which it is properly applicable'.[8]

This view sees metaphor as the result of substitution. You may wish to say that a man eats too much. Instead you say that he is a pig. Since the context, an affirmation about a man, shows that the full sense of 'pig' cannot be meant, the interpreter searches for some secondary or derived use of 'pig' that will fit the context. He finds it in the common association of greedy eating with the pig, and concludes that he is meant to understand that the man is a glutton.

Why, then, did not the communicator say what he meant in the first place? Why require the receptor to do a double-take? Various reasons may be given. Perhaps the more vivid language will keep the hearer awake. The fleeting vision of the man in question undergoing a porcine metamorphosis could be mildly entertaining. Or perhaps the stimulus is more to analysis than to imagination. We like to work puzzles, and the quick solution of this one makes the hearer a satisfied participant in the language game.

In any case, the substitution view focuses on the word and makes a strong case for the definable meaning of metaphorical expressions. At the same time, it is a case against their necessity. We need only insert the language for which the metaphor is substituted and we have the meaning without the metaphor.

If metaphor has only a rhetorical justification, its use in scientific language may well be challenged. Max Black describes the scorn of the French physicist Pierre Duhem for the models used in British physical theory. Duhem considers Faraday's model of electrostatic action to be a fantastic assemblage of glued rubber bands; he concludes that theory for the English physicist is 'neither an explanation nor a rational classification, but a model of these laws, a model not built for the satisfying of reason but for the pleasure of the imagination. Hence, it escapes the domination of logic.'[9]

Duhem's objection to models in science would apply with greater force against the use of substitution metaphors in scientific language.

Yet even when a metaphor is defined in terms of the use of a word rather than in terms of the predication of a sentence it may function as more than a rhetorical decoration. C. S. Lewis proposed a useful distinction between a master's metaphor and a pupil's metaphor.[10] In the first, a teacher who understands what he wishes to communicate uses a metaphor to make it vivid and concrete (or to assist communication in some other way). In the second, a 'pupil' who does not understand a subject struggles to grasp it by using the analogy of metaphorical expression. When Jesus says, 'I am the door', he understands what he wishes to express about his unique role in admitting people to fellowship with God and with others who have been brought into that fellowship. His is a master's metaphor. But we could imagine someone trying to understand how diversity of spiritual gifts could produce unity in the church. 'How can the church be like that?' he might ask. 'Oh, I see', he could exclaim, with a flash of insight, 'the church is not a collection of cards, it is a *body*!'

As Lewis points out, the master can dispense with his metaphor and express his meaning directly. But for the pupil, the metaphor is indispensable. He cannot paraphrase it because he cannot find any other means of expressing the understanding for which it is the key.

The metaphor in this case functions as a model. It organizes and redescribes a state of affairs by an analogy. The fictional model of people being organs in a physical body offers a new way of interpreting how they relate to one another in the church. As a model, the figure is more than a picture. It is a simplified structure that serves to relate and interpret what could not otherwise be grasped.

Since metaphors and models depend upon the function of analogy, involving both identity and difference, there are those who would go to an opposite extreme. Rather than limiting metaphor to dispensable decoration, they would extend it to cover all language and thought. Sallie TeSelle urges that metaphorical language does not simply have a place in human knowing, but that it is 'the human method of investigating the universe'.[11] Indeed, metaphorical groping describes the movement of the human organism in all its areas of discovery, whether they be 'scientific, religious, poetic, social, political or personal'. The basis of the movement is 'undoubtedly erotic', the desire to be united with 'what is'.[12] The human organism is itself the great metaphor that makes all understanding autobiographical. We 'figure' the unknown with ourselves. Herwi Rikhof objects to Te Selle's definition of metaphor, and to the vagueness of her sweeping claims. His key objection, however, is the absence of criteria. If all thought is metaphorical, 'everything is possible and everything is permissible, which leads to a Christianity void of content and rightly denounced as ideology'.[13]

Indeed, the very fact that metaphorical expression can be made a subject of argument and that sweeping claims can be made for it would seem to show that metaphors do have a place, and do not fill the entire horizon of language and thought. Without an accepted order of reality to which conceptual language refers, the deviation that constitutes the metaphor could not be recognized.

Still another position regarding metaphor denies that all language is metaphorical, but affirms that theological language is necessarily metaphorical. Alan Richardson says: 'Much depends on our understanding of the necessarily symbolical character of all theological language. It would surely be wiser to say that such a phrase as "the body of Christ" (meaning the church) is used realistically, ontologically, and *therefore* metaphorically or symbolically or analogically.'[14]

One of the commonplaces of post-Kantian theological thought has been that our language for describing the noumenal cannot operate with the categories used by scientific thought in analyzing the phenomenal world. Kant developed his critical philosophy to gain a secure base for Newtonian physics in the face of the skepticism of David Hume. At the same time, he sought a separate epistemological ground for reflection on God, freedom, and immortality. His refutation of the classic proofs for the existence of God was an effort to show that theoretical categories could not be used for the transcendent.

The Kantian dualism has broken down from both sides. On the one side, theological liberalism has made painfully evident the consequences of divorcing Christian faith from scientific fact and historical understanding. Christian belief hangs upon the truth-claim made for the physical resurrection of Jesus Christ. On the other side, the positivistic understanding of Newtonian physics has dissolved. The physicist finds himself compelled to recognize the inadequacy of his models and to debate the function of metaphor and analogy in the paradigms around which scientific research is organized.[15]

To be sure, the Kantian division is not healed in contemporary phenomenology on the one hand, or logical positivism on the other. For logical positivists religious talk may be seen as a language game that we play according to our arbitrary rules without reference to the God who is there. Phenomenology as adapted by Rudolf Bultmann rejects ontology in the biblical sense. For Bultmann the biblical conception of God in heaven is mythological. The meaning of the myth is to be found in our existential decision.

In any case, Christian theology must challenge all immanentism. From the assumption that human experience must be our only starting point we cannot give an account of either that experience or of the God who gives it. For that reason we cannot be content with philosophies that deed a playing field to religion provided that it keeps in bounds and knows its place (whether mythological or metaphorical). To say this, of course, does not answer the question as to the place of analogy in our created understanding. Nor does it deny that there is distinctiveness to religious language. 'But religious language is distinctive not because it deals with some narrow, peculiar subject matter, nor because it is properly used only in certain restricted areas of life. It is distinctive precisely because it is presuppositional, and thus demands authority over all life.'[16]

One other sweeping claim about metaphorical language should be noted. It is sometimes said that the Bible reflects an imagistic culture that is alien to our analytic and scientific understanding of life.[17] This may be taken to be the difference between Eastern and Western thought, or between ancient and modern thought, rather than the difference between religious and secular thought. At its extreme, this approach may liken Hebrew thought to the 'primitive mentality' imagined by anthropologists before the days of field experience. Those ancient Hebrews, it was thought, could not distinguish the individual from the collective personality of the tribe, nor could they distinguish word from event (since *dābār* means both). James Barr has laid to rest the foolishness about Hebrew mentality deduced from the meaning of *dābār*.[18] We may hope that just as anthropologists have gained a profound appreciation for the reasoning ability evident in tribal life,[19] so, too, Bible scholars will continue to produce convincing evidence of the wealth of discursive thought that the Scriptures contain. The book of Romans contains many images, but they are embedded in a conceptually coherent structure of analysis and reasoning.

Whatever difficulties interpretation may encounter in relating 'meaning-then' to 'meaning-now', the two horizons share perspectives common to human beings made in God's image living in a world God created. When the experience of God's salvation is also in common both horizons come under the rainbow of God's revelation.

2.   Metaphor and Meaning

Before we turn to biblical figures for the church we should draw together some key observations on metaphor and meaning. Some of these points have already been stated in setting aside the sweeping assumptions we have just considered.

First, the metaphor is found in the sentence, not in a single word. The 'substitution' view, as we have seen, finds the metaphor in an improper word that has been inserted. Instead of saying, 'He is a glutton', we say, 'He is a pig'. But as Rikhof points out, this understanding of metaphor confuses usage with use.[20] Dictionaries define word usage; they cannot define or describe possible use. The metaphor appears in the use; the terms of a metaphorical statement must carry their normal reference for the metaphor to convey its meaning. Indeed, if a term is used in a trite metaphor, it may acquire an unusual meaning that the dictionary will list. 'Pig', for example, in Webster's Seventh Collegiate Dictionary has among its definitions, 'one resembling a pig' and '*slang*: an immoral woman'.[21] When we use the word 'pig' in one of its possible dictionary meanings (established by usage) we are no longer speaking metaphorically, if metaphor is word substitution.

In so brief a metaphorical expression as 'he is a tiger', it may seem that the metaphor is entirely in the word, for if another word is substituted the metaphor may disappear. 'He is aggressive' is not metaphorical. When the metaphor is more complex, the substitution paraphrase becomes more difficult, although not impossible. The prophet Amos cries, 'The lion has roared; who will not fear?' He proceeds to give a paraphrase: 'The Lord God has spoken, who can but prophesy?' (Amos 3:8). But the complexity becomes overwhelming when Jesus says, 'I am the true vine, and my Father is the husbandman. Every branch in me that does not bear fruit, he takes away; and every branch that bears fruit, he cleanses it, that it may bear more fruit' (Jn.15:1,2).

The image of the vine as it is used in the sentence recalls the prophetic figure of Israel as the vine and God as the vinedresser (Isa.5:1-7). The adjective 'true' in John can mean the real in contrast to symbol or type. It therefore controls our understanding of the metaphorical expression. Jesus is the true Israel, and God's care plants and nurtures him. Only as his disciples are united to him are they part of the true Israel of God. As soon as we begin to paraphrase, however, we become aware of how much more is implied. The metaphorical expression relates the Father to the Son, and the disciples to both. The further thought of the life of the branches coming from the vine is also involved in the original expression. We begin to perceive that the metaphor is not simply a colourful synonym. Rather it brings together two realms of concepts that the rules of language would normally keep distinct. A man cannot be identified with a plant, nor God with a gardener. Rikhof argues that the rules of language are not violated or discarded. To do so would be to produce nonsense, and the metaphor must be distinguished from nonsense as well as from non-metaphorical statements. The rules are not cancelled but relaxed for the time being.[22]

The 'openness' of a metaphorical statement, the possibility of an expanding interpretation, is a result of this relaxing of the rules. As the metaphor brings together two conceptual realms, we are invited to explore one in terms of the other. Max Black likens the subsidiary subject (in the example above, the vine and the gardener) to a filter through which the principal subject is seen.[23] The relations of the Father to the Son and of the Son to the disciples are seen in terms of the relations of a vine to its branches and to the gardener who trims them.

As Black points out, the principal subject also interacts with the subsidiary subject. The distinction between Christ and his disciples pushes the hearer to reflect on the distinction between the stem of the vine (to which it is cut back annually) and the branches that grow from the stem.

The metaphor, then, is not found in one word, whether the word be a noun or another part of speech. Rather, the metaphor is formed by the sentence. Paul Ricoeur pushes beyond this, to consider the place of metaphor in discourse.[24] In the vine and branches example, our interpretation of the metaphor depends not only on the statements quoted above, but on the context of the discourse of Jesus recorded in John's gospel, and on the universe of discourse that includes the Old Testament background and the use of the metaphor there.

This brings us to a second key observation regarding metaphor. Ricoeur argues that even taking account of the discourse does not adequately account for the function of metaphor. By creating a fictional structure of reference the metaphor may redescribe reality, and in that way express a poetic truth that stands in tension with the truth of ordinary understanding in a way that may be compared to the tension in the structure of the metaphor itself. Ricoeur summarizes:

> From this conjunction of fiction and re-description I conclude that the 'place' of metaphor, its most intimate and ultimate abode, is neither the name, nor the sentence, nor even discourse, but the copula of the verb *to be*. The metaphorical 'is' at once signifies both 'is not' and 'is like'. If this is really so, we are allowed to speak of metaphorical truth, but in an equally 'tensive' sense of the word 'truth'.[25]

Rikhof makes a similar point by describing the purpose of metaphor as a 'proposal to redescribe reality'.[26]

One may question, of course, whether so drastic an implication may be attached to the simplest of metaphors. Max Black distinguishes between simple word-substitution metaphors and more complex inter-active metaphors.[27] The latter carry a cognitive content that cannot be fully conveyed by paraphrase. Yet even the simplest metaphors exist in the tension of the sentence. In principle they draw together two horizons and propose, however modestly, to redescribe reality.

A third observation is closely related to this: the relation of model to metaphor. Especially since the publication of Thomas S. Kuhn's *The Structure of Scientific Revolutions*[28] the discussion of the role of models in science has spread far beyond the fields of the philosophy and history of science. In particular, the place of models in theology has become a renewed issue. Do the metaphors for the church in the Bible offer a basis for the elaboration of models that may function in ecclesiology in a way similar to the function of models in science?

Max Black sees models as closely related to metaphors. There is similarity, he says, between the use of a model and of a metaphor—'perhaps we should say, of a sustained and systematic metaphor'.[29] Like metaphors, models in science bring together two separate cognitive domains to produce insight. Models are used in science as instruments for discovery, not just as means for description.

At the same time, Black acknowledges differences between models and metaphors. Metaphor is best limited to relatively brief statements, while the model is extended and elaborated. The metaphor operates with commonplace implications, while the model brings into relation with the principal subject a subsidiary subject that is already framed as a well-knit theory. Black raises a further possible difference when he points out that a scientific model may be checked for validity. A deductive correspondence cannot be expected, but in principle at least the quality of the 'fit' can be investigated apart from the pragmatic test of fruitfulness in discovery.[30]

Rikhof strongly objects to the identification of model with metaphor. He holds that it rests in part on a misunderstanding of metaphor. The 'extension of meaning' in a model implies, he thinks, the substitution view of metaphor. He argues that scientific models redescribe reality in a way that is not metaphorical. The scientific imagination, whether operating in the field of perception or of reality beyond perception, is seeking 'to reach a scientific explanation, a theory of causal mechanism'.[31] Precisely in the area of reality that can never be experienced (the area of metaphysics), we cannot visualize or represent. What is necessary is not metaphor, but precise, technical, theoretical language.

Ricoeur, on the other hand, sees an analogy between models in science and metaphor in poetry. In scientific language, 'the model is essentially a heuristic instrument that seeks, by means of fiction, to break down an inadequate interpretation and to lay the way for a new, more adequate interpretation.'[32] With Black, Ricoeur sees the model as an instrument of discovery, using a rational method with its own principles. In using the model, the scientific mind is not being distracted by images, but it is given an instrument to try out new relationships that have their rationale in an isomorphism of relationships between the original domain and the domain described in the model. Since the domain of the model is not constructed by deduction from that which is to be explained, but has its own coherence, the 'approximate fit' of the model situates it closer to metaphorical language than to pure deduction.[33]

Further, the scientific model involves a 'redescription of reality'. The model enables us to see that which is to be explained in a different light. There is danger, of course, that the redescription will be carried too far by adopting a provisional model as the 'real' explanation. Maxwell first proposed 'an imaginary fluid' as a model to explain an electrical field. He described it as 'a collection of imaginary properties' including incompressiblity. Later he and others began to speak of ether in a realistic idiom.[34] But the mistake in supposing that ether existed was not a necessary consequence of the model that was used. Nor was the original model the hypothesis that such a fluid existed.

With Black, Ricoeur sees the literary parallel to the scientific model not in the brief metaphor but in its extension: the allegory or tale of fiction. He appeals to Aristotle's analysis of tragedy. Tragic poetry, Aristotle said, is an imitation (*mimesis*) of human life, but this imitation passes through the creation of a tale (*mythos*), which has a structure and order not found in the dramas of daily life. The *mythos*, Ricoeur suggests, is metaphorical much as a model is. He compares it to the 'root metaphor' of which Black speaks, a master metaphor, or archetype that stands as a model, offering a network of organization in terms of which we may gain a new perspective on what we seek to understand, the events of life. The model of the *mythos* is at the service of the redescription, the *mimesis*. The 'imitation' is the denotative dimension of the *mythos*.[35]

Ricoeur uses the parallel of metaphor with model to bring to light a further implication of metaphor, the concept of 'metaphorical truth'. He presents this not only as a defensible but as a necessary implication of metaphor, springing from its redescription of reality. At the same time he clearly shows the tension that must exist between the metaphorical redescription and the description that it replaces or seeks to disclose.

In the vast range of metaphorical expressions presenting the relation of God with his people, the concept of 'metaphorical truth' seems to meet us on every hand. The 'redescription of reality' that shows God, then Christ, as the Shepherd and us as the sheep provides such rich insight that we often lose sight of its metaphorical structure. Then we learn, for example, that oriental shepherds were known to sleep across the only opening of a stone sheepfold where wood for a door was not available. Jesus' statement 'I am the door' after he has identified himself as the good Shepherd suddenly acquires fresh metaphorical power.[36]

B.   METAPHORS FOR THE CHURCH

1.   Richness of Metaphorical Expression

With these observations on metaphor and meaning in mind, let us consider the question of scriptural metaphors for the church. If we classify them in terms of their subordinate subjects rather than in terms of the aspects of the church that they reveal, we see that the major spheres of life have been harvested. Paul Minear remarks on the 'diverse origins of the analogies: in home life, in wedding customs, in farm and lake, in city streets and temple, in kitchen and in courtroom, in ancient legends and contemporary events'.[37] Certainly the major areas of human life are drawn from: family life, for we are described as the family of God (Eph.3:14), his sons and daughters (Deut.14:1; Hos.1:10; Isa.43:6; 2 Cor.6:18) and therefore brothers and sisters in our relations to one another (Matt.12:49,50; 23:8; 1 Jn.4:21); community life, for the tabernacle and temple symbolize God's dwelling in the midst of his people (1 Ki.8:12,13,27). Marriage is used, for Israel appears as the unfaithful bride of Yahweh (Hos.2:14–20) and the N.T. church is presented as the bride of Christ (2 Cor.11:2; Eph.5:32). The language of covenant uses the figure of the suzerainty treaty to describe the bond that God establishes with his people (cf 1 Sam.11:1; Exod.24:7,8). The world of agriculture is well represented: bread and wine (1 Cor.10:16–18), the vine and vineyards (Jn.15:5; Matt.21:33–44), the fig and olive trees (Mk.11:13,14; Rom.11:17–24), God's field and his planting (1 Cor.3:9), the sowing and the reaping of the Lord (Matt.13:1–30; Jn.4:35). Often linked with agriculture is the world of construction. The church is the house and temple of God (Eph.2:20; 1 Cor.3:16,17), an edifice built on a rock (Matt.16:18), the pillar and ground of truth (1 Tim.3:15), God's building of living stones (1 Pet.2:3–5).[38] The very organism of our bodies becomes a major metaphor, for we are members of the body of Christ, formed to minister to one another in union with him.

As we review the plethora of images, we must remember that these are not simply word-metaphors to be substituted for 'Christ' or 'church'. Rather, they represent worlds of human experience. Here a distinctive principle comes to view in the understanding of Christian faith. The worlds of human experience reflect man's own nature, for he is made in the image of God. The principle of analogy, so fruitful in the operation of our thought, is not an alien mold stamped upon a meaningless universe. Rather, analogy is fruitful because God has established a universe with analogical structure.

Further, as we consider the scriptural metaphors for the church, we find, as Paul Minear rightly insists, that they are always directly theological.[39] That is, they continually relate the church to the triune God. The church is not simply a body as the citizens of a Greek city might be a body; it is the body of Christ. Israel is not just a people, one among the peoples of the earth; it is the people of God. The church is a house or a temple, not as an architectural image in itself, but as the dwelling of God, his habitation in the Spirit.

The God-relatedness of the figures is more consistently perceived if we recognize the structure and operation of metaphor.

We do not have only images or pictures of the church. We have metaphorical affirmations in which the daily realities of life in the created world are brought into a tensive but fruitful relation to the realities of God's revelation of his name and his works.

By recognizing this principle we can better understand the flexibility and interfacing of the metaphors concerning the church. The body metaphor, for example, is closely connected with the temple metaphor (1 Cor.6:19). This is not the case because of an extension of the organic figure in itself. The way in which the diverse functions of the individual members contribute to the unity of the body does not suggest that the body is a dwelling to be inhabited. Rather, it is the relation of the body of Christ that opens the metaphor in that direction. So, too, the relation of the body figure to cohabitation (1 Cor.6:15–20) and to marriage (Eph.5:23,28–32; 1 Cor.11:3) finds its explanation not by way of word substitution, but by way of metaphorical discourse in which the life of the body is drawn into relation with Christ and his union with the church.

A further implication of the 'metaphorical truth' aspect of scriptural metaphors is the difficulty that appears in distinguishing the literal from the metaphorical as the world of the metaphor rises from the inorganic and the organic to the highest relationships of human life. To speak of our bodies as temples of the Holy Spirit is still to use a metaphor; it is obviously metaphorical to speak of the church as the bride of Christ. But when Paul says that the members of our bodies are members of Christ, the metaphorical element in the expression is much less obvious. Such is the case, too, with the figure of the church as the family of God or the people of God. Evidently there can be danger in ignoring the 'tensive' character of the metaphor, or forgetting that the expression is metaphorical, or of ignoring the scriptural context of the world of the metaphor. Precisely because a metaphor carries emotional as well as cognitive content, precisely because the scriptural metaphors reach into the world of daily experience and are applied to the affairs of daily life, it may be easy to forget the common understandings of family and societal structures that form the basis of the subordinate subjects of the metaphors. For example, we may be puzzled to find 'father' rather than 'king' in correlation with 'kingdom' in the gospels. We forget that the father image in the metaphor of father applied to God is the patriarchal father who is the final law and governor as well as progenitor of the tribal unit.

We have seen something of the richness and flexibility of the metaphors for the church in Scripture and we have noted how important it is to perceive metaphorical use in context and not to think narrowly of word-metaphors.

2. Metaphors and Models of the Church

We may now focus on the question of major metaphors of the church and their relation to models in ecclesiology. As we have seen, two metaphors for the church are used in a prominent way in the *Lumen Gentium* of Vatican II. 'Body of Christ' and 'People of God' are metaphors that have been used as models. Yet when Avery Dulles designates the major models in Roman Catholic ecclesiology, he does not work directly or exclusively from the scriptural metaphors. The models he examines are: the church as institution, as mystical communion, as sacrament, as herald, and as servant. He sees these models as representing different mind-sets having wider application than to ecclesiology. Dulles develops the models with a view to serving the cause of Roman Catholic ecumenical dialogue. He is committed to theological pluralism, believes the Roman Catholic church has really allowed this more than it may recognize, and hopes that by describing these models dispassionately he may encourage others to see that, 'by a kind of mental juggling act, we have to keep several models in the air at once.'[40] His listing of pros and cons in the book makes it clear that he has preferences among the models, but he would argue that each has value as a perspective on the church.

The pluralist argument does not actually square with Kuhn's description of the use of models in science. Pluralistic theologians regularly appeal to the wave and corpuscular models in the scientific theories about light. Yet Kuhn's study of the history of science is not an account of how discrepant models learned to live together in scientific theory. Rather Kuhn's thesis is that scientific revolutions are brought about when one model or paradigm in science is succeeded by another. A paradigm is established in relation to key experiments. It provides the framework in which facts are interpreted and sets the agenda for 'normal science'. When the paradigm begins to break up it is never abandoned, according to Kuhn, until a new one is offered to take its place. A period of transition follows during which scientists shift to the new paradigm.[41]

Dulles, too traces a somewhat similar development in the history of Roman Catholic ecclesiology. The institutional model he sees as deeply rooted in the Middle Ages but much strengthened in the Counter-Reformation. The strengthening came about by a 'conservative' movement in the church. Dulles does not deal directly with the history of the challenge to Roman Catholic ecclesiology by the theology of the Reformation. The institutional model was succeeded by the 'mystical body' model, often combined with the sacramental. The 'herald' model brings in, belatedly enough, some aspects of reformation ecclesiology in neo-orthodox form, and the servant model represents the challenge of World Council of Churches theology to the Roman Catholic church.

Certainly a survey of the history of the competitive models does not reassure us as to the skill of theologians in keeping a half-dozen balls in the air at once. Indeed, we may fear that the best jugglers are ecclesiastical politicians like one of the drafters of *Lumen Gentium* who told Edward Schillebeeckx: 'We have intentionally formulated some texts in an ambivalent way, so that the minority can accept the principle of collegiality.'[42]

When Schillebeeckx objected that the minority of traditionalists would use their official positions to put their interpretation on the ambiguous texts, he was told, 'Compromise is the only way to reach a degree of consensus'.[43]

Certainly we all must acknowledge a vast pluralism of metaphors regarding the church in the Bible. This does not necessarily indicate that we must work with a pluralism of models, however. That may depend upon our understanding and use of a model. Paul Minear says about the figures of the church: 'No one figure can be selected as the dominating base line.'[44] In his judgment no one figure of the church will serve as an adequate model.

As we have seen, a model offers a redescription of reality. It offers organization that incorporates what is known and by analogy suggests exploration that promises new understanding.

'Root models' or archetypes as described by Max Black have their rationale as exclusive models. They serve the purpose of providing a framework. Such models must seek to incorporate other models within themselves. When they can no longer do this they will be replaced. Those working within a model will tend to extend its boundaries, to carry its basic figure as far as possible to cover areas that seem alien to its idiom.

This has happened in the various models used for the church. For example, the figure of the body for the church serves beautifully to describe the relation of Christians with diverse gifts to one another. It may also serve to show the collective growth and maturing of the church in the life of Christians together. But it is an awkward model to use for the missionary expansion of the church. In the organic realm of plant life the figure may include this by the rather drastic image of grafting. So Paul speaks of the grafting of the wild olive branches into the cultivated olive tree (Rom.11:16–24). But the hellenistic world knew nothing of bodily organ transplants, and the notion of the body growing by feeding on the nations would scarcely be an appropriate metaphor for world missions![45]

Catholic theologians who prefer the model 'body of Christ' to 'the people of God' often defend their choice by arguing that the people of God model is essentially O.T. in its provenance, while the 'body of Christ' is a distinctively N.T. figure. Reformed theologians have favoured the 'people of God' image partly because of its comprehensive reference, uniting O.T. and N.T. believers. The development of 'people of God' as a model has also been advanced by the reformed doctrine of the covenant, a figure that can be applied to marriage and to the bonds of friendship as well as to a people united under a suzerainty treaty. Yet here, too, the figure must be pushed beyond its normal limits to serve as a model for the relation of the triune God to the church. It is awkward to express sonship or divine dwelling in strictly covenantal terms, even though covenantal theology at its best has well described how the covenant is transformed as well as fulfilled in the new covenant and union with Christ.

Models may also be used eclectically, of course. It is quite possible to think of images like the body of Christ and the people of God as major metaphors without assuming that they be used as archetypes providing a framework for the whole of ecclesiology. The interrelation of such major metaphors will then become a significant theological task. Such interrelation may sometimes be accomplished in the idiom of the metaphor itself. The apostle Paul does this when he relates the organic figure of the body to the figure of marriage by means of the concept of bodily union: the O.T. image that man and wife become 'one flesh' (Eph.5:31; Gen.2:24). The interrelation may also be done in theoretical language that makes no direct use of metaphorical expressions.

On the other hand, there are combinations of metaphors that violate the 'grid' of the original metaphorical predication. For example, Anders Nygren uses the 'body of Christ' figure to suggest that just as a body without a head is dead, so a head without a body can accomplish nothing.[46] The suggestion that Christ is helpless without the church would surely never have occurred to the apostle Paul. It arises as a deduction from an improper combination of two distinct metaphors: the image of the head and of the body.

Paul uses the term 'head' (κεφαλή Hebrew *rosh*) to describe the supremacy of Christ over all things and all ages (Eph.1:22; Col.2:10). His usage is shaped from the O.T. in Greek, where κεφαλή is associated with ἀρχή in translating the Hebrew *rŏ'š*. The 'head' has primacy, origination, honour, authority, summation. Here usage has so faded the original metaphor that there is no necessary implication whatever that the head stands in any organic connection with the body. Christ is head of all powers in heaven and earth as well as head of the church (Col.2:10; 1:18). Neither the universe nor the powers are thought of as the body of Christ.[47] Even when Christ as 'head' is brought in close connection with the body the independence of the metaphor remains. When Paul describes the members of the body of Christ, he does not hesitate to use the eye and the ear as sample members of the body. If he thought in composite terms, of Christ as the head and the body as the torso, he would not have chosen parts of the head to illustrate members of the body. Efforts to explain the physiology of Paul's supposed composite metaphor in Eph.4:11–16 have been in vain. How does the body grow up into the head? How is the body framed and knit together by the head? The point is that Paul's image of the church as a body is the image of a whole body, head included, a new man in Christ. Christ is the head over the whole body as the husband is the head over the wife (cf 1 Cor.11:3; Eph.5:23). Only by keeping the metaphors distinct can they be properly understood.[48] Paul does not conceive of

Christ the head of the church after the fashion of the 'Head' in C. S. Lewis's novel, *That Hideous Strength*!

The harvest of metaphorical teaching is to be reaped, not only in preaching and teaching, but also in theology. But the effort to construct one model as an archetype from a scriptural metaphor has not succeeded. It is conceivable that a particular metaphor could be so used, but we begin to see the dangers that would threaten the project.

The formation of an archetypal model requires a distinct process of construction. The metaphors of Scripture are employed occasionally, not systematically or comprehensively. The metaphor that would be extended for use as a model must be such that other scriptural metaphors and non-metaphorical statements can be included in it. It must also be such that it suggests new ways of understanding the riches of scriptural teaching about the church.

In the process that constructed models in the past drastic alterations were made. Yves Congar, in an essay on defining the church, calls attention to the differences between those using 'the body of Christ' as a model for defining the church and the exegetes who were concerned with the N.T. passages. (The exegetes, Congar notes, recognized the separation of the 'head' metaphor from that of the body.)[49]

In the traditional Roman Catholic 'body of Christ' theology, as represented by *Mystici Corporis*, there are included the concepts of the Spirit as the 'soul' of the body, of the body as sacramental, and of the church as hierarchically organized, on the assumption that the body is hierarchically organized.[50] This is carried to the point of representing the pope as the head of the body in his role as the vicar of Christ.[51] The sacramental view of the church is, of course, connected with the Roman Catholic view of sacraments. As the bread of the sacrament incorporates the heavenly presence in the earthly, so does the church incorporate the presence of Christ as his mystical body.[52] Christ's incarnation is continued not only in the elements on the altar, but also in the church. The emphasis put by some theologians on the 'people of God' metaphor at Vatican II was an effort to reduce the hierarchical and sacramentalist interpretation that the body of Christ figure had received.

As Paul Minear shows,[53] the apostle Paul did not think of the 'body of Christ' in application to the church as a physical body, as though it represented the temporal aspect to be supplemented by the Spirit as the heavenly presence. The body is spiritual, constituted by the presence and gifts of the Spirit.

The dangers of reconstructing a metaphor into a model are increased as one model is isolated from others. We have seen the awkwardness that comes when a model is stretched to include teaching that it cannot readily 'code'. But if an isolated model is *not* stretched, an imbalanced view of the church will result. Certainly the institutional view of the medieval church described by Dulles fell into this error. The figure of the kingdom, misinterpreted in the doctrine of the 'two swords', was made the basis for viewing the church as the city of God in a fashion that made it an ecclesiastical counterpart to imperial Rome. The often quoted dictum of Cardinal Bellarmine was that the church is a society 'as visible and palpable as the community of the Roman people, or the Kingdom of France, or the Republic of Venice'.[54] One wonders whether the comparisons are merely illustrative or whether the secular empire came close to being a model for the Rome of the Papal States and even Vatican City.

In a curious way the temple also became a model for the medieval church. A sacramental theology might be incorporated into the model for the church in one locality as well as for the church universal. The cathedral at Chartres gave overwhelming architectural form to the sacramental mysteries at one place where the mystery was made visible. Would any worshipper there in the days of its glory think of the church as anything but a temple? We need not go back to medieval Chartres to find the church understood in the model of a temple! What is more common among contemporary Protestants than to speak of the building as a 'church'?

C. THEOLOGICAL USE OF METAPHORS FOR THE CHURCH

Our review of the effort to derive an archetypal model of the church from one of the metaphors has certainly not covered all the possibilities, but a case against the effort has been taking shape. We have noted the deficiencies and dangers of making such major models as 'body of Christ' or even 'people of God' into archetypes.

1. How Metaphors are Understood

How, then, are metaphors to be grasped and related? For Christians who acknowledge the authority of the Word of God, it is clear that the metaphors of Scripture are in no different position from any other forms of inspired text. They are to be understood in their context by careful exegesis. We have already seen the check that Scripture puts on certain reconstructions of the metaphorical expressions.

Since Scripture characteristically blends images together, exegesis will be sensitive to both their independent structure and their interrelation. For example, when Jesus speaks his foundational word regarding the church to Simon Peter as recorded in Matthew 16, we find in one short pericope the figures of building, assembly, rock foundation, the gates of Sheol, the keys of the kingdom, and binding and loosing, not to speak of the messianic role that Jesus fills as the eternal Son of God. Surprisingly, the literature of the Qumran community has shed light on many of these figures, not only by the community's own use of similar metaphors, but by the prominence that the Qumran scrolls give to metaphors from the O.T.[55] We are reminded, too, that ἐκκλησία is the Septuagint translation of *qāhāl*, and we are led back to the great assembly at Mount Sinai where God constituted his covenant people before him after the exodus deliverance. It is not just a word that makes this connection. (James Barr can rightly protest the habit of making indefinite words definite so that they may bear a technical meaning.)[56] Rather, it is the interplay of the messianic activity of building and that which is constructed, not just the tabernacle of David that was fallen down (Amos 9:11; Acts 15:16–18), but the people of God in the latter days. As in the Qumran literature, the community is founded upon the truth, truth not accessible to the flesh, but revealed of God. The confessing apostle, articulating by revelation the distinctive faith of the Christian church, is made a rock of foundation.[57]

The image of the rushing flood of death and destruction issuing forth from the gates of Sheol is one that the Qumran writers took from the O.T. The church that Jesus establishes is built upon the rock and the floods cannot carry it away (Isa.28:14–18).[58]

The keys of the kingdom are given to those called to exercise authority in the church (Matt.16:18,19; 18:18). The church is therefore brought into close relation to the kingdom of heaven, a relationship that must be clarified by careful examination of many other N.T. passages.

We cannot here consider the exegesis of this passage,[59] but perhaps it is already evident that we cannot interpret scriptural metaphors by imaginatively applying our own associations. The 'commonplace' associations of our culture may be quite different from those that existed in the original context of the Scriptures. When Jesus spoke of his 'assembly', the associations evoked by ἐκκλησία or *qāhāl* were 'the great day of the assembly' at Sinai, the feast-day assemblies at the temple, and national assemblies of covenant renewal. They were not the associations of a modern interpreter who might think of an assembly as a New England town meeting, or as a gathering of students at a secondary school to hear the principal's announcements.

Another example is Paul's use of the 'body of Christ' figure. Scholars have sometimes expended more effort in seeking the origins of this figure than in exploring its meaning. Almost every part of Paul's religious and cultural background has been isolated as the source of his use of the body figure. The Stoics described the cosmos as a σῶμα; in gnostic mythology the body of Anthropos, the primordial man, was cosmic; rabbinical speculation spoke of the nations of the world springing from parts of Adam's body. H. Wheeler Robinson found the origin in the Hebrew conception of corporate personality. Many would point to the body figure in the sacrament of the Lord's supper: 'This is my body' (cf 1 Cor.10:17; 11:24).[60]

We cannot categorically exclude any of these proposals, since we do not know what contacts may have first suggested the figure to Paul. But we can observe Paul's use of the figure and recognize what is decisive in its formulation. Paul sees Christ as the second Adam, the head of a new humanity. The principle involved is that of covenantal representation. The 'corporate personality' explanation of Robinson does not adequately distinguish the covenantal representation of the O.T. from the Oriental and Greek notions of embodiment. The O.T. reveals God as the personal creator and sets aside all pantheistic identification. The living God is not a cosmic ocean, the womb and tomb of the universe. Fellowship with God has the pattern of lord and servant, husband and wife, father and son. The images are personal, not material. Even the 'embodiment' of descendants in a patriarch is not simply physical, because it takes place before God and by his appointment.

Markus Barth well summarizes this principle:

> Yet it is a peculiarity of Israel's writings, that only the one God in his free election, not different gods, or men, or human deeds, or criteria decides who has to be respected or distinguished as representative of the many. Israel's chosen men are representatives of the people only along with the call to speak, to act, to suffer for *God*, as representatives of *God's* will, in the midst of the people. This is the theological nature of biblical representation.[61]

The key to Paul's use of the metaphor 'body of Christ' lies in this representative principle as it is applied to the *literal* body of Christ. Paul speaks of our 'being reconciled in the body of his flesh through death' (Col.1:22). He also refers to Christ's physical body when he says we are 'dead to the law through the body of Christ' (Rom.7:4). Whoever partakes of the sacrament unworthily is 'guilty of the body and blood of the Lord' (1 Cor.11:27). Here the crucified body of Christ is in view. The apostolic doctrine is that Christ 'bore our sins in his own body on the tree' (1 Pet.2:24). We are justified by the blood of Christ (Rom.5:9).

The close connection in Paul's thought between the physical body of Christ (who died as our representative) and the church as the body of Christ is evident in Eph.2:13–16. The representative efficacy of Christ's death is emphasized. Gentiles are brought near 'in the blood of Christ'. The enmity between Jew and Gentile is abolished 'in his flesh'. Jews and Gentiles are reconciled 'in one body unto God through the cross'.

Notice the possible reference of the 'one body' in that last clause (v 16). Does the 'one body' refer to the church, the one new man of v 15? Or does it refer to the physical body of Christ ('the blood of Christ', v 13; 'in his flesh', v 16)? The difficulty in answering this question demonstrates how closely Paul draws together the physical, representative body of Christ and the figure of the church as his body. Since we are saved by union with Christ, a union that is both representative and vital, we can understand that Paul calls those who are joined to the body of Christ by that very name. Christians are one in Christ's body; they are one body in Christ (Rom.12:5); they are a body of Christ (without the article: 1 Cor.12:27). They are *the* body of Christ (Eph.4:12).

Having this root for the metaphor, Paul elaborates it. He makes use of the organic simile of the body to describe the way in which the ministry of differing spiritual gifts does not divide, but rather unites Christians in fellowship. The organic simile provides the key for that unity.

Again we see the necessity of exegesis in the interpretation of these metaphors. Only in the full discourse in which the metaphor appears will we find the proper context for its interpretation.

Another instance of this is the interpretation of the temple image in the Gospel of John. John presents the fulfilment of the tabernacle/temple in Jesus Christ.[62] In him is found the reality of which the O.T. figure of God's dwelling with man was the type.

2. Metaphors in the History of Revelation

As we take account of the setting of metaphors in biblical discourse we will be struck by their richness and the orchestration of their interrelation. Paul Minear uses the apt figure of the kaleidoscope to point up the striking difference between looking at a figure in isolation (like a chip of coloured glass from a kaleidoscope) and looking at the ever-changing kaleidoscopic patterns of the figures as we find them in the interplay of biblical use.[63]

The patterns of biblical revelation, however, do not change at random like the patterns of a kaleidoscope. They are ordered by the progressiveness of the history of redemption and of revelation. Not only must we consider the context of the immediate discourse in which a metaphorical expression appears, we must also take account of the horizon of the history of redemption in which the discourse is found. Major metaphors found in the O.T. are transformed as they move forward to their fulfilment in Christ. Various metaphors are interrelated; the patterns that they form unfold through the epochs of the history of redemption.

Take, for example, the grand concept of the dwelling of God with his people. The garden of Eden contains the tree of life with its symbolism, but the garden itself is symbolical. It is the 'garden of God' (Ezek.28:13;31:8), not only a prepared place for *man's* dwelling, but a place of *God's* dwelling where he may walk in fellowship with the pair created in his image. The motif of the garden as a sanctuary is heightened by the appearance of the cherubim at the east gate of the garden to keep the way of the tree of life (Gen.3:24). The symbolism of the embroidered cherubim on the veil of the holy of holies (Exod.26:31) reflects this background, for the tabernacle (and the later temple), with gates to the east, symbolize the way of approach to God's dwelling.

As the history of redemption unfolds, the 'dwelling of God' theme is developed in the contrast between the tower of Babel (Gen.11:1–9) and the stairway of Jacob's dream (Gen.28:10–22). In both cases the phrase is used of the top reaching to heaven. Such was the goal of the tower builders (Gen.11:4); such was the realization of the stairway in Jacob's dream (Gen 28:12). The parallel is closer than one might suppose; the *sullam* of the dream was not a wooden ladder but a stone stairway.[64] We may think of both as reflecting the ziggurat concept in which the tower offered a stairway for the gods.[65] God does come down at Babel (Gen.11:7), but in judgment. Men cannot in pride construct their place for God's dwelling.[66] But God comes down to Jacob in grace, to affirm his promise of covenant mercy.[67] Because God does come down the stairway to stand over him, Jacob says, 'Surely the Lord is in this place; and I knew it not.' He is afraid, and adds, 'How dreadful is this place! This is none other than the house of God, and this is the gate of heaven' (Gen.28:16,17).

The theme of God's dwelling with his people is central to the book of Exodus. In Mount Sinai Moses received the plan for the tabernacle, God's tent of dwelling to be pitched in the midst of the camp of Israel. But while Moses was on the mountain the people were feasting before the golden calf. In the judgment that followed, God threatened to abandon the tabernacle project. If he were to tabernacle in the midst of this stiff-necked people, surely they would provoke his judgment and he would consume them (Exod.33:3,5). Instead, God promised to go before them in the presence of his angel, drive out the Canaanites and give them the land of his promise. In place of the tabernacle in the midst of the camp, Moses was to pitch a tent of meeting outside the camp where God would be available for counsel (Exod.33:7-1 l).

Moses rejected that proposal in despair: 'If your presence does not go with us, do not carry us up hence' (Exod.33:15). It was not enough for God to go before them in his angel. He must go in the midst of them, reveal himself to them, be present as their God whose dwelling is among his people. Moses prayed, 'Show me, I pray, your glory' (Exod.33:18). God heard the prayer of Moses, declared his name as Yahweh, the God of grace and truth, and the tabernacle was built.

The symbolism of the tabernacle had two aspects flowing from this central figure of God's dwelling in the midst of a sinful people. One was the aspect of a barrier, of insulation as it were, between the holy God and sinners. The veils cordoned off the holy of holies, the holy place, and the courtyard around the tabernacle. The other aspect was that of a way of approach. Through the sacrificial blood of the great altar and the water of the laver the priests could enter the holy place. The high priest could enter the inmost sanctuary on the day of atonement to represent the people in approaching the mercy-seat, the golden cover of the ark of the covenant that symbolized God's throne.

The cloud of glory was the divinely provided symbol of God's presence and dwelling. It appeared over the tabernacle and again over the temple in Jerusalem. In Ezekiel's vision it was seen departing to the east and returning again (Ezek.10:18,19; 11:23; 43:2). The return of the cloud of glory, symbolizing the dwelling of God with his people, is part of a broad use of the symbolism of the temple in the prophets. The restoration will be so unimaginably full and glorious that it will become a renewal. God himself will come to his people and the glory of his coming will surpass all description. The very pots of Jerusalem will be like temple vessels, the least of its citizens will be like David, and in the place of King David will be the angel of the Lord's presence (cf Isa.19:18–25; Zech.14:20–21; 12:8,9).

The history of redemption in the O.T. carries along a rich pattern of figures centering on the dwelling of God with his people. This leads to the N.T. revelation. God came at last to dwell with men: not in a tent, nor in a temple of stone and cedar, but in the temple of the body of the Son of God (Jn.2:19). In the first chapter of his Gospel, John refers repeatedly and explicitly to Exodus 33,34. 'The law was given through Moses . . .' (v 17). 'No man has seen God at any time' (v 18). John reminds us that

Moses saw only God's back. 'The word became flesh, and tabernacled among us (and we beheld his glory, glory as of the only begotten from the Father), full of grace and truth' (v 14). John alludes not only to the cloud of glory over the tabernacle, but to Moses' vision of the glory of the Lord, and to the Lord's proclamation of himself as 'full of grace and truth' (Exod.34:6; Jn.1:14).

Further, the history of redemption is more than a carrier for the symbolism of the cultus. It furnishes in its occurrences metaphors that point to the fulfilment of God's promises. The exodus, for example, is more than an act of social and political deliverance. It is a sign of the full and spiritual salvation of the Lord. As Walther Eichrodt points out, the prophets themselves see the exodus as typical of God's great future deliverance when he will again come marching through the wilderness as the saviour of his people: 'Prepare in the desert a highway for our God!' (Isa.40:3).[68]

The N.T. interpretation of the Old is grounded in this typological structure.[69] The O.T. history is not complete in itself, but provides analogies that anticipate the greater realization of the New. Jesus is not just another David or Solomon, but the one whose calling is prefigured by the Lord's anointed in the O.T. 'A greater than Solomon is here' (Matt.12:42).

We may represent the history of revelation as a horizontal line. Along that line concepts such as the 'dwelling of God' motif move forward. Many figures and metaphors are used to represent these concepts. The figures add to the elaboration and communication of the concepts. We may therefore project a line of symbolism in which a particular event, ceremony, or role points to the concept being revealed. In the fullness of revelation the concept reaches its realization in Jesus Christ. Therefore wherever the line of symbolism exists in the history of revelation, the line of typology can also be validly drawn. There are no concepts that drop out of the plan of redemption. In one way or another all point forward to Christ. A concept in the first stages of revelation we may call C^1 (C to the first power). That concept as fulfilled in Christ is C^n (C to the nth power). The significance of the event for our understanding is not to be read directly across the bottom of the rectangle. That does not take seriously the presence or absence of symbolism in the O.T. text, nor the development of

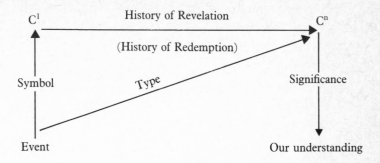

the history of revelation. Similarly, the full significance of the concept C^1 will escape us if we fail to carry it forward to its realization and fulfilment in Christ.

Paul Ricoeur likens a scientific model to tragic poetry.[70] The fiction of the plot of the tragedy corresponds to the extended metaphor of a scientific model. This is the myth that is retold in the poetry. In the retelling, however, there is *mimesis*, imitation of real life. The story is told with details taken from daily life with which we can identfy. This imitation in the tragedy Ricoeur compares to the redescription of the model by which account is taken of the data it seeks to explain. The power of the poetry is the remodeling of human life on the theme of fate and tragedy.

In a very different way the O.T. accounts model life and its meaning. The O.T. contains stories. These are not myths fleshed out by fictional imagination. They are events in the history of God's dealings with his people. Yet they do have significant form. They show the judgments and triumphing grace of God as he overcomes the unfaithfulness of his people. At the same time these accounts reflect daily human experience. Indeed, they offer matchless descriptions of human life in theological perspective.

Much as we may appreciate these descriptions of human life (the jealousy of Joseph's brothers, the sporting wagers of Samson), we may not understand the significance of O.T. history by isolating this aspect. The 'plot line' is crucial. It is outlined, for example, in Deuteronomy 30. There we learn of the blessings God will give his people, the curses that will follow as a result of their rebellion, and the final restoration, renewal and blessing when God will circumcise their hearts.

The plot line of the biblical 'typos' model differs radically from the Greek 'mythos' model. It is a model of hope rather than despair, of promise rather than fate. Further, because the O.T. tells the story of God's salvation, it presents the work of God in the perspective of his promise. God continually anticipates and foreshadows his final and full salvation in his incarnate Son.

The 'modelling' of the O.T. is the modelling of God's own work. The servants God calls fulfil particular roles that anticipate the Savior he will send. Judges, kings, priests, prophets, suffering righteous men—these all are given, not first as 'examples' to us, but as 'models' showing what Christ must do. They are more than symbols, for in living faith they serve God in their generation, and in faith they are examples to us.

This is the explanation of the problem as to whether the designation of the church as the 'people of God' is a metaphorical or literal description. It is both. The church in both the N.T. and the Old *is* the people of God, yet O.T. Israel is also a model, a type, in its earthly form, of the spiritual and heavenly reality of the church. Abraham, Isaac, Jacob, and David all participate by faith in that reality, but their history is embedded in the preparatory forms of that time before Christ came. The mystery was hidden from ages and generations to be revealed in Christ and the church of the new covenant.

In the use of metaphors for the church in the N.T. we find a transformation of figures drawn from the O.T. At times the transformation is by way of contrast: for example, the change from the passover meal to the Lord's supper, or from circumcision to baptism as the initiatory rite of the people of God. The sudden discontinuance of the cultic language of the O.T. in the New is explained by the argument of the book of Hebrews.

An appreciation of the history of redemption is needed to be sensitive to both the connections and the dynamic of transformation.

At this point we may ask, 'Does not the passage from promise to fulfilment bring the end to all models and metaphors?' This question is raised in John's Gospel in the upper room discourse. Jesus says that he has spoken to the disciples in 'parables' but that 'the hour comes when I shall no more speak to you in parables, but shall tell you plainly of the Father' (Jn.16:25). The term translated 'parable' is παροιμία which means a byword or proverb (2 Pet.2:22; Prov.26:11). Aristotle classes παροιμίαι as metaphors,[71] and in John's Gospel (10:6; 16:25,29) the term refers to figurative discourse. The disciples respond, 'Now you are speaking plainly, and without figure of speech [paroimia]' (16:29).

Friedrich Hauck holds that the future time in view is not Easter or Pentecost, but the παρουσία when unconcealed revelation will be given, which will be for the first time fully objective speech concerning heavenly things. When the disciples say that he is now speaking plainly, 'it is as it were a dawning of this time.'[72]

Heinrich Schlier in his article on παροιμία, the term for 'plain speaking', says that the promised time when metaphor and riddle will be past is the time when the disciples will pray in the name of Jesus and receive answer directly from God, the day when the Spirit of truth comes (16:13).[73]

It is characteristic of John's Gospel to stress the realization that comes with the resurrection of Jesus and the coming of the Spirit. Hauck is right in referring the final παροιμία to the παρουσία, but Schlier properly shows that, according to the discourse of Jesus, it does not wait until then. Rather, the 'plain speaking' comes with the Spirit. What is at issue is not the form of the words but their effect. The apostle Paul used great plainness of speech in declaring the whole counsel of God, but that did not cause him to abstain from figurative language. We may recall C. S. Lewis' distinction between master metaphors and pupil metaphors. We must add, however, another kind of 'master metaphor'. Jesus spoke in parables with a double purpose. The metaphorical language provided a spur and means of discovery to those who believed, while at the same time the truth was hidden from those who were not prepared to appreciate it (Matt.13:10–15,34,35). To be sure, the disciples were sometimes in this category when they should not have been, and Jesus found it necessary to explain the metaphors to them (Mk.7:17,18). In both cases it was not ignorance of the secondary subject that presented the barrier to understanding. The disciples and the Pharisees alike understood the metaphors of sowing, fishing, and vine-tending. It was ignorance of the principal subject that left them baffled.

In the case of the disciples, however, 'hearing ears' are given by the blessing of God (Matt.13:16,17), and Jesus explains the parables to them. Even when they deserve rebuke, Jesus teaches

THE BODY OF CHRIST, THE CHRISTIAN, THE CHURCH

CHRIST'S BODY IN THE FLESH	THE CHRISTIAN'S BODY	CHRIST'S BODY THE CHURCH
Organically one (the assumption of 1 Cor.1:13;12:12)	*Organically one* 1. May be defiled by one member 1 Cor.6:15 2. May be cleansed by removing the offending part Matt.5:29,30; 18:7–9; Mk.9:43	*Organically one* 1. May be defiled by one member 1 Cor.3:17; 5:5,6,9–13; cf Matt.18:5–20 2. May be cleansed by removing the offending member Refs. above; Jn.15:2 3. Operates in organic harmony 1 Cor.12:12–27; Rom.12:4–8
Indwelt of the Spirit Therefore: 1. A temple Jn.1:14; 2:19 (Incarnation) 2. A renewed temple Mk.14:58; Jn.2:19 (Resurrection)	*Indwelt of the Spirit* 1. A temple 1 Cor.6:19 2. A new temple 2 Cor.5:1	*Indwelt of the Spirit* 1. A temple Eph.2:13–22 1 Cor.3:16,17 cf. 1 Tim.3:15 2. A new temple 1 Pet.2:5; 2 Cor.6:16
Offered for sin Col.1:22; Eph.5:2; Heb.9:14 Symbolized in the Lord's Supper 1 Cor.11:27	*Offered in gratitiude* Rom.12:1,2 Discerning the Lord's body in the Supper 1 Cor.11:28,29	*Offered in gratitude* Rom.15:16 Communion in the Supper 1 Cor.10:16–18
Raised in new life 1 Cor.15:20; Col.1:18 As the second Adam 1 Cor.15:20–28; Rom.5:15	*Redeemed for new life* 2 Cor.4:10; Rom.8:10,11 Joined to Christ 1 Cor.6:15; Eph.5:30; Col.1:28 New creation 2 Cor. 5:17 Gal.6:15	*'Fullness' of risen Lord* Eph.1:23; 4:13; Col.2:9,10 Joined to Christ as wife Eph.5:22-33; 2 Cor.11:2 New Man Col.3:9-11; Eph.2:15;4:24

them (Mk.7:18,19). In Mark's Gospel the insensitivity of the disciples appears in their failure to discern the metaphorical character of Jesus' words (the 'leaven of the Pharisees', Mk.8:15,16) and of Jesus' miracles (as heavenly signs, to be understood in their meaning, Mk.8:21). The disciples have eyes but do not see, and ears, but do not hear (Mk.8:18). Jesus, however, will restore spiritual as well as physical hearing and sight (Mk.7:35; 8:25).

3. *Metaphors and Definitions*

This consideration of metaphors in the context of redemptive history has brought us back to the basic question. How do we understand the metaphors for the church in Scripture? Are these metaphors irreducible, or can they be paraphrased in literal language? Do they enable us to frame a definition of the church in systematic form, or do they remain distinct perspectives on the church that cannot be translated into one another or into abstract language?

No single metaphor used in Scripture provides an adequate model to incorporate the cognitive elements of all the other metaphors. The two best candidates, 'people of God' and 'body of Christ', demonstrate this by their very juxtaposition, for neither is adequate to express the full content of the other.

We have seen, too, the difficulty in maintaining that all language is metaphorical and therefore that paraphrasing can mean only translating from one metaphor into another. Jesus set about paraphrasing his parables to his disciples in order to reveal their meaning, and the disciples rejoiced at the promise of his speaking 'plainly' rather than figuratively. If meaninglessness is to be avoided, there must be criteria by which the 'fit' of a metaphor or model can be judged.

Further, even a brief reference to some of the metaphors for the church in Scripture calls attention to the importance of understanding not simply various possible connotations of a metaphor but its strong denotative force. This is revealed as metaphors are developed in contexts of discourse. We are required as interpreters to consider carefully the subordinate subject in its cultural context (Hittite treaty forms, Near Eastern customs in shepherding, a *series* of tabernacle/temple forms, fatherhood in the patriarchal sense). We are also required to observe the direct contextual explications and qualifications (the *true* vine, the *heavenly* Father). These contextual modifications include the placing of the metaphor in the history of redemption. For example, when the seven churches appear as lampstands in the opening vision of Revelation, the metaphor alludes to the furniture of the temple. So specific are the metaphors in the description of the glorified Christ in this vision that they function almost as quotations from the O.T. The metaphors do not form one imaginative *Gestalt*, but accumulate statements regarding the divine glory possessed by Christ.

On the other hand, however, to say that we must perceive meaning in the metaphors, that they are not irreducible, is not to say that they can be readily paraphrased or that their implications can be quickly traced. Andrew Burgess has called attention to the conditions in which a metaphor is understood.[74] He proposes that 'wherever there is the danger of conceptual confusion we be reminded that a metaphor includes a reference to the person for whom it is a metaphor.'[75] This carries further the point made by Max Black that a set of 'commonplaces' is assumed about the secondary subject.[76] As we have noted, the 'commonplaces' of Ezekiel's contemporaries about shepherds, or of Hosea's about fathers, or of Paul's about dogs are not necessarily those of our contemporaries. Further the principal subject may also be misunderstood, as it was by the Pharisees and to an extent, the disciples, in attending to Jesus' parables.

If our theory of metaphors were simple word-substitution, we might demand a simple answer to the question of paraphrase. But since metaphorical statement draws together two horizons, and in a sense, two views of reality, we rightly anticipate that the implications may be open-ended. To paraphrase the central meaning of a metaphor in an understandable way may not be too difficult (even if both the Pharisees and the disciples failed). But to draw out the fullness of meaning may prove to be an ongoing process.

This conclusion cuts two ways. We cannot abandon or regard as illegitimate the endeavour to generalize and systematize the understanding gained from scriptural metaphors. The task of systematic theology is essential for the teaching ministry in Christ's church. This enterprise is not self-sufficient, but rests upon and continually returns to the instruction that Scripture gives in metaphorical language as well as in 'plain speech'. On the other hand, we can never discard the metaphors of Scripture. The metaphorical form is not chaff to be blown away once the wheat of meaning has been harvested. No, the metaphors remain, not only to compel us to re-check our conclusions, but also to lead us into further understanding produced by the power of their truth.

We may note the way in which the Westminster Assembly *Confession of Faith* forms its definition of the church. It states in non-figurative language whom the church consists of, and then in figurative language what the church is. It does both from two aspects, the church as invisible and as visible. For the church invisible, the figurative terms spouse, body, and fullness of Christ are used. For the church visible, the figures are: kingdom of Christ, house and family of God.

The figures are carefully chosen to express the distinction between the church as God alone forms it and the church as it is made apparent to us. Yet, while these emphases may be shown to be uppermost, the figures cannot be strictly categorized in this way. The metaphor of the house of God, for example, may be used so as to include non-elect people (under the further figure of clay pots for dishonour, 2 Tim.2:20). But the same figure of the house may also be used to describe the temple of living stones (1 Pet.2:4), a figure in which a hypocrite would find as little place as in the body of Christ metaphor. (There is no suggestion of surgery on the body of Christ.)

The procedure followed in the Westminster Confession does keep in balance theoretical and metaphorical forms of definition. Apart from the unifying perceptions of theoretical analysis we would be vulnerable to a relativistic pluralism in which any image is legitimate. Krister Stendahl has said, 'Over against stringent logic (the way of thinking of later theology) stands Jewish thinking in images, where contradictory facts and conceptions can be put together in a kind of significant mosaic.'[77]

If we assume that scriptural images present to us contradictory conceptions that cannot be related or reconciled, theological pluralism will be the outcome. We will have not a mosaic but a mêlée.

But if the metaphors are ignored, a closed systematic structure will lock us in to definitions that gain a specious clarity at the expense of the rich mystery that is revealed. Yves Congar shows

how this has happened. When the church is conceived sociologi-
cally as a society with certain rights and powers, it is possible to
ignore the scriptural figure of the body of Christ and to view the
church as one society among others, a Christian species of a
well-known human genus. As Congar says, the 'society' of the
church is not distinguished by something that is added to a
human social entity. 'It is in that very thing that appears to be
relatively in common that the Church is substantially supernatural, and represents a mystery.'[78]

As Minear found in his study of the N.T. images, the
dimension of depth in defining the church always appears in its
theological reality.[79] The church cannot be understood apart from
the person, presence, and work of the triune God. The church is
the congregation, in heaven and on earth, of those whom God has
united to Jesus Christ through the work of the Spirit and in the
fellowship of the Spirit. A God-centred definition of the church
must recognize God's choosing in Christ before the world began,
as well as of his begetting 'us again unto a living hope by the
resurrection of Jesus Christ from the dead' (1 Pet.1:3b), and his
making us alive who were children of wrath, dead in trespasses
and sins (Eph.2:1–10). The term 'invisible' is perhaps unfortunate in its suggestion of Platonic idealism, but the Reformers
developed it against Rome precisely to defend a conception of the
church grounded in the free grace of God.

The church must be understood from the side of God's
presence and work; and the scriptural metaphors emphasize this.
The church is a people of God's own possession, called by him,
redeemed by him, assembled to him. It is to be holy because he is
holy. It is his house, temple, field; his vine, olive tree; his city
and kingdom; his flock. It is the bride and body of Christ, the
fullness of him who fills all in all.

Yet these same metaphors both allow for and provide for the
manifestation of God's saving work in the world. A definition
limited to the theological nature of the church in the narrow
sense will not do justice to the structure of the new covenant.

Because of this richness of relation, much of ecclesiology has
been occupied with the unpacking of a fuller definition of the
church: not only the relation of the church as invisible to the
church as visible, but of the church as organism to the church as
organization, of the church militant and triumphant, local and

catholic—all before the consideration of the Nicene attributes to one, holy, catholic, apostolic church.

To isolate even so rich a concept as communion for as brief a definition as Rikhof proposes—'the *communio* of the faithful'—is not in the long run the most fruitful course. (Note that the *Westminster Confession* presents a chapter on the 'Communion of the Saints' immediately after its chapter on the church.) Definitions and summary statements are more useful if they open into the metaphors as well as gleaning understanding and structure from them.

D.   INSIGHTS FOR HERMENEUTICS

In the brief summary we may consider some implications for hermeneutics of this study of metaphors and models in the church.

1.   Literal or Figurative?

All interpretation requires an assumption of meaning in that which is to be interpreted. That meaning may be interpreted correctly or incorrectly. The irony implict in the denial of this is illustrated by Eric D. Hirsch, Jr., who writes: 'I was once told by a theorist who denied the possibility of correct interpretation that I had not interpreted his writings correctly.'[80]

In biblical interpretation the literal meaning of a passage has been identified with the meaning intended by the author.[81] This is debated: apart from inspiration we must allow for the possibility that the author or speaker did not say what he intended. In the case of inspiration the possibility opens at the other end: he may have said more than he intended, as Caiaphas obviously did (Jn.11:49–52). Then, too, we must take account of the audience to whom the words were originally directed, and the situation and context of the discourse.[82]

In any case, the 'literal' meaning is usually taken to include figurative language. 'For example, when a writer or speaker makes use of common figures of speech, a "literal" interpretation accepts the figures of speech as figures.'[83]

But as our consideration of metaphors has suggested, there are degrees and shadings of metaphorical use. Simple metaphors that could plausibly be explained by word substitution may be taken 'literally', but we encounter complex metaphors, discourse metaphors, and models within Scripture (like the tabernacle/ temple and the accompanying cultus). Further, we discover that biblical history, since it points forward to fulfilment in Jesus Christ, is structured prophetically. Its literal meaning as a report of God's dealings with Israel does not exhaust its significance in the context of the history of redemption. This we have seen in the 'people of God' analogy for the church. In a sense, this is not a metaphor and therefore not a type, because there is a continuity between the 'elect nation' under the old covenant and the new. Yet the form given to Israel in the O.T. anticipates in its outward structure the spiritual reality of the New Covenant church. Its kingship, its ceremonial cleanness, its inheritance of the land, all this and much more is typical of the blessings given to the new Israel.

We dare not, like Origen and some of his modern counterparts, reject the historicity of God's redemptive work in favour of its spiritual teaching.[84] To do so is to reject the historical reality that distinguishes the salvation of the living God. But neither should we miss the *significance* of God's salvation in its preparatory forms.

In appreciating the depth of God's revelation we do not reject the literal. Yet we must appreciate that the literal can be taken up in a fulfilment that is more than literal. This is evident in Zechariah's description of the glory of Jerusalem in the latter days, when every wash-pot will be like a temple vessel, when horses will be wearing the inscription from the high priest's tiara, 'Holiness to the Lord' (Zech.14:20), and when the lowliest citizen will be as King David. Whom then will the king be like? 'The house of David shall be as God, as the angel of the Lord before them' (Zech.13:8). The figures are stretched to bursting as they point to their fulfilment in the coming of the Lord (cf Isa.19:19–25).

The glory of the church as the realization of the O.T. symbolism implies that we are given a key for understanding the figurative language. The key is in Christ himself, who fulfils all the promises of the O.T., who breaks down the barriers in that fulfilment, and who seals in the gift of the Spirit all the blessings promised to Abraham, Moses, and David (Gal.3:13,14,29; Phil.3:3; Acts 15:14–18).

The structure of metaphor brings together two world views and forces us to rethink what we think we know by requiring us to use a perspective that seems absurd. Yet what metaphor does in its distinctive and radical way is characteristic of all significant learning. We continually bring together diverse horizons, see the significance of meaning as we find it set in a new context. We ought not to be dismayed, therefore, by the abundance of figurative language that God uses in his revelation. In part, we must learn from figures what we can grasp in no other way. The 'pupil metaphors' are our windows on God's world.

We may be reminded, too, that God who has made us in his image has created a world in which analogy abounds. Vern Poythress has described the cosmos as God's choric poem.[85] It is not only poetry and painting that reflect the allusiveness of God's created analogies. All human thought, science too, must take account of the echoes that resound through the structures of the universe and resonate in the hearts of God's image-bearers.

2. Hermeneutics and Imagination

When the depth of metaphorical expression is appreciated we will not think of metaphors as mere decoration. We will appreciate their power. Rikhof repeatedly insists on the distinction between religious and theoretical language.[86] His argument is that metaphorical language is religious but that it must be paraphrased for theoretical expression. Theology is to be cognitive, not emotional.

Certainly metaphors are emotionally moving. Paul presents the church as a pure virgin to Christ (2 Cor.11:2). He warns a man tempted to fornication that he cannot take the members of Christ and make them members of a harlot (1 Cor.6:15). God's temple, the church, is not to be defiled (1 Cor.3:16,17). These metaphors do carry emotional overtones—i.e. an emotional response that is evoked by the secondary subject may be transferred to the principal subject. Indeed in the parables this transference is often focal. Jesus expects indignation at the behaviour of the wicked husbandmen (Matt.21:40); he pictures vividly the joy of the shepherd, the woman, the father in finding that which was lost (Lk.15).

Yet in the secondary subject, that which evokes emotion is understanding of a situation. The transference is legitimate where, as in these parables of Jesus, the analogy of the principal situation calls for a similar or greater response. The theoretical understanding implied in interpreting the parable is that which can secure the intended response. This is the case with Nathan's parable to David (2 Sam.12:1–15).

The divorce that Rikhof assumes between theology and preaching does not do justice to either. Theology involves analysis, clarity of statement, and economy of expression. Yet theology is not an intellectual exercise divorced from the service of God. It is done before God and unto God. The scriptural ideal is wisdom, an ideal that unites the theoretical and practical in the ordering of thought and life in God's truth. Theology explores the Word of God to understand its significance for belief and life. It is done in the service of the Word of God and through the illumination of the Spirit of God, but it is done in a situation that God has providentially ordained: *our* situation, in which some truths of revelation will be perceived more readily than others, and in which our own understanding of ourselves and our world will be reshaped as we struggle to understand and interpret the Word God has addressed to us.

Again, the fact that the metaphors for the church stretch our understanding beyond our ability to paraphrase them exhaustively is not to be seen as a defeat but as a challenge. We cannot discount the imaginative force and emotive power of metaphors as irrelevant to hermeneutics. The whole impact of the figures contributes to the understanding that we gain from them. As we are challenged in our view of the world and ourselves by the metaphor/model of the body of Christ, we reflect on the implications of this intimate organic union with him and with one another. Our imagination is not freed to re-direct the metaphorical expression into other channels, but to pursue the depths of the biblical analogy. Indeed, since preaching engages in this pursuit before God and in address to the people of God, preaching not only has need of theology, it also develops theology, as Luther and Calvin have shown us.

3. Metaphors and Theology in Context

We have seen that metaphors are to be understood and interpreted in context. The metaphor itself draws together two dissimilar contexts. Further, it is to be interpreted in the context of discourse; first, the immediate discourse of the text in which it is found, and then the wider discourse of the author's other writings and the situation in which he wrote. Hirsch has distinguished between meaning and significance, recognizing both the necessity of establishing the original meaning of a text and interpreting its significance in any number of broader contexts.[87] This distinction is important for biblical interpretation.

Only by a complete rejection of the Bible's claims for itself can we use it as a picture file from which to clip illustrations to fit our own copy. Biblical interpretation must understand biblical figures in their immediate context. At the same time, the wider contexts of the progressive history of redemption must be taken with equal seriousness. Only when this is done may we legitimately explore the significance of the revelation for our own context.

Unfortunately, under the buzz word of 'theology in context' all of these principles may be violated. For example, the historical metaphor of the exodus from Egypt may be taken from its context by ignoring the stated purpose of God's exodus deliverance.[88] True, God did declare, 'I have broken the bars of your yoke, and made you go upright' (Lev.26:13). But God's purpose of deliverance is that 'I will walk among you, and will be your God, and you shall be my people' (Lev.26:12). God delivers Israel from bondage to Pharaoh so that Israel might serve him in his covenant (Exod.4:22,23). God not only brought Israel out, but brought them unto himself (Exod.19:4–6). The theology of Exodus is not simply a theology of liberation, but of redemption. As we move through the covenantal history of the O.T. and into the New, we find that Israel's failure to perceive the meaning of redemption lay at the root of all its troubles. The political deliverance was not an end in itself, but a sign and claim of a new relation with God.

In much the same way the medieval institutional ecclesiology, reaffirmed in the Counter-Reformation, both isolated and distorted one image: the church as city and kingdom, with the sad consequence acknowledged by Dulles and others.[89]

But if it is not desirable, is it not nevertheless inevitable that every cultural context will feature one metaphor of the church, convert it into a model and ignore less pleasing or convenient images? Does this not account in a measure for denominational divisions? Must we not expect that people in social or political bondage will take most seriously the liberation aspect of the exodus figure? Do not the reflections of tribal life in the life and laws of Israel provide an attractive model in tribal areas of Africa, where legalistic mores are inherent in tribal culture?

Or may not cultural factors operate by contrast: will not a factory worker be drawn to the freedom of the church as fellowship of the Spirit, just as the chaotic Middle Ages sought structure and stability in a hierarchical institute?

Our inquiry into the structure of metaphors has led to the acknowledgment that two horizons are brought unexpectedly together in the working of the metaphor. For its interpretation the horizon of the secondary subject must be regained if it is to serve its valid metaphorical function. This, and not a contemporary understanding of the secondary subject must be used as the 'grid' in interpreting the meaning of the metaphor.

Yet interpretation is possible because regaining the horizon of the secondary subject is possible—possible because of our common human nature made in the image of God, because of our common universe created by God and the resulting commonalities of human experience, and because of the continuing work of the Creator Spirit in maintaining our life and our understanding.

Often, however, the secondary subject will be closely akin to knowledge and experience in the context of a particular culture. Or the principal subject may relate directly to a need that is perceived or to a structure that is acknowledged in that culture. In this way cultural perspectives assist in the hermeneutical task. They bring to light positively or by contrast the *meaning* that the figure had in its original context and the *significance* that it has in the context of the contemporary culture in question.

This is the contribution of 'contextualized' theology; to recognize it is to acknowledge that every cultural context will offer both barriers and avenues of approach in a formal sense, even though the sinner's heart is hostile to the truth of God.

But the task of biblical interpretation is to support the proclamation of the whole counsel of God. Indeed, the interpreter carries a particular responsibility to present those metaphors that may be misunderstood or found offensive. Only in this way can balance be gained, and only in this way can the misinterpretation of favourite models be avoided.

The denominational divisions of the church do exist in part because of hermeneutical failure. Consider the effects of those isolated and distorted models of the church that Dulles describes in his survey. Think not only of the sacramentalist and hierarchical model of the Middle Ages, but of the universalist 'servant church' of ecumenical theology. So long as one metaphor is isolated and made a model, men are free to tailor the church to their errors and prejudices. The answer, however, is not a pluralistic theology grounded in a hermeneutical principle of relativism. The answer is found in comparing Scripture with Scripture, relating metaphor to metaphor, and gaining that growing understanding that leads to the unity of the Spirit in the bond of peace as we discern one body and one Spirit in one hope of our calling.

NOTES

1. Paul Minear, *Images of the Church in the New Testament* (Philadelphia 1960) 28.
2. Austin Flannery, O.P., ed., *Vatican Council II: The Conciliar and Post Conciliar Documents* (Northport, N.Y. 1975, reprinted 1980, Wm. B. Eerdmans, Grand Rapids) 350–426. For a discussion of the drafting and revision process, see Herwi Rikhof, *The Concept of Church: A Methodological Inquiry into the Use of Metaphors in Ecclesiology* (London 1981) 13–38.
3. *Lumen Gentium* I:5 (Flannery, *Vatican Council* 353).
4. Pius XII, *Mystici Corporis Christi* in Claudia Carlen, ed., *The Papal Encyclicals 1939–1958* (Wilmington, N.C. 1981) 37–62 as cited in Rikhof, *The Concept of Church* 45, and in Avery Dulles, *Models of the Church* (Garden City, N.Y. 1974) 27.
5. (London, Shepherdstown, W.Va. 1981).
6. See, for example, his summary paragraph on p.205.
7. p.233.
8. Max Black cites the *Oxford English Dictionary* definition in his essay 'Metaphor' in *Models and Metaphors* (Ithaca 1962) 31.
9. ibid. 234. The quotation is from Pierre Duhem, *The Aim and Structure of Physical Theory*, trans. Philip P. Wiener (Princeton, N.J. 1954) 81.

10. C.S.Lewis, 'Bluspels and Flalansferes', in *The Importance of Language*, ed. Max Black (Englewood Cliffs, N.J. 1962) 36–50.
11. Sallie McFague TeSelle, *Speaking in Parables: A Study in Metaphor and Theology* (Philadelphia 1975) 59.
12. ibid. 58.
13. Rikhof, *The Concept of Church* 141.
14. A. Richardson, *Introduction to the Theology of the New Testament* (London 1958) 257. Cited in Minear, *Images of the Church* 21.
15. This is evident in the issues raised by Thomas S. Kuhn, *The Structure of Scientific Revolutions* (Chicago 1970^2). See the analysis by Paul Feyerabend, 'How to Defend Society against Science', in Ian Hacking, ed., *Scientific Revolutions* (New York 1981) 156–167. Kuhn's position is debated in Imre Lakatos and Alan Musgrave, eds., *Criticism and the Growth of Knowledge* (Cambridge 1970).
16. John M. Frame, 'Christianity and the Great Debates' (Course syllabus, Westminster Theological Seminary, Philadelphia n.d.) 24.
17. Paul Minear discusses the problem briefly, noting 'the radical discontinuity between the mind of the New Testament and our own mind.' He refers to 'the archaic mythology of the New Testament with its fantastic concepts of heaven, the angels, the demons, and hell—all repugnant to the scientific world views of modern churchgoers' (*Images of the Church* 16,17).
18. James Barr, *The Semantics of Biblical Language* (London 1961). See chap.2, 'The Current Contrast of Greek and Hebrew Thought' (8–20) and '*Dabar* "Word, Matter"' (129–140).
19. For example, Paul Radin, *Primitive Man as Philospher* (New York 1927). So, too, Claude Lévi-Strauss speaks of 'the false antinomy between logical and pre-logical mentality'. 'The savage mind is logical in the same sense and the same fashion as ours, though as our own it is only when it is applied to knowledge of a universe in which it recognizes physical and semantic properties simultaneously' (*The Savage Mind* [Chicago 1966] 268).
20. Rikhof, *The Concept of Church* 69.
21. (Springfield, MA 1965) 640.
22. Rikhof, *The Concept of Church* 83: 'in using and understanding language metaphorically, the rules governing the use of the sets of concepts or the conceptual realms involved are relaxed for this particular occasion, and on that level a combination is allowed which under normal circumstances would not be permitted.' See also pp. 119–121.
23. Max Black, *Models and Metaphors* 41ff.
24. Paul Ricoeur, *The Rule of Metaphor*, trans. Robert Czerny (Toronto 1977) 173–215.
25. ibid. 7.
26. Rikhof, *The Concept of Church* 121.
27. Black, *Models and Metaphors* 38ff.
28. See note 15.
29. Black, *Models and Metaphors* 236.
30. ibid. 238.
31. Rikhof, *The Concept of Church* 159.
32. Ricoeur, *The Rule of Metaphor* 240.

33. ibid. 242.
34. Black, *Models and Metaphors* 226, 228.
35. Ricoeur, *The Rule of Metaphor* 244, 245.
36. cf Kenneth E. Bailey, *Poet and Peasant* (Grand Rapids 1976).
37. Minear, *Images of the Church* 221.
38. For the use of these images see Paul Minear, ibid. chap.2.
39. ibid. 223.
40. Dulles, *Models of the Church* 8.
41. Thomas S. Kuhn, *Structure passim.*
42. Rikhof, *The Concept of Church* xii.
43. ibid.
44. Minear, *Images of the Church* 222.
45. Minear disputes the observation of Ernest Best that the body figure does not include the thought of expansion or service (ibid. 239f).
46. Anders Nygren, *Christ and His Church* (Philadelphia 1956) 89–100. Nygren qualifies this. It is shockingly put in *Mystici Corporis Christi* (par. 44), where 'The head cannot say to the feet: I have no need of you' is applied to Christ the Head needing his members!
47. Lucien Cerfaux, *The Church in the Theology of St. Paul* (New York 1959) 338–341. Cerfaux opposes W.L. Knox, *St. Paul and the Church of the Gentiles* (Cambridge 1939) 160ff., and others.
48. See Cerfaux, *The Church* 370; Pierre Benoit, 'Corps, Tête et Plérôme dans les Epîtres de la Captivité', *RB* 63 (1956) 26; Stephen Bedale, 'The Meaning of κεφαλή in the Pauline Epistles', *JTS* 5 (1954) 211–215; Herman Ridderbos, *Paul: An Outline of His Theology* (Grand Rapids 1975) 376–387; Yves M.-J. Congar, *Sainte Eglise* (Paris 1964) 29.
49. Congar, 'Peut-on définir l'église?', in *Sainte Eglise: Etudes et approches ecclésiologiques* (Paris 1964) 29.
50. *Mystici Corporis Christi* in Claudia Carlen, ed. *The Papal Encyclicals 1939–1958* (Wilmington, N.C. 1981) 37–62.
51. ibid. par.40,45: 'That Christ and His Vicar constitute one only Head is the solemn teaching of Our predecessor of immortal memory Boniface VIII in the Apostolic Letter *Unam Sanctam*; and his successors have never ceased to repeat the same.' Cf also par.44.
52. See Bonaventure Kloppenburg, *The Ecclesiology of Vatican II*, trans. Matthew J. O'Connell (Chicago 1974) 78 n.15. As late as the eleventh century, the 'mystical body' meant the eucharist. When it was used of the church it 'initially simply emphasized the traditional doctrine that the Eucharist signifies the Church and the ecclesial body is symbolized by the Eucharistic body.'
53. Minear, *Images of the Church* 238.
54. Dulles, *Models of the Church* 32.
55. See E.P. Clowney, *The Biblical Doctrine of the Church* (Phillipsburg, N.J. 1979) 87–92.
56. James Barr, *Semantics* 122. Barr attacks the linguistic error of 'unjustified determination'.
57. See E.P. Clowney, 'Note on *Sodh* and *Yesodh* in Qumran Literature,' in *Biblical Doctrine* 183–184.

58. ibid. 106–107.
59. I have attempted this in the work just cited.
60. ibid. 150ff.
61. Markus Barth, 'A Chapter on the Church—The Body of Christ', *Int* 12 (1958) 139 n.19.
62. E.P. Clowney, 'The Final Temple', *WTJ* 35 (1973) 156–189.
63. Minear, *Images of the Church* 226–227.
64. See KB 660; William L. Holladay, *A Concise Hebrew and Aramaic Lexicon of the O.T.* (Grand Rapids 1971) 257.
65. See André Parrot, *The Tower of Babel* (New York 1955) for a defence of the religious character of the Mesopotamian ziggurat: a small temple was built at the top of the stairway, a larger one at the bottom.
66. See Edmond Jacob's review of Parrot in *RHPR* 30 (1950) 137–141. 'In the O.T. man does not mount toward God but by an express command, as Moses did on Sinai; and he does not do it without trembling. Yahweh, to descend to the earth, does not have need for men to construct for him ways of access' (p. 140).
67. The Hebrew word in Gen.28:13 should be translated 'beside him' rather than 'above it'. The same phrase is found in the second appearance of God to Jacob at Bethel in Gen.35:13, 'God went up from beside him.' The preposition '*al*' ('above' or 'upon') is used to describe someone standing above one who is recumbent.
68. Walter Eichrodt, 'Is Typological Exegesis an Appropriate Method?' in Claus Westermann, ed., *Essays on Old Testament Hermeneutics* (Richmond, VA 1963) 234.
69. The typical interpretation assumed in the N.T. is studied in Leonhard Goppelt, *Typos: The Typological Interpretation of the Old Testament in the New* (Grand Rapids 1982).
70. Ricoeur, *The Rule of Metaphor* 244,245.
71. *Rhetorica* (Academia Regia Bouissica ed., 1831ff) III,11,1413a,1414. Cited in Friedrich Hauck, art. παροιμία, *TDNT*.5.854.
72. ibid. 856.
73. Schlier, art. παρρησία, *TDNT*.5.881.
74. Andrew J. Burgess, 'Irreducible Religious Metaphors', *Religious Studies* 8 (1972) 335–366.
75. ibid. 364.
76. Black, *Models and Metaphors* 40.
77. K. Stendahl in A. J. Fridrichsen, ed., *The Root of the Vine* (New York 1953) 67, quoted in Minear, *Models and Metaphors* 252.
78. Congar, *Sainte Eglise* 42.
79. Minear, *Images of the Church* 223.
80. E. D. Hirsch, Jr., *The Aims of Interpretation* (Chicago 1976) 6.
81. William Sanford LaSor, 'Interpretation of Prophecy', in Bernard L. Ramm *et al.*, *Hermeneutics* (Grand Rapids 1971) 98.
82. Vern S. Poythress, 'Analyzing a Biblical Text: Some Important Linguistic Distinctions', *SJT* 32 (1979) 113–137.
83. LaSor, 'Interpretation', 99.

84. Robert M. Grant, *A Short History of the Interpretation of the Bible* (New York 1963) 82ff.
85. Unpublished article, 'Science as Allegory'.
86. Rikhof, *The Concept of Church* 4–6.
87. Hirsch, *Aims* 2–6.
88. This tendency is described and critiqued by Rosemary Ruether, *Liberation Theology* (New York 1972) 10ff.
89. Dulles, *Models of the Church* 40–42.

5

Principalities and Powers
Opponents of the Church

P.T. O'BRIEN

A.   INTRODUCTION

The following study is an exegetical exercise which attempts to determine what the New Testament writers and Paul in particular meant by the phrase, 'principalities and powers', and its equivalents. At the same time the paper is a study in hermeneutics and the history of interpretation, for these and related phrases have been widely used in a variety of ways within contemporary theology. They function to define the concerns and mission of the church and are currently being applied in diverse political, cultural and ideological circumstances. Ronald Sider, for example, recently commented: 'To announce Christ's Lordship to the principalities and powers is to tell governments that they are not sovereign.'[1] Earlier in the same article Sider had noted: 'There is growing agreement that when St. Paul speaks of the principalities and powers . . . he refers *both* to the socio-political structures of human society *and* to unseen spiritual forces that undergird, lie behind and in some mysterious way help shape human socio-political structures.'[2] Sider's references to governments, and the principalities being identified, in part at least, with 'the socio-political structures of human society' are consistent with a recent trend among contemporary theologians. Are this and other diverse interpretations of the New Testament references to the powers legitimate? And what hermeneutical presuppositions are (implicitly or explicitly) appealed to in order to generate such conclusions?

The purpose of this study, which seeks to probe into these and related questions, is fivefold. First we shall provide a brief history of interpretation indicating how major interpreters since the end of the nineteenth century have understood Paul's references to the powers. Second, special attention will be paid to the significant hermeneutical presuppositions of these writers as well as to the principles of interpretation used by them. Next we shall attempt to enunciate the main lines of the New Testament teaching on the powers, though in the nature of the case our comments will necessarily be by way of summary. Fourth, some brief remarks will be made about the relationship of the powers to the structures. And finally, in the light of the preceding, some of the Christian's ongoing responsibilities will be set forth.

B. THE DEBATE OVER THE POWERS IN RECENT THEOLOGY

1. *Isolated References in the Nineteenth Century*

During the nineteenth century litle attention was paid to the principalities and powers as part of Paul's teaching. Statements about the powers were either read as a confirmation of the conventional orthodox doctrine about angels and devils, or else they were seen as the last vestiges of an antiquated mythology in Pauline thought on which more enlightened ages need waste no time. The statement of Otto Everling[3] is pertinent: 'The utterly subordinate significance of this segment of Paul's thought world seems to have become too generally axiomatic for one to give serious attention to it.'[4]

Other liberal theologians of the nineteenth century, regarding the cosmology of the New Testament as essentially mythical and obsolete in character, thought they could safely eliminate it along with all other mythological elements. They distinguished between the essence of religion and the temporary garb which it assumed. The kerygma was reduced by Harnack, as a representative example, to a few basic principles of religion and ethics which are timeless and eternal. Although it is only within concrete historical processes that they are realized, we are all capable of verifying them in our own experience in whatever period we happen to live. References, then, to the principalities and powers in Pauline thought were eliminated as part of that antiquated mythology.

2. The History of Religions School

Representatives of the history of religions school were the first to discover the extent to which the New Testament is permeated by mythology.[5] For them the importance of these documents lay not in their *teaching* about religion and ethics but in the *actual* religion and piety. All the mythological imagery with its apparent objectivity was either of secondary importance or else completely negligible. Martin Dibelius's work on the spirit-world in the thought of Paul[6] was a product of this school. In a detailed piece of scholarship he placed Paul's expressions in the context of contemporary religious thought. Following Everling, Dibelius sought to show that a world dominated by supernatural forces was central to Paul's thinking, that these forces were hostile to mankind, and that this was the framework within which Paul developed his views about man's existence and the work of Christ. Dibelius considered Paul's uniqueness to lie in his belief that the powers were conquered in Christ. But the mythological imagery itself was of value only from the viewpoint of comparative religion. Since in our time 'ideas of spirits and devils' are 'in the process of disappearing' the language of the powers has no meaning for us. So we must get to the essence of Paul's message concerning man's existence and Christ's work. The high-water mark of the apostle's teaching was the experience of mystical union with Christ, in whom God took symbolic form.

3. Bultmann and the Existentialist Approach

If little attention was paid to the powers in Pauline thought during the nineteenth century and early part of the twentieth, then in the 1930s a change occurred. A number of German theologians, after the rise of Nazism, began reading the relevant Pauline texts in a new way. Heinrich Schlier, one of the first to consider that these passages found a strong resonance in the atmosphere of the times, as early as 1930 observed that although the background of the Pauline conception of the powers had been studied in the context of comparative religion, 'we have generally neglected even to ask whether Scripture and Christian tradition might be thinking of definite life experiences when they speak of the devil and the demons'.[7] For Schlier the powers were not objective realities but projections of what we might call, with Bultmann, man's 'self-understanding'. Schlier was later to change his own theological position[8] but his contribution at this point of time was important since it gave expression to an existential understanding of the principalities and powers.

Bultmann himself had understood the powers as expressions, on the one hand, of man's inability to control his world and the future, and, on the other, in terms of the New Testament's call for existential emancipation.[9] What hermeneutical principles had led Bultmann to arrive at these conclusions? Central to his hermeneutic in relation to the New Testament was his understanding of myth.[10] For Bultmann the gospel is not separate or distinct from myth; rather, it is embodied in the mythical language of the New Testament. To discard the myth is to discard the gospel itself. Bultmann uses myth in three distinct though related ways (these are not necessarily fully compatible with each other): first, myth is a way of speaking 'of the other world in terms of this world, and of the gods in terms derived from human life'.[11] Second, myth explains unusual phenomena in terms of the invasion of supernatural forces. It is necessarily bound up with a primitive or pre-scientific way of looking at the world. So Bultmann writes:

> The cosmology of the New Testament is essentially mythical in character. The world is viewed as a three-storeyed structure, with the earth in the centre, the heaven above, and the world underneath. Heaven is the abode of God and of celestial beings. . . . The underworld is hell. . . . The earth . . . is the scene of the supernatural activity of God and his angels on the one hand, and of Satan and his demons on the other. These supernatural forces intervene in the course of nature and in all that men think and will and do.[12]

This particular view of myth had a long history, stemming from the period of the enlightenment, and it persisted in the intellectual circles in which Bultmann moved. Mythical thinking, then, was essentially uncritical thinking.

Bultmann's third concept of myth may be discerned in his statement: 'The real purpose of myth is not to present an

objective picture of the world, but to express man's understanding of himself in the world in which he lives. Myth should be
interpreted not cosmologically, but anthropologically, or better
still, existentially.'[13] These three distinguishable accounts of
myth Bultmann sought to hold together. As understood by him
myth is almost all-embracing and includes, for example, not only
the three-decker view of the universe, miracles, God's sending
his Son in the fullness of time, the resurrection of Christ as an
event, and all statements about future eschatology, but also those
motifs which have particular reference to our theme, viz. demon
possession and the notion that supernatural powers influence the
course of history.

Bultmann next enunciates the task facing the Christian interpreter of the New Testament. It is not that of trying to 'save the
kerygma by selecting some of its features and subtracting others,
and thus reduce the amount of mythology in it'.[14] Nor is it with
the older liberal theologians to regard mythology as relative and
temporary and therefore to eliminate it altogether while retaining
only the broad, basic principles of religion and ethics. Instead,
the New Testament itself, for the following reasons, compels us
to engage in the task of demythologization,[15] that is, of reinter-
preting the mythological elements along existential lines: first, its
mythological language is really intended to speak of human
existence and to challenge men to a new self-understanding and
existential decision. Second, various myths within the New
Testament contradict each other, thus demonstrating that myth
is no more than a way of speaking. Third, the process of
demythologizing has already begun in the New Testament itself,
especially in the way eschatological language is handled. So to
engage in the hermeneutical task of demythologizing is not to
reject Scripture but the world-view of Scripture, which is the
world-view of a past epoch. By demythologizing the interpreter
will eliminate false stumbling-blocks and 'bring into sharp focus
the real stumbling-block, the word of the cross'.[16]

Käsemann in his paper entitled 'The Eschatological Royal
Reign of God', which he read at the 1980 Melbourne W.C.C.
conference, carried through Bultmann's hermeneutical principles consistently with reference to the principalities and powers.
He acknowledged that when the New Testament referred to
these authorities it seemed to indicate that they were personal. It

was necessary, however, according to Käsemann, to 'criticize and demythologize the language and ideas of an antique world-view as out of date . . . since only in this way can we have a true perception of the reality of our contemporary life and present world' (p.4). Käsemann then reinterpreted the Pauline statements and understood them of *particular* demonic structures which need to be exorcized in the name of Christ.

By way of response it is not our intention to attempt a comprehensive critique of Bultmann's hermeneutics. Our aims are much more limited. But the following need to be noted in as much as they bear on contemporary interpretation of the Pauline references to the principalities and powers. In many respects Bultmann's existentialist interpretation crystallizes, though it develops beyond, previous scholarly assessments of the powers. At the same time the current debate cannot be adequately understood apart from his contribution. We may not be entirely satisfied with Bultmann's answers. But there is no doubt that he has raised some relevent questions in their most acute form.

(i) On the positive side, it is noted that Bultmann's hermeneutics is 'never *only* a matter of understanding, but also of *hearing* and of *appropriation*'.[17] Its purpose is to bring about encounter and dialogue. And although one may have serious questions about his demythologizing, the presupposition of such a reconstruction is that the New Testament writings have something to say to the present.

(ii) Bultmann has undoubtedly made a significant contribution to the issue of the interpreter's 'pre-understanding' as he approaches the text of the New Testament. He has argued that there is no neutral or presupposition-less exegesis, so that the hermeneutical task is a circular one, with constant interaction between object and subject, text and interpreter. In this dialectical process he claims there can be no finality, only an approximation to the truth of the Word of God in a particular culture or situation. The interpreter's pre-understanding is the critical factor in this process.[18] But Bultmann himself has been criticized by N. A. Dahl for 'absolutiz(ing) . . . his philosophical "pre-understanding" in such a way that he decides in advance what the New Testament writings may or may not really say'.[19] Even if Dahl's criticism is not wholly correct regarding Bultmann's *view* of pre-understanding (and the latter recognizes that preunderstanding is a starting point which must be corrected in the light of the text), the way in which he has let his own pre-understanding be shaped in *practice* is certainly open to criticism.[20] In effect his pre-understanding is essentially a pre-commitment to an existentialist interpretation of the gospel, resurrection, eschatology, and the powers, etc., in a twentieth-century Western cultural context.

(iii) Serious questions and criticisms have been raised about Bultmann's three-fold understanding of myth. On the one hand many consider his *concept* of myth to be too all-embracing.[21] It confuses myth and analogy and if pressed makes it in effect impossible to speak of God at all. Bultmann recognized that it was legitimate to talk of 'God as Creator' by analogy, but once he allows this, is it not possible to argue that much of the so-called 'mythological language' of the New Testament is metaphor, symbol or analogy after all? Several scholars have cautioned us about assuming the biblical writers necessarily used mythical imagery uncritically. Albright, for example, insists that they no more thought of heaven as literally 'up' than the modern man thinks of the sun as literally 'rising'. Minear has concluded that the author of the Apocalypse did not believe naïvely in a three-decker universe, while others have argued that myth is to be understood not as an outmoded primitive world-view, but as vivid imagery which functions with an inner logic. It is 'not a thing of the past, but characterizes man in any epoch'.[22] Further, the belief about supernatural interventions in the affairs of men is not necessarily primitive or pre-scientific, as the Enlightenment view of myth would imply. Pannenberg has rightly asserted: 'The acceptance of divine intervention in the course of events . . . is fundamental to every religious understanding of the world, including one which is not mythical in the sense in which comparative religion uses the term.'[23] And pertinently he adds that even belief in demons is not specifically mythical. It is clear that these last points are particularly significant for other interpreters besides those within the Bultmannian existentialist school.

(iv) On the other hand, if Bultmann's definition of myth is too all-embracing, then paradoxically his *understanding* of the *truth* of myth is too narrow. He has been attacked by his more radical disciples for not carrying through his demythologizing program further. If 'the self understanding of the man of faith is really the constant in the New Testament'[24] then where does Christology really fit in? If faith relates to man's possibility of authentic existence then this cannot be tied exclusively to Christ. Critics from the right have argued that Bultmann has reduced theology to anthropology, or at the least Christology to soteriology. And as far as the Pauline principalities are concerned Bultmann's reductionist interpretation leads him to assert:

> He (Paul) is thereby only expressing a *certain understanding of existence*: The spirit powers *represent* the reality into which man is placed as one full of conflicts and struggle, a reality which threatens and tempts.[25]

The objective, malevolent activity of Satan and his minions has been effectively reduced, even removed, through this demythologizing program.

4. *Cullmann's Two-Fold Interpretation: Angelic Powers and Civil Authorities*

We next turn to the important and influential contribution of Oscar Cullmann to the subject. Cullmann addressed himself to the question of the ἐξουσίαι ('authorities') in Rom.13:1.[26] To whom does this term refer? It is, of course, clear that the civil authorities are being spoken about. What has been in dispute is whether there is in ἐξουσίαι a double reference—that is, not only to the civil authorities but also the angelic powers standing behind and acting through these civil authorities. The suggestion of a double reference goes back to Martin Dibelius (who, however, later abandoned it) and, in addition to Cullmann, it was taken up by K. L. Schmidt, G. Dehn, K. Barth and others. Cullmann argued that the two-fold interpretation was 'thoroughly justified as an hypothesis, from the standpoints of philosophy, Judaistic concepts, and the early Christian and Pauline theology'.[27] His reasons[28] were as follows:

(i)   Whenever ἐξουσίαι occurs in the Pauline letters in the plural or in the plurally used singular with πᾶσα (except for Tit.3:1) it clearly signifies invisible angelic powers (1 Cor.15:24; Eph.1:21; 3:10; 6:12; Col.1:16; 2:10,15; cf 1 Pet.3:22).

(ii)   The subjection of the powers is a central dogma of the primitive Christian confession and therefore of Pauline thought.

(iii)   1 Cor.2:8 is a strong ground for the double reference to both spiritual and human forces, while in 1 Cor.6:1ff. the mention of angels in connection with the litigation by Christians in the civil courts is best explained by reference to the idea of the civil authorities as the executive agents of angel powers.

(iv)   Early Christianity shared with late Judaism the belief that invisible powers were at work behind the earthly phenomena; especially there was a firm belief in the angels of the nations.

Considerable opposition to Cullmann's theory was voiced by a number of critics on linguistic, exegetical, historical and dogmatic grounds. C. D. Morrison[29] charted the course of the debate, and the more important objects brought against the theory are as follows:

(i)   The term ἐξουσίαι is not accompanied here by ἀρχή nor does it form part of a list of (at least two) terms. The occurrence at Rom.13:1 thus differs from all others in the Pauline corpus whenever it refers to spiritual powers.

(ii)   Unlike other passages in Paul that have references to the powers, Romans 13 is not explicitly concerned with the work of Christ.

(iii)   Cullmann has drawn too much out of the text of 1 Cor.2:8 in understanding the rulers as both human and spiritual forces.[30]

(iv)   There is no evidence in the New Testament that the hostile spiritual powers were re-commissioned, after being subdued, to a positive service of Christ. If this was followed logically it would suggest that in Christ the powers themselves rule the believer. Quite the reverse. In being united to Christ believers are no longer subject to the spiritual powers of the world (cf. Col.2:20).

(v)   Paul's teaching in Rom.13:1–7 is best understood against an Old Testament prophetic, apocalyptic and wisdom tradition of God's appointment and use of human rulers for his own purposes.

Although Morrison[31] furthered Cullmann's hypothesis by seeking to prove that 'a common Graeco-Roman concept of the State' by which rulers were 'divinely appointed in relation to a cosmic system of spiritual powers' was shared alike by the

Graeco-Roman world, Hellenistic Jews and early Christians and therefore is an assumption lying behind Paul's use of ἐξουσίαι in Rom.13:1, serious doubts have been raised against it. The fact that nowhere in the New Testament is the relationship between civil rulers and spiritual powers explicitly affirmed stands against Morrison, and constitutes reason for doubting its presence.[32]

5. *Ethical and Socio-Political Structures*

We have already noted that a number of German theologians, during the period between the two world wars and especially after the rise of Nazism, began reading the Pauline texts about the powers in a new light. In the English-speaking context this discussion arose after World War II. As a post-war theory it assumed that when the apostle Paul spoke of the 'principalities and powers', as well as equivalent terms, he was alluding to structures of thought such as tradition, convention, law, authority and even religion, particularly as embodied in the state and its institutions, rather than to demonic intelligences. The exponents of this increasingly fashionable theory were all Western or Western-trained theologians, and this of course raises the question as to whether they were predisposed culturally to interpret the expressions of Paul along definite structural lines. Certainly the number of third world theologians writing on and reflecting this viewpoint was not large.

On this recent view Paul's obscure references to the heavenly powers speak relevantly to our own earthly situations. On the other hand, advocates of this new line have admitted they have had great difficulty in finding in the New Testament any allusions to social structures, which have become a significant modern preoccupation. The new theory now solves both problems simultaneously. 'We lose the demons and gain the structures, for the principalities and powers are structures in disguise.'[33]

In the following analysis we shall draw attention to the major contributions and later comment on the relevant hermeneutical principles.

(i)   Gordon Rupp[34] writing in the aftermath of the second World War drew attention to the Pauline expression 'principalities and powers' at the beginning of one of his books. By this phrase, borrowed from late Jewish apocalyptic thought, Paul meant 'supernatural cosmic forces, a vast hierarchy of angelic and demonic beings who inhabited the stars and . . . were the arbiters of human destiny', enslaving men 'beneath a cosmic totalitarianism'.[35] However, without any exegetical justification he simply transferred the expression to economic, social and political forces. Rupp spoke of the 'little people' who in every era had felt themselves to be nothing more than the playthings of great historical forces and now in the twentieth century believed they were the victims of 'great economic and sociological pressures'. Down the centuries, according to Dr. Rupp, the principalities and powers have assumed many disguises. Today, as terrifying and as deadly as ever, they are the economic, social and political forces.[36]

(ii)   Hendrik Berkhof's monograph, *Christ and the Powers*,[37] has been influential in this debate (for example, note Yoder's indebtedness). His thesis is that Paul borrowed the vocabulary of the powers from Jewish apocalyptic, yet his understanding of them was different. Jewish apocalypses thought primarily of the principalities and powers as heavenly angels; Paul regarded them as structures of earthly existence.[38] He demythologized them! Although the apostle may have 'conceived of the Powers as personal beings . . . this aspect is so secondary that it makes little difference whether he did or not'.[39] According to Berkhof such powers are to be identified with the στοιχεῖα τοῦ κόσμου ('elemental spirits of the universe') of Gal.4:3,9 and Col.2:8,20. He translates the expression as 'world powers' and considers they are seen in human traditions as well as religious and ethical rules. The powers (e.g. tradition, morality, justice and order) which were created by God have become tyrannical and the objects of worship. They both preserve and corrupt society. But Christ has overcome them, for in his cross and resurrection they have been 'unmasked as false gods' and 'the power of illusion' has been struck from their hands.[40] As a result Christians see through the deception of the powers and refuse, in principle at least, to be enslaved or intimidated by them. The 'Holy Spirit "shrinks" the powers before the eye of faith'[41] so that the believer sees their true creaturely existence. Also the church announces to the powers that their unbroken dominion has come to an end and wages a defensive warfare against them. It is thus along these lines that Berkhof sought to explain Eph.3:10 and 6:10–17.

(iii) The contribution of Amos N. Wilder to this debate, an article entitled 'Kerygma, Eschatology and Social Ethics',[42] has given a fresh and clear rationale for the place of the principalities and powers in a 'kerygmatic social ethic'. Wilder concedes that quantitatively the New Testament says little about politics, economics and the structure of social institutions. Qualitatively, however, it contains highly significant material. Wilder is concerned to find a truly scriptural basis for social ethics. He is not satisfied with a 'general undifferentiated summons to obedience or love', which he says is 'an impoverishment of the biblical ethic' and 'an unwarrantable assumption'. Recent biblical theological insights have placed this matter of social ethics in a new light so that it is now possible to set forth a kerygmatic social ethic using the whole Bible as a basis rather than some narrow dimension such as the social ideals of the prophets or Jesus. The kerygma with its appeal to the saving events of the divine operation in history and to the promise and fulfilment motif provides a genuinely biblical basis for this social ethics. Wilder then turns specifically to the Pauline statements about 'the principalities and powers' and 'the rulers of the world'. He claims the apostle is using mythological language to describe 'the victory of the gospel over the tyrants of this world, its false authorities'.[43] The apostle's language and perspective must be demythologized or 'translated into contemporary terms without forfeiting the evangelical substance'.[44] Wilder, however, distinguishes this demythologizing from Bultmann's programme of 'existential interpretation', because he believes the latter's individualistic and ahistorical approach cannot do justice to the full dimensions of the New Testament message.

For Wilder the mythological-eschatological victory over the cosmic tyrants in the cross of Christ (Col.2:15) is not concluded. 'This struggle continues in the eschatological experience of the church itself, to have its final conclusion only at the return of Christ.'[45] And how can this struggle be described? To answer in non-mythological terms, it is a conflict with 'the structural elements of unregenerate society, the false authorities of culture. The dethroning of such authorities and the weakening of such power principles constitute the central tasks of Christian social action.'[46]

Paul has used the language of his time to describe what we call secular error, secular false gods, the idols of the market place,

etc. These are 'the rulers of this age which are passing away'.
When the Christian church attacks these false authorities in
culture and politics it is engaged in a strategic attack upon the
corrupted structures of society, that is, against 'the world-rulers
of this darkness' (Eph.6:12).

6.   *Structures and Unseen Spiritual Forces – A Conservative Viewpoint*

Under this broad category several recent writers representing a
conservative theological standpoint need to be considered. Each
has been influenced by the work of Berkhof; at the same time
they take the debate still further in a 'political' direction. Each
interprets the powers in a two-fold way, i.e. the principalities are
regarded as *both* the socio-political structures of human society
and the unseen spiritual forces lying behind these structures. In
observing a double significance they differ formally from the
position of Rupp, Wilder and others. Materially, however, the
differences with these latter writers are not great, for although
they concede Paul's 'powers' refer *also* to unseen spiritual
forces,[47] their whole emphasis falls upon the principalities as
structures, especially of a political kind.

(i)   The treatment of the Pauline principalities and powers
by John Howard Yoder[48] is set within a wider context of
Christian social ethics in which the author advocates a specific
kind of pacifism (which he calls 'revolutionary subordination')
and 'a theologically coherent radical attitude toward society'.
Yoder argues that biblical scholarship over the last generation
has come to a striking degree of clarity and unanimity[49] regarding the 'powers'. He thus seeks 'not to (explicate) . . . the
Pauline doctrine of the powers . . . but to (illuminate) . . . the
way in which this doctrine meshes with modern understandings
and questions'.[50] His study, then, is not a work of exegesis,
though he would claim it is exegetically based and hermeneutically valid.

Yoder decisively rejects the view, held by so many earlier and
present day scholars, that Paul's teaching on the powers is
'archaic or meaningless. . . . (Rather it) reveals itself to be a very
refined analysis of the problems of society and history.' In fact, it
is 'far more refined than the other ways in which theologians have

sought to describe the same realities in terms only of "creation" or "personality"'.[51] Paul, in his references to 'principalities and powers', 'thrones and dominions', etc., was using language of political colour. The relevance of this language to 'the institutions and ideologies of our times need not imply the rejection of all the more literal meanings which the language of the demonic and of bondage can also have'.[52] But such a statement appears to be simply a concession on Yoder's part. For him the powers are pre-eminently the structures, institutions and ideologies of our times, a point which comes out clearly in his later exposition.

The author examines the issue of political involvement in the context of the Christian's attitude towards the civil order. In his dealing with the issue of a responsible political involvement which is compatible with the Anabaptist understanding of discipleship, Yoder speaks of 'revolutionary subordination' and 'accepting powerlessness'. The liberating power of the gospel eradicates the patterns of domination and submission. 'Revolutionary subordination', the proper Christian posture toward the civil order, is based in part on the Pauline advice to women and slaves as well as the manner in which he advises Christians to relate to the state. Significant for our purposes, however, is that the whole question of the Christian's political involvement, with its 'revolutionary subordination' and 'accepting powerlessness', is integrally related to the confrontation with the powers which took place in the death and resurrection of Jesus Christ. According to Yoder 'the proper Christian posture toward the civil order cannot be decided on the basis of a theocratic conception or an appeal to general political obligations. . . . [These] patterns must finally be judged in the light of the cross of Christ.'[53] The Christian's submission to the state grows out of an attempt to imitate the work of Christ on the cross. He adds that 'only at one point, only on one subject — but then consistently, universally — is Jesus our example: in his cross'.[54]

Space prevents us from examining Yoder's position in detail. However, three brief criticisms relating to the overall purposes of this essay may be made. First, we cannot 'consistently and universally' imitate the work of Christ on the cross.[55] Second, it may be seriously questioned whether Christ's death on the cross provides a pattern for the Christian's political involvement at all. Third, Yoder describes Jesus' relationship to the powers as one of 'subordination'. His work is characterized by 'the voluntary subordination of one who knows that another regime is normative'.[56] But 'subordination' describes Jesus' relationship to the Father. He was victorious over the powers in his cross, not subordinate to them in some revolutionary way. The New Testament consistently interprets the clash with the forces of darkness at the cross as denoting Jesus' victory over them (Col.2:15; cf Jn.12:30; Heb.2:14). One wonders whether Yoder has been influenced by his own background and, in particular, Mennonite notions of pacifism when he views our Lord's death in this way.

(ii) Richard Mouw's treatment of the powers, like that of Yoder, is set within the context of political questions. In his volume, *Politics and the Biblical Drama*,[57] he contends that to discuss theology is to raise political issues. In particular the questions he raises (What is the 'kingly' task of the Christian community? and, Is it permissible for Christians to attempt to gain political power?) lead him to an examination of the Pauline references to 'principalities and powers'. He then helpfully surveys the literature produced on this theme in the two decades prior to 1976, noting the following points of consensus: (a) Paul believed in a plurality of created spiritual powers. (b) Although drawing on a biblical tradition the apostle went beyond the Old Testament by 'depersonalizing' the powers, partially at least (note the indebtedness to Berkhof).[58] They may now be identified with national or racial groupings, religious doctrine, moral rules, technology, sexual desires, altruism, etc. However, Mouw does recognize the problems of demythologizing Paul's language and wonders whether the apostle's statements 'commit us to the belief that there is an "ontological" or "causal" residue that exists "over and above" observable individual and sociological factors'.[59] In other words, to what extent does Paul's language commit us to regarding them as personal spiritual beings? (c) The powers exercise their influence in the regular patterns and structures of social life. This is not to suggest, however, that 'political leaders are demon possessed or communing with the spirits in some popular sense of these phrases'.[60] As created instruments of God the powers were intended to assist man's orderly existence, but now subsequent to the fall they present themselves to us as possible objects of idolatry.

Mouw also recognizes several areas of disagreement in the current debate over the powers: (a) How many references does Paul actually make to the principalities? (b) How has the redemptive work of Christ affected the status of the powers? That is, in what sense have they been overthrown and yet continue to exist, inimical to man and his interests? (c) How does the Christian community relate to the powers in the light of Christ's redemptive work?

The author notes that in previous discussions of the powers writers begin by describing the scope of the topic in very general terms; but they almost always apply it to the political realm alone. While Mouw himself recognizes the need for study and application in other areas he proceeds to do the same thing! Finally, in a lengthy section dealing with the powers and political involvement Mouw interacts in detail with Yoder's presentation. This debate is set within the Anabaptist-Reformed dialogue and, while rejecting Yoder's specific recommendations regarding 're-volutionary subordination' and 'accepting powerlessness', he concedes the latter's work, *The Politics of Jesus*, with its treatment of the Pauline powers, adds significantly to our understanding of the political message of the New Testament. Mouw concludes that we do not need to face death in the way Jesus did, nor confront the powers after the manner of his work on the cross. 'His was *the* confrontation with the Powers — the means of their ultimate defeat.'[61] What then is the responsibility of the Christian in the light of Christ's victory? We do not need to fear the powers because of Christ's encounter with them; rather, we can now enter their domain and engage in political activity 'seeking to promote justice and righteousness in the confidence that they cannot separate us from God's love'. But what has happened to the preaching of the gospel and the turning of people from darkness to light and from the power of Satan to God? Is all this subsumed under a political message?

7. *Principalities and Powers: Angels Serving God, not Hostile Supernatural Authorities*

The most recent examination of our subject is also the most thorough and comprehensive exegetical treatment to date. I refer to the Cambridge S.N.T.S. Monograph of Wesley Carr, entitled

Angels and Principalities and published by Cambridge University Press in 1981. As the sub-title suggests this work is concerned with the background, meaning and development of Paul's phrase 'the powers and authorities'. Carr challenges the commonly accepted scholarly opinion that Paul and his contemporaries inhabited a world thought to be dominated by hostile superhuman powers, of whom Jews and Gentiles alike lived in fear. Like many previous scholars Carr began his study with an examination of the pre-Christian Jewish and pagan background to the apostle's thought. But his conclusions are very different from those of his predecessors. He claims that in the Jewish writings up to the mid-first century A.D. terms such as ἀρχαί, ἐξουσίαι and δυνάμεις are confined to the angels and archangels of Yahweh and never are used of demonic forces. The few references in paganism during this period to angels and powers have no clear point of contact with Paul's work. From his study of the background material Carr concludes that 'the concept of mighty forces that are hostile to man, from which he sought relief, was not prevalent in the thought world of the first century A.D.'[62]

In the central part of his book Carr examines the major Pauline texts under the headings: the powers and Christ triumphant (Col.1:16; 2:14f.,18; Phil.2:10; the 'enemies' of Ps.110:1), the powers and the spiritual world (Rom.8:38f. and references in Ephesians), and the powers in relation to the political world (Rom.13:1–7; 1 Cor.2:6–8; 6:1ff.). The principalities and powers, according to Carr, are to be understood in a good sense of spiritual beings which are in a positive relationship to God. The references in Colossians and Ephesians (except 6:12) contribute to the Christology of the two letters 'not by pointing to any achievement of Christ in battle against hostile powers, but by associating him with God as the one who receives the recognition and worship of the heavenly host'.[63] In Romans 13 and 1 Corinthians 2 ἐξουσίαι refers simply to human authorities, while 1 Cor.6:1ff., with its reference to angels, in no way contributes to the interpretation of Rom.13:1. Carr argues that Paul's usage of the language of the powers and associated terms conforms to basic Jewish usage. Further, this terminology would have conveyed to the Gentile readers of Paul's letters notions of power and authority that are associated with God rather than with hostile forces.

However, according to Carr, a development took place in Christian thinking about the powers after the time of Paul. The interpretation of the work of Christ as a defeat of hostile powers is certainly found in Christian thought by the end of the second century A.D. There is a humanizing and psychologizing of the powers after the mid-first century in which magic, divination, idols, planets and fate played their part. The climax of this development occurred in Origen with whom there is a reinterpretation of the Pauline texts and development in the doctrine of the atonement. But, Carr concludes, this was far from being a fundamental part of the background and proclamation of the Christian message. The idea of mighty forces of evil being ranged against man was not part of the earliest Christian understanding of the world and the gospel.

If Carr's conclusions are correct, then his study has important ramifications for the contemporary debate about the meaning and relevance of the Pauline powers. Bultmann and many of his followers concluded Paul's language needed to be demythologized. Berkhof suggested Paul himself had demythologized Jewish language. Carr contends, in effect, that the language of evil powers does not need to be demythologized at all, since the principalities are good, not evil.

In spite of the many fresh insights of Carr's monograph one must conclude that his work is not convincing for the following reasons:

(i)   There is still no consensus among scholars regarding the precise significance of the Jewish and pagan background material to the Pauline statements about the powers. All sorts of contrasting conclusions have been drawn from the time of Dibelius through Cullmann and Morrison up to the present with Carr's monograph. This most recent work makes claims that, at best, are only provisional (see below). Certainly Carr's reading of the texts runs counter to the commonly accepted scholarly opinion that Paul and his contemporaries inhabited a world believed to be dominated by hostile superhuman powers, of whom Jews and Gentiles alike lived in fear.

(ii)   A major weakness of many of the studies on this Pauline theme of the powers is the limited nature of their investigation, and Carr's work is no exception. The issue of the Pauline principalities ought to be set not only against the contemporary background of first century Palestine but also within the wider framework of the holy war tradition in Scripture, including both the Old Testament relating to the God who fights and the renewal of that war tradition in the ministry of Jesus in the New. The author's inability to see that the demons which Jesus confronted in the Gospels have anything to do with the principalities and powers of Paul's letters is a serious weakness (see below). Carr's monograph fails because it is not set within or checked against an integrated biblical theology.[64]

(iii) At an exegetical level Carr's handling of Col.2:14f.[65] and other Pauline texts is in our judgment unsatisfactory. Admittedly Col.2:14f. is a notoriously difficult crux and on a number of exegetical issues scholars have been divided, e.g. the relationship of the forgiveness in v 13 to what follows; whether or not we have a hymnic fragment; if so, its relatinship to the context; the meaning and the nature of the χειρόγραφον, etc. But Carr has erred in removing every note of conflict from the passage and therefore in rejecting any idea of victory over or defeat of alien enemy powers.

(iv)　This criticism is confirmed when we note the author's handling of Eph.6:12. He is obliged to say that the verse is unlikely to have been part of the original Pauline text since it represents a departure or declension from his notion of the Christian life and of the nature of the world. There is no textual evidence in support of this contention. Since the text as it stands does not fit Carr's reconstruction we must conclude that his understanding of Paul's thought, at this point, is incorrect. Not all the powers are 'goodies' even though Carr thinks they are.

(v)　Finally, questions must therefore be raised as to whether Carr has really grasped correctly the Pauline world view at all. And since this conflict and victory motif is taught in other documents of the New Testament (see above), as Carr himself concedes, it would seem that the notion of mighty forces of evil ranged against man was consistently part of the earliest Christian understanding of the world and the gospel.

C.　HERMENEUTICAL ASSUMPTIONS AND METHODS

In the previous sketch we sought to indicate how major exponents since the end of the nineteenth century have understood Paul's references to the powers. Comments and criticisms have been made along the way. The area of study is a limited [66] though significant one. There is considerable value in examining a narrow theme such as the principalities and powers since it is then possible to focus on significant hermeneutical factors. We now turn to evaluate the important assumptions of these writers as well as the interpretational methods employed by them.

1. Mythical Language and an Outmoded World-View

Any study of the principalities and powers quickly runs into problems of language, for the apostle Paul (not to mention other New Testament writers) uses terminology that is strange to us. The majority of theologians examined above thus *assume* that such statements about spiritual powers were last vestiges of an antiquated mythology in Pauline thought which needed to be removed by one method or another. Everling in the nineteenth century believed no serious attention ought to be given to it. The older liberal theologians said these mythological elements could be safely eliminated as part of the temporary garb, rather than essence of religion. Dibelius recognized that a world dominated by evil supernatural forces was central to Paul's thinking, but nowadays ideas of spirits and devils have no meaning for us. Bultmann, on the other hand, did not seek to discard the mythological language for this would involve discarding the kerygma itself. He too assumed that mythical thinking was uncritical and necessarily bound up with a primitive or pre-scientific way of looking at the world. But the mythical elements were to be reinterpreted along existential lines.

More recent writers from a variety of theological standpoints (including an evangelical one), presumably embarrassed by the mythical language of the apostle, also speak of demythologizing the powers. Rupp and Stringfellow simply transfer the expression to economic, social and political forces; Wilder, who rejects Bultmann's individualistic and ahistorical approach of existential interpretation, nevertheless claims that the apostle's language and perspective must be 'demythologized' or translated into contemporary terms without forfeiting the evangelical substance.

Berkhof, whose writings have been influential in evangelical circles, argues that Paul himself 'demythologized' the powers, regarding them as structures of earthly existence. His understanding, at this point, is different from that of late Jewish apocalyptic which thought of the powers as heavenly angels.

Mouw, writing from a Reformed background, recognizes the need to 'demythologize' the principalities, though he does concede that there may be an 'ontological or causal residue' over and above what results from the demythologizing process.

We have already examined the question of myth and the mythological language of the New Testament in the context of Bultmann's existential interpretation. Several have noted: (i) that myth is not to be understood as part of an outmoded primitive world-view, but characterizes man in any epoch; (ii) that belief about supernatural interventions in the affairs of men is neither mythical, naïve nor pre-scientific (as the Enlightenment view would imply); (iii) and that belief in demons is not specifically mythical, as Pannenberg rightly points out.

Further, it is most important to note that certain third world theologians have often claimed that a biblical, and especially Pauline, perspective on the powers is perfectly intelligible in their own cultural contexts. The present writer had this point forcibly brought home to him on more than one occasion when teaching (over a ten year period) in an Indian theological college at a graduate and post-graduate level: a number of those from southern Asia who were studying in the college expressed their dissatisfaction with some Western commentaries on the Gospels and the Epistles because of their failure to take seriously the accounts about demons, exorcism, or Christ's defeat of them. The biblical and Pauline world view did not present a stumbling block to these younger third world scholars.

The problem lies with many contemporary Western theologians and their cultural conditioning; they have allowed the latter to dictate their understanding of the biblical texts with the result that an increasingly fashionable view, viz., that the Pauline powers designate modern socio-political structures, has become the new orthodoxy. One way or another they have come to regard the apostle's statements as a concession or accommodation to his own milieu which we must then lay aside, rather than as reflecting a divine view of reality.

2.   Interpretation of Background as a Hermeneutical Principle

Our investigation into the scholarly study of the Pauline principalities has raised in a particularly acute form a series of distinct though related hermeneutical questions about the cultural context of or background to the apostle's statements. Pressing issues arise: what where the Jewish and pagan backgrounds to the Pauline teaching? Was Paul influenced by them, or did he modify them? If so, in what ways? And are we committed to such a viewpoint as part of the apostolic teaching? As we have noted, Dibelius, Cullmann and Carr give varying answers to the first question. Furthermore, their particular interpretations of the background to the apostle's thought greatly influences, even controls, their exegesis of the Pauline texts. So Cullmann sees a double reference to angelic powers and civil authorities in ἐξουσίαι ('authorities') at Rom.13:1, because he believes, in part at least, that this was confirmed by the common view early Christianity shared with late Judaism about invisible powers being at work behind the earthly phenomena. The double reference was present, even when not explicitly stated by Paul, since it underlay his thinking. Carr, on the other hand, interprets the background material about the supernatural powers in quite another way—they are good, not evil—and so he arrives at quite different conclusions from his study of the Pauline texts. Berkhof's view is different again: Paul took over the language of the powers and the notion that they influence events on earth from his intellectual and religious environment. But the apostle himself 'demythologized' the principalities so that they were structures of earthly existence rather than heavenly angels or the like. We do not wish to suggest that a careful scholarly study of each of the possible backgrounds to the Pauline statements concerning the powers is unnecessary. Quite the reverse. My own view is that insufficient attention has been paid to the terminology of the Book of Daniel (esp. chap.7), and that it provides a basis for much of the New Testament, and in particular Pauline, teaching on the principalities and powers.[67] But in the context of the current debate the cynic might be tempted to say that, in some cases at least, the interpreter has read his pre-understanding into the first century background material and from this source into the Pauline teaching itself.

3. Pre-Understanding and the Text

In the recent hermeneutical debate, particularly since the contribution of Bultmann, the issue of the interpreter's pre-understanding as he approaches the text of the New Testament has been regarded as extremely important. Bultmann is right in arguing there is no neutral or presupposition-less exegesis. There is a constant interaction between subject and object, text and interpreter. But this does not mean there can be only an approximation to the truth of the Word of God in a particular culture or situation.

The interpreter's pre-understanding is not to be regarded as definitive, but nor is he to lay aside his own preliminary understanding, becoming a kind of *tabula rasa* who then indulges in some form of pneumatic exegesis. Instead, he must allow his own presuppositions and pre-understanding to be modified or even completely reshaped by the text itself. An exegesis guided rigidly by pre-understanding will be able to establish only what the interpreter already knows. So there must be constant dialogue between interpreter and text. The hermeneutical circle (or spiral, as some have recently suggested) is not only unavoidable but also desirable. As the text is given priority so it will interpret the interpreter; the authority of Scripture is taken seriously and God's Word speaks to me in my situation.[68]

As far as the Pauline teaching on the powers is concerned, many expositors, as we have already seen, cannot accept the notion that these principalities are personal, supernatural beings who were defeated by Christ in his death. One way or another writers on this theme representing all shades of theological opinion have sought to evade this conclusion. Now if by careful grammatical and historical exegesis it can be shown that the Pauline language is not speaking of such beings, well and good. But in most cases the arguments have been along other lines, and one wonders whether the pre-understandings are not at best presuppositions which have not adequately been tested, or at worst prejudices.

The same kind of question might be levelled against the complementary notion that the powers are to be identified with the structures of human society, particularly of a political kind. The hermeneutical methods employed vary (cf. Käsemann and Mouw)[69] but the conclusions are the same. It might of course be argued that the general consistency of the final results points to the correctness of the conclusions. But our contention is that the destination had already been chosen and it did not particularly matter which route was taken to reach this single goal! A particular vision of social justice (which on other grounds may be quite appropriate) has become so strong that it begins to exercise a hermeneutical control.

4. Interpretation and Biblical Theology

In evaluating the work of Wesley Carr we have already noted that a major weakness of many studies on this Pauline theme has been the limited nature of their investigation. I refer to the wider framework of the holy war tradition in Scripture, from Old Testament to New, within the prophetic tradition and the ministry of Jesus. In short, the Pauline powers are not studied within an integrated biblical theology in which the ultimate purposes of God for his creation are expounded. The victory of Christ over Satan and his minions can properly be understood within those revealed purposes of God, and at the same time the ongoing responsibilities of Christian people *vis-à-vis* the powers can be discerned. Questions as to whether the Christian has any political responsibilities can then be answered in the light of this integrated biblical theology rather than through some slick identification of the powers with political structures. Mouw and to a lesser extent Wilder have indicated an awareness of this need, but neither has developed the point nor effectively checked his own pre-understanding in the light of it.

D. THE MAIN LINES OF NEW TESTAMENT TEACHING ON THE POWERS

A variety of viewpoints about the powers in Paul has been presented in our historical survey. In significant instances these results have reflected differing hermeneutical assumptions and methods. Conscious of some of the hermeneutical pitfalls, we propose to look at the main lines of the New Testament teaching on the theme, especially in the light of the dominant view that the principalities are concrete historical, social or psychic structures or institutions.

1. Texts in Ephesians and Colossians

The three main references in Ephesians to the principalities and powers are 1:20–21; 3:10 and 6:10ff.[70] In the first, Christ is said to have been raised by God 'far above all rule and authority, power and dominion. . . . ' The difficulty with interpreting this to mean 'far above all earthly rulers and institutions' is that the realm in which Christ has been supremely exalted is specifically designated as 'in the heavenlies'[71] at God's right hand. Earthly structures do not fit this context. At chap.3:10, again because of the allusion to 'the heavenly places', the interpretation which considers Paul to be asserting that God's manifold wisdom is made known through the church to the power structures on earth is very strange indeed. Finally in chap.6:10ff. the Christian's spiritual warfare is said to be 'not with flesh and blood, but with principalities and powers. . . .' On the more recent view this must mean that the believer does not war against human forces, but demonic structures. However there are several serious weaknesses with this understanding: first, as in the two previous references, there is the awkward addition of the phrase 'in the heavenly places'. These principalities and powers are in the heavenly realm. Second, the references to 'the world rulers of this present darkness' and 'the spiritual hosts of wickedness', as well as to the kind of armour needed to withstand them, fit supernatural powers more easily, particularly when it is noted that the devil is mentioned twice (vv 11,16) in this context. The view that the phrase means 'not with human but with demonic forces', which until recent times has been universally held, is still more satisfactory on exegetical grounds. Stott,[72] after his exegetical critique, claims, 'I have not come across a new theorist who takes into adequate account the fact that all three references to the principalities and powers in Ephesians also contain a reference to the heavenly places, that is, the unseen world of spiritual reality.' Perhaps this is also why both Caird and Barth, when writing their commentaries on the Letter to the Ephesians, modified their earlier positions in the direction of supernatural spiritual forces.

The evidence of Colossians is best understood along similar lines. At chap.1:16 the principalities and powers, together with thrones and dominions as part of 'all things', have been created in Christ, as well as through him and for him. These same authorities are said to have been reconciled to him (v 20) so that the universe is again placed under its head and cosmic peace has been restored. When Paul speaks of reconciliation on this wide front he probably includes the notion of pacification, since some of the principalities and powers are not depicted as gladly surrendering to God's grace but as submitting against their wills to a power they cannot oppose.[73] Although the point cannot be established decisively from vv 16 and 20, the most natural interpretation is that four classes ('thrones, dominions, principalities and powers') of spiritual and supernatural forces (possibly representing the highest orders of the angelic realm) are in view.[74] In our judgment this personal interpretation also makes the most sense out of chap.2:15. In a statement full of picturesque language and graphic metaphors Paul asserts that God stripped the principalities and powers—who kept men and women in their dreadful clutches because they possessed the damning indictment, man's signed acknowledgment of his indebtedness—of their authority and dignity. Not only so, but having divested these principalities on the cross God exposed to the universe their utter helplessness. He has paraded these powerless 'powers and principalities' in his triumphal procession in Christ, making plain to all the magnitude of his victory. Their period of rule is finished; they must worship and serve the victor. They have been pacified (1:20); overcome and reconciled, yet not finally destroyed or appeased. They continue to exist, opposed to man and his interests (Rom.8:38,39). But they cannot finally harm the person who is in Christ, and their ultimate overthrow though future is certain (1 Cor.15:24–28). Such language describes supernatural cosmic forces, a vast hierarchy of angelic and demonic beings, as Käsemann acknowledges when he admits that the language and ideas need to be demythologized.

Before leaving Colossians a comment should be made regarding the expression 'the elements of the world' στοιχεῖα του κόσμος (Col.2:8,20; Gal.4:3; cf v 9). The precise meaning of this phrase has puzzled Christian interpreters since very early times, as Bandstra has shown in his stimulating study on the history of the exegesis of these passages.[75] One line of interpretation has been to regard κόσμος as denoting the material, physical world, with στοιχεία pointing to the elemental parts of that world. Eduard Schweizer,[76] a recent commentator on Colossians, has pursued this line of the physical elements. He suggests that the Colossian 'philosophy', which Paul was seeking to correct in his letter, had been influenced by Pythagorean ideas in which cosmic speculation about the elements had been ethicized. The elements exercised power in much the same way as the law did. Purification of the soul took place by abstaining from meat, etc. To behave in accordance with these elements was a matter of life and death, but in fact led to a kind of slavery to innumerable legalistic demands. Whether Schweizer's detailed arguments with reference to a Pythagorean background convince contemporary New Testament scholars or not, he has certainly opted for an impersonal understanding of στοιχεῖα, meaning 'elements' or 'elemental principles', and such a view lends itself more easily to being reinterpreted with reference to a structural understanding of the principalities and powers. However, the majority of commentators this century have understood the στοιχεῖα τοῦ κόσμου in Galatians and Colossians as denoting spiritual beings, regarded as personal and active in the physical and heavenly elements. It is probable that in the syncretistic teaching being advocated at Colossae these στοιχεῖα were grouped with the angels and seen as controlling the heavenly realm and man's access to God's presence.[77] (Jewish apocalyptic literature had already associated angels closely with the heavenly powers. According to Jubilees 2:2 each of the elements had its own angel to rule over it, while in Enoch 60:11,12 reference is made to the spirits of the various natural elements. In the New Testament at Acts 7:53; Gal.3:19; and Heb.2:2 the Jewish tradition regarding the angelic mediation of the law is mentioned, and in Gal.4:3 some close connection between, or identification of, these angels and the στοιχεῖα is required.)

2.   *A Survey of the Wider New Testament Teaching*

Up to this point our critical comments have been made with reference to the evidence of Ephesians and Colossians only. It is now necessary to survey the wider New Testament teaching, though in the nature of the case our remarks will necessarily be brief.

The powers of evil are referred to by an unexpected variety of names in the New Testament, and they appear in the Synoptic Gospels, John, many of the epistles and the Book of Revelation, thereby showing that a concern with these spiritual forces was a very important matter to the New Testament writers, a concern that continued in the subapostolic age. In addition to 'principalities' and 'powers' we read of 'authorities', 'dominions', 'thrones', 'princes', 'lords', 'angels', 'devils', and 'unclean or wicked spirits'. In the singular there is also mention of 'Satan' or 'the devil', who is called 'Beelzebul', 'Belial', 'the evil one', 'the accuser', 'the destroyer', 'the adversary' and 'the enemy'.[78] He also appears as 'the prince of demons', 'the prince of this world', and 'the prince of the power of the air'. Despite the variety in nomenclature, the overall picture is the same: a variety of evil forces under a unified head. The New Testament is reserved in its statements about the principalities; it has no theoretical or speculative interest in them. It provides no description of the phenomena, and makes no attempt to differentiate among them or to arrange the names or appearances systematically. It would appear that the names given to the powers of evil are in large measure interchangeable. Unlike their Jewish and pagan predecessors the New Testament writers had no interest in building up demonologies; they enumerated at random, only in order to show that these enemy forces were one and all disarmed by Jesus Christ. The prevailing belief in the demonic throughout the ancient world is significant. Nowhere does Jesus have to explain himself when exorcising demons, either on Jewish or on Gentile soil. The same is true of the apostles as well as in the subapostolic age. One distinction, however, is clearly drawn in the New Testament, viz. that the demons, spirits, angels, principalities and powers are regarded as subordinate to Satan or the devil. They are his innumerable powers seen as organized into a single empire (note especially Mk.3:22–30; cf Lk.10:17f.; Rev.12:9; 16:13ff.). They are manifestations of the devil's power.

The New Testament teaches that the principalities and powers are kinds of personal beings. This is obvious from the names that they bear (they are called gods, princes and angels, while Satan is the prince of this world, the god of the world, the accuser, the adversary, the destroyer, etc.), and from the nature of their operations and activities. To speak of 'personal beings' means that they 'manifest themselves as beings of intellect and will, which can speak and be spoken to. They are something which is capable of purposeful activity.'[79] This is not to suggest that they are always encountered as individuals. Sometimes they are examples of a species (cf Mk.5:9, 'My name is Legion for we are many.'). The principalities are not only kinds of personal beings with will and intelligence, but also beings of power.

There are, in the New Testament, five stages in the drama of the principalities and powers, and it may be convenient for us to mention these in order:

(i)   Their original creation

In a passage already referred to, Col.1:16, we noted that all things were created through Christ. The statement is amplified in the following words: 'whether thrones or powers or rulers or authorities; all things were created by him and for him'. The forces of tyranny that hold sway over men's lives—and perhaps some of the Colossians were troubled by this—are, in fact, a part of creation and subject to Christ as Lord (cf Rom.8:38,39).

(ii)   Their subsequent fall

Several passages in the New Testament refer to the subsequent fall of these supernatural authorities, e.g. Jude 6 and 2 Pet.2:4. At the same time the hymnic passage of Col.1:15–20 implies a serious dislocation or breach. Although there is no specific mention of it, a cosmic rupture of enormous proportions is implied, since the high point of the hymn refers to the reconciling work of Christ, by which 'all things' that have been created are now pacified in Christ's death. Col.2:15 is to be understood along similar lines, for the principalities needed to be disarmed and their utter helplessness made plain to all since they had rebelled against their creator. They became independent and autonomous, manifesting a self-centredness that is in opposition to God and his power.

(iii)   Christ's defeat of the powers of evil

In most of the New Testament references to the powers of evil there is some mention of God or Christ's supremacy or victory over them. 1 Jn.3:8 succinctly summarizes the reason for our Lord's coming: 'The reason the Son of God appeared was to destroy the works of the devil.' 'During those thirty odd years the key battle of the history of the universe was being conducted, and both sides knew it.'[80] Moreover, Jesus' triumph over the principalities and powers of evil is a major theme of the New

Testament. Our Lord is supreme in the temptation, when, driven by the Spirit into the wilderness, he overcomes the Satanic onslaught (Mk.1:13; Matt.4:1–11; Lk.4:1–13). He is victorious as he chooses the mission committed to him by God and which will finally be vindicated by the Father, even though it leads through suffering and humiliation. This victory over Satanic temptation is held up as an example and an encouragement to Christians in their perseverance in suffering (Heb.2:18; 4:15).

Jesus is supreme over evil spirits. In the Beelzebul controversy it is made plain that by the finger (Lk.11:20) or Spirit of God (Matt.12:38), not by the power of Beelzebul, Jesus exorcizes the unclean spirits. He is the one through whom the kingdom of God operates to destroy the power of Satan (Mk.3:23–26; Matt.12:26; Lk.11:18). He is able to enter the strong man's house and plunder his goods (Mk.3:27). Every exorcism is a further spoiling of Satan's goods and signifies his defeat. Jesus is also shown as delegating his power over evil spirits to his followers who then exercise it as his representatives (Mk.3:14f.; 6:7; Matt.10:1; Lk.9:1f.; 10:1).

Christ's victory over Satan and the powers of darkness occurs pre-eminently in his death, resurrection and exaltation. In John's Gospel there is a clear and obvious connection between the defeat of Satan and the death of Jesus: '"Now is the time for judgement on this world; now the prince of this world will be driven out. But I, when I am lifted up from the earth, will draw all men to myself." He said this to show the kind of death he was going to die' (Jn.12:31–33, NIV). The same point about the victory over the evil powers at the cross is brought out in Col.2:14,15 (cf 1:20; Heb.2:14,15), as we have observed above. In Eph.1:20–23; 4:7–11, the exaltation of Christ is proof that he is superior to the powers of darkness: he is Lord. Cf 1 Pet.3:18ff. where it is asserted that in the period between his death and resurrection Christ descended into the underworld where supernatural evil powers, the spirits, were held imprisoned; they were the archetypal sinners of Gen.6:1–4 who have now heard the proclamation of his achievement.

In these cases the victory of Christ over the powers of evil is asserted as a fact, and believers are called on to recognize it and live accordingly. So Col.2:20; 3:1ff. make it plain that the Christians at Colossae have died and were raised with Christ out from the sphere of influence of the powers, and ought to live as those free from binding rules and regulations.

The triumph of Christ over the principalities is a frequent theme of the New Testament. They have been overcome by him and condemned to await the final ruin of their power.

(iv)   Their continued hostility

For the time being, however, the triumph of the crucified, risen and glorified Jesus Christ over the principalities is hidden. It is not yet final as far as the world is concerned. At this present moment the whole world lies in the power of the evil one, or to put it in the language of Ephesians the prince of the power of the air is the spirit who is now at work in those who are disobedient (2:2).

Although defeated foes the principalities and powers continue to exist, inimical to man and his interests. This is a reality even for the believer. The recipients of Peter's first letter are exhorted to resist the devil and stand firm in the faith for he, their enemy, 'prowls around like a roaring lion looking for someone to devour' (1 Pet.5:8). Eph.6:12 underscores the reality of our engagement with the powers of darkness. There will be no cessation of hostilities until our departure to be with Christ or his return, whichever is the sooner. Our struggle is not with human beings but with supernatural intelligences. Our enemies are not human but demonic, and they are powerful, wicked and cunning. But the power of God is stronger and we are to make use of it to the full (Eph.6:10ff.), knowing that neither these powers nor anything else in the whole of creation will be able to separate us from God's love (Rom.8:38f.).

(v)   Their final overthrow

If Satan and his hosts continue to exist in order to make war on the saints, then their time is short (Rev.20:3). It is not as though the principalities and powers continue just as they were prior to Christ's victory at the cross. Their defeat though hidden is no less real for all that. They have no other expectation than final ruin. Their ultimate overthrow has been fixed by God, as 1 Cor.15:24–28 and the many references in Revelation make plain: 'And the devil, who deceived them, was thrown into the lake of fire, where the beast and the false prophet had been thrown. They will be tormented day and night for ever and ever' (Rev.20:10).

E. THE PRINCIPALITIES AND THE STRUCTURES

The powers of evil, then, are to be regarded as personal, supernatural agencies. We have argued that the 'new orthodoxy' by equating the principalities and powers with impersonal structures, traditions and the like has failed to understand correctly the Pauline teaching.

Further, simply to identify 'the powers' with human structures leads to several erroneous consequences. First, we do not have an adequate explanation as to why structures do not always become tyrannical. Second, we unjustifiably restrict our understanding of the malevolent activity of Satan, whereas he is too versatile to be limited to the structural. And this is the great weakness of the new theory with its identification (by some of its advocates) of the principalities with multi-national corporations and the like. Third, we become too negative towards society and its structures. For if we identify the powers of evil with the structures we will seek to dethrone them, or to fight against them. What will happen if some structures are changed for good? How would the new theology of the powers respond to such changes? Advocates of the new theory may warn against defying the structures; they have to be warned against demonizing them. Both are extremes to be avoided.

But we still need to ask the pressing question: What is the relationship of the biblical powers to the structures, traditions or institutions?[81] Can they use these things? We may not identify the powers with the structures, but can they work through such human agencies, given that the New Testament asserts that the whole world lies in the power of the evil one?

Before directly answering these questions a note of warning needs to be sounded. Care must be exercised when using the term 'structures'. If an impersonal entity is meant then this may result in the removal of responsibility for action from those who are responsible human agents. Impersonal structures may be blamed for wrongdoing when, in fact, evil men and women are culpable.[82]

Satan and his hosts exist by influencing the world and mankind at every level. Satanic power, though hidden, is no less real for all that. The evil one works through the events of history: at 1 Thess. 2:18 Paul asserts that his intended visits to the Thessalonians were stopped by Satan; while in the Book of Job it is clear that the Adversary was actively at work in the circumstances surrounding Job's life—though Satan was still subject to divine control: cf Job 1 and 2. According to Rev.2:10 the devil will cast some believers into prison since he had a particular grip on the circumstances in Pergamum, the seat of political power in Asia. Historical manifestations like this come close to the meaning of the 'beast' in Daniel and Revelation, according to Green and Caragounis.[83]

The inherent distresses of life according to Rom.8:38 are related to the evil powers mentioned in the same verse, while in the Gospels illness is occasionally due to Satanic or demonic activity (cf.Matt.9:32 the dumb man; 12:22, blindness; Lk.9:42, epilepsy). (The biblical writers do not attribute all illness to direct satanic activity: Luke, for example, distinguishes between 'healing' and 'casting out demons', 13:32; 4:40f.; 9:1f.; demons are expelled, diseases are healed.)

Christian teachers and their teaching are subject to attack and distortion by the principalities and powers. Paul speaks of false apostles who have entered the churches, disguising themselves as apostles of Christ. 'And no wonder, for even Satan disguises himself as an angel of light. So it is not strange if his servants also disguise themselves as servants of righteousness' (2 Cor.11:13–15). Heresy too is clearly assigned to their activity. 'The Spirit expressly says that in the last times some will depart from the faith by giving heed to seducing spirits and doctrines of demons' (1 Tim.4:1; cf. 1 Jn.4:1). According to Col.2:20f. the elemental spirits of the univer   made use of the legal demands of the false teachers in order to bring the Christians at Colossae into bondage. It would appear that social, political, judicial and economic structures can become demonic. This seems evident to anyone who has considered the state: in Rom.13 it is the minister of God, while in Rev.13 it has become the ally of the devil.

The last and greatest enemy to which man is exposed by Satan and his minions is death. Men 'through fear of death are in lifetime bondage to him who has the power over death, that is the devil' (Heb.2:14). 'Death is, accordingly, the supreme focus of these enemy forces. They smell of death. They revel in it. They spread it'[84]

Satan and his principalities exist for the purpose of bringing their evil and destructive influences to bear on the world and mankind at every level. In the chapter, 'Principalities and Powers' of his book *I believe in Satan's Downfall*, Michael Green draws attention to a whole range of factors in our modern society which suggest superhuman evil forces are at work. René Padilla[85] states that 'man's situation in the world [is] in terms of enslavement to a spiritual realm from which he must be liberated.'

F.   THE CHRISTIAN'S PRESENT RESPONSIBILITIES

Given that the principalities and powers continue to exist, inimical to man and his interests, hell-bent on carrying out their tyrant's destructive plans, how should the Christian respond, knowing that these supernatural authorities have been overcome by Christ and condemned to await the final ruin of their power? Granted that there is a range of injunctions in the New Testament covering a variety of issues, what specific exhortations are found in this context?

First, believers are to live in the light of Christ's victory over the powers of darkness, demonstrating *confidence and boldness*. Satan is a defeated foe. No weapon formed against Christ and his people can ultimately prosper. The king of death has had his domain ravaged, and its gates, locked since the dawn of time, have been thrown open decisively by Jesus our Lord.[86] At Romans 8, where trouble, hardship and persecution are mentioned as well as death and evil powers, the apostle Paul asserts that we are 'super-conquerors' through him who loved us and that no power, human or otherwise, can separate us from God's love in Christ Jesus our Lord (vv 37–39). Paul prayed that the Colossian Christians might give thanks joyfully to the Father because he had rescued them from a tyranny of darkness and transferred them into a kingdom in which his beloved Son holds sway. They have already received redemption and the forgiveness of sins in him (Col.1:12–14). God wiped out their trespasses and nailed the signed document of their indebtedness, i.e. the IOU, to the cross when Christ died. Further, he stripped the principalities and powers, who had kept us in their grip through their possession of this document, divesting them of their dignity and might. God exposed to the universe their utter helplessness, leading them in Christ in his triumphal procession. He paraded these powerless 'powers and principalities' so that all the world might see the magnitude of his victory (Col.2:13–15). John encourages the readers of his first letter to be confident and buoyant in their conflict with the world, the flesh and the devil on the grounds that those born of God will be kept by him and the evil one cannot touch them (1 Jn.2:13; 4:4; 5:4,18).

Second, Christians are to *recognize* the *nature* and the *dimension* of the *spiritual conflict* in which they are engaged. Many church members seem to be unaware that there is a war in progress, or if they are they consider it is being fought at a purely human level and therefore earthly resources will be entirely adequate for conducting the campaigns. We live in the overlap of the ages and the triumph of the crucified, risen and glorified Jesus Christ over the principalities remains hidden. Satan's ultimate overthrow along with the destruction of death lies in the future. In the meantime the evil one prowls around like a roaring lion (1 Pet.5:8) endeavouring to destroy men and women. His aims are partially achieved if he is able to convince some that he does not really exist and others that their opposition, struggles and difficulties really come from other people. The New Testament, on the other hand, warns us that we are engaged in a deadly warfare against the god of this world and his minions, and that our struggle is *not* against flesh and blood, or other people, but against spiritual forces of evil headed up by Satan himself.

In the light of this spiritual warfare we are to resist vigorously the onslaughts of the evil one (cf Jas.4:7), or to use the words of Eph.6:11, to 'take your stand against the devil's schemes'. God's own armour has been forged and furnished by him for our use so that we may obey his injunction to stand firm. Only spiritual weapons are of value in this deadly struggle (6:10ff.). To stand firm will commit us to:

1. Prayer and Watchfulness

(Eph. 6:18) Both are vital in Christian warfare. The apostle knew that prayer is 'the supreme expression of our dependence on God'.[87] When we call upon him in prayer the principalities and powers are restrained. To be truly Christian prayer which is offered in the Spirit of God, it will be regular and constant, accompanied by 'all perseverance', for like good soldiers we are to keep alert, neither giving up nor falling asleep. Such prayer will include intercession 'for all the saints' (v 18).

We are to watch out for the devil's assaults (cf 1 Cor.16:13; 1 Pet.5:8; 1 Thes.5:6) especially as he masquerades as an angel of light and his servants disguise themselves as apostles of Christ, as servants of righteousness (2 Cor.11:13–15). Such watchfulness will involve being on guard against heresy in the church (note Acts 20:31), and it will include a spiritual wakefulness so that we do not enter into temptation (Matt.26:41). It is particularly important to note, however, that being watchful has been interpreted in the New Testament in a more technical sense of believers, the children of light, being awake and renouncing the sleep of this world of darkness, with the mind directed towards Christ's return[88] (Matt.24:42; 25:13; Lk.12:37; and note Rev.16:15, 'Lo, I am coming like a thief! Blessed is he who is watchful. . . .').

2. The Word of God

(Eph. 6:17). A significant piece of the divine armour, fashioned for our use in the spiritual struggle against our supernatural enemies, is the word of God, described in Ephesians 6 as 'the sword of the Spirit'. Of the six pieces of weaponry listed, this sword is the only one that can be used for attack as well as defence. This weapon of the word is to be used in several different ways. First, we are to hold fast to it for it is the truth (cf Col.1:5). By it we are saved (1 Cor.15:2), and also it is the yardstick by which instruction may be tested. False teachers and their doctrine are to be rebutted by the word of God. Then too, this same word of God, which focuses upon the death and resurrection of Jesus Christ is to be proclaimed fearlessly in the power of God's Spirit. Men and women, in their own natural condition, are described as being dead in trespasses and sins, and captive to 'the prince of the power of the air' (Eph.2:2; cf Col.1:21). Through the proclamation of this word of God, the gospel, God calls men and women out of darkness into his marvellous light, to share in his Son's glory (2 Thess.2:14). By this means the Colossians were delivered from a tyranny of darkness and transferred into a kingdom where God's beloved Son rules (Col.1:13). Paul was commissioned to preach that gospel for the purpose of opening the eyes of Gentiles and turning them from darkness to light, from the power of Satan to God (Acts 26:18). Satan and his emissaries are implacably opposed to the gospel of the Lord Jesus Christ for by it those enslaved are liberated from the evil one's clutches. Through Christ's own death the sting of death has been drawn and those held in lifetime bondage through the fear of death are able to be freed.

At Rev.12:11 the apostle John draws our attention to Christians who had overcome the evil one. They had, of course, recognized and resisted the great accuser (rather than demythologized or neglected him), and they overcame him: (a) 'by the blood of the lamb'—that is, their confidence lay in the victory won by the Lord Jesus over Satan at the cross; (b) 'by the word of their testimony'—commissioned as Christ's ambassadors they bore fearless and continuous testimony to their risen Master. Satan was driven back each time faithful testimony was given and whenever men and women were snatched from his evil clutches. They were totally committed to their Lord, for: (c) 'they did not love their lives so much as to shrink from death'. Knowing that Satan was a defeated foe they also knew that the cause of the Lord Jesus, whatever the reverses, could not be stopped.

In the light of the concerns of this paper, viz. that the principalities and powers be understood as personal, supernatural intelligences, emissaries of the god of this world, which seek to influence the world and mankind for ill at every level, using every resource at their disposal, it is highly significant that the Christian's responsibilities in this ongoing warfare are, according to the New Testament, what we might call, spiritual ones. We are exhorted to resist the devil, stand firm, watch and pray, use the word of God, not be brought into the bondage of man made rules, forgive one another so that Satan may not gain control over us, preserve the unity of the brothers and so on. Thus the question must fairly be asked: Have we as the people of God made use of the divine resources placed at our disposal, or taken the weapons God has so graciously provided and heeded his clear injunctions? Perhaps on too many occasions we have engaged in other activities instead. However, the measure of our victory over these 'opponents of the church' will be the measure of our obedience.

NOTES

1. R. J. Sider, 'Christ and Power', *IRM* 69 (1980) 17.
2. ibid. 12.
3. In the introduction to his *Die paulinische Angelologie und Dämonologie* (Göttingen 1888) 4.
4. Quoted by H. Berkhof, *Christ and the Powers* (ET Scottdale, PA 1962) 72.
5. Many influential scholars representing this viewpoint came to the conclusion that not only did Christianity have its own myths, but also it had been significantly influenced at its formative stage by particular myths of other religions, esp. those of Jewish apocalyptic, of Gnosticism and of the Hellenistic mystery religions; note the treatment by J. D. G. Dunn, 'Demythologizing—the Problems of Myth in the New Testament', in *New Testament Interpretation. Essays in Principles and Methods*, ed. I. H. Marshall (Exeter 1977) 285–307.
6. *Die Geisterwelt im Glauben des Paulus* (Göttingen 1909).
7. Cited by Berkhof, *Christ and the Powers* 73.
8. The above-mentioned statement does not appear in the later English translation, *Principalities and Powers in the New Testament* (Freiburg 1961).
9. R. Bultmann, *Theology of the New Testament*, vol. 1 (ET London 1952) 258–259; cf the recent article, part of which is devoted to the theme of the Pauline powers, by L. Bautista, H. B. Garcia and Sze-Kar Wan, 'The Asian Way of Thinking in Theology', *ERT* 6 (1982) 37–49, esp. p.43.
10. In this analysis of Bultmann's hermeneutics I am especially indebted to A. C. Thiselton's writings, especially *The Two Horizons* (Exeter 1980) 252ff.
11. ibid. 252.
12. 'New Testament and Mythology', in *Kerygma and Myth. A Theological Debate*, ed. H. W. Bartsch (ET London 1972) 1.
13. ibid. 10.
14. ibid. 9.
15. On the antecedents to Bultmann's demythologizing see especially Thiselton, *Two Horizons* 205ff., and Dunn, 'Demythologizing', 289.
16. R. Bultmann, *Jesus Christ and Mythology* (ET London 1960) 35–36.
17. Thiselton, *Two Horizons* 287.
18. On the importance of pre-understanding in relation to the New Testament text, together with important safeguards, see G. N. Stanton, 'Presuppositions in New Testament Criticism', in *New Testament Interpretation* 60–71; cf also B. J. Nicholls, *Contextualization: A Theology of Gospel and Culture* (Exeter 1979) 40ff.
19. N. A. Dahl, *The Crucified Christ and Other Essays* (ET Minneapolis 1974) 97, cited by Thiselton, *Two Horizons* 283.
20. Thiselton, *Two Horizons* 283.

21. Dunn, 'Demythologizing', 297.
22. So Karl Jaspers, cited by Thiselton, *Two Horizons* 289.
23. ibid. 290.
24. H. Braun, cited by Dunn, 'Demythologizing', 298.
25. *Theology* vol. 1, p.259, our italics.
26. He expressed his views in *Christ and Time* (ET Longon 1951) and subsequently in *The State in the New Testament* (ET London 1957). Note especially the excursus in the latter volume, pp.95–114.
27. *State* 114.
28. Note C. E. B. Cranfield's treatment in *A Commentary on Romans 12–13* (Edinburgh 1965) 66f., and more recently *The Epistle to the Romans* vol. 2 (Edinburgh 1979) 657–658.
29. *The Powers That Be. Earthly Rulers and Demonic Powers in Romans 13:1-7* (London 1966) esp. pp.40ff.
30. Note the recent assessment by W. Carr, *Angels and Pincipalities. The Background, meaning and development of the Pauline phrase* hai archai kai hai exousiai (Cambridge 1981) 118–120.
31. pp.63–101.
32. Cranfield in his more recent *Romans* p.659 has stated that he now regards the double reference interpretation as less probable than the view that Paul had in mind simply the civil authorities at Rom.13:1.
33. J. R. W. Stott, *God's new society. The message of Ephesians* (Leicester 1979) 271.
34. *Principalities and Powers. Studies in the Christian Conflict in History* (London 1952).
35. pp.11–12.
36. cf also the writings of W. Stringfellow, especially *Free in Obedience. The Radical Christian Life* (New York 1964) 49ff.
37. (ET Scottdale, PA 1962).
38. ibid. 23.
39. ibid. 24.
40. ibid. 38–39. Note also Stott, *God's New Society* p.269, and especially his clear and incisive analysis of the recent debate (pp.267–275) about the Pauline powers being interpreted as ethical and socio-political structures.
41. Stott, p.269.
42. First published in *The Background of the New Testament and Its Eschatology*, ed. W. D. Davies and D. Daube (Cambridge 1964) 509–536. Reprinted as *Kerygma, Eschatology and Social Ethics* (Philadelphia 1966). References below are to the later edition.
43. ibid. 23.
44. ibid. 30.
45. ibid. 24.
46. ibid.
47. G. B. Caird, *Principalities and Powers. A Study in Pauline Theology.* (Oxford 1956) drew attention to three structures: first, 'pagan religion and pagan power' including the state; second, the law which is good in itself, since it is God's, becomes demonic when it is 'exalted into an independent system of religion'; the third power is those recalcitrant elements in nature

which resist God's rule, e.g. wild animals, diseases, storms and even the whole of creation's bondage to corruption. But twenty years later, in his more recent commentary on Ephesians (*Paul's Letters from Prison* [Oxford 1976] 91), Caird shifted his ground by conceding that Paul was referring to 'spiritual beings' which operated in and through the structures. Similarly, Markus Barth in *The Broken Wall. A Study of the Epistle to the Ephesians* (London 1960) identified the principalities with structures, but later said the terms referred to spiritual entities as well (*Ephesians* vol. 2 [Garden City, NY 1974] 800). For further reading see G. H. C. Macgregor, 'Principalities and Powers: The Cosmic Background of Paul's Thought', *NTS* 1 (1954–55) 17–28, and A. van den Heuvel, *These Rebellious Powers* (London 1966).

48. *The Politics of Jesus* (Grand Rapids 1972).
49. ibid. 137–38, 142.
50. ibid. 138.
51. ibid. 146.
52. ibid. 141–142.
53. R. J. Mouw, *Politics and the Biblical Drama* (Grand Rapids 1976) 111.
54. Yoder, *Politics* 97; cf Mouw, *Politics* 112.
55. Note Mouw's detailed criticisms, *Politics* 112–116.
56. Yoder, *Politics* 192.
57. (Grand Rapids 1976).
58. Mouw, *Politics* 87.
59. ibid. 97.
60. ibid. 88.
61. ibid. 115.
62. Carr, *Angels and Principalities* 43.
63. ibid. 123.
64. cf the recent work of C. H. Sherlock, 'The God Who Fights. The War-Tradition in Holy Scripture' (unpublished Th.D. thesis, Australian College of Theology, 1980) which seeks to remedy this deficiency.
65. pp.52–66.
66. We have avoided the temptation to add names of other writers to the list simply for the sake of completeness, particularly when their treatments and the hermeneutical principles underlying them have already been examined in connection with others. Paul Tillich's study on the theme of 'power', for example, might have been included. Although various liberation theologians could have been surveyed, their contributions frequently related to the exodus motif while their references to the Pauline powers were, on the whole, few. René Padilla's treatment in *The New Face of Evangelicalism* is a significant contribution from a Latin American context.
67. Note C. C. Caragounis, *The Ephesian* Mysterion. *Meaning and Content* (Lund 1977) 157–161.
68. Stanton, 'Presuppositions', 68.
69. See above.
70. The issue of the Pauline or post-Pauline authorship is not particularly relevant to the exegetical issues and need not be examined.
71. Note A. T. Lincoln, 'A Re-Examination of "the Heavenlies" in Ephesians',

NTS 19 (1972–73) 468–483, esp. p.472, and Caragounis, *Ephesian* 146–152.

72. p. 273.
73. For a discussion of this crux see my article, 'Col.1:20 and the Reconciliation of All Things', *RTR* 33 (1974) 45–53.
74. For details see E. Lohse, *Colossians and Philemon* (ET Philadelphia 1971) 51.
75. A. J. Bandstra, *The Law and the Elements of the World* (Kampen 1964).
76. *Der Brief an die Kolosser* (Zürich 1976) 101–102.
77. For a survey of the ways this expression has been understood by Christian interpreters see my *Colossians and Philemon* (Waco, TX 1982) 129–132.
78. For details see H. Schlier, *Principalities and Powers in the New Testament* (ET Herder 1961), and R. Yates, 'The Powers of Evil in the New Testament', *EQ* 52 (1980) 97–111.
79. Schlier, *Principalities* 18.
80. M. Green, *I believe in Satan's Downfall* (London 1981) 92.
81. Note the treatment by Green, ibid. 86ff.
82. I am not opposing the use of the term 'structures'. Rather, I am concerned we do not assume that our term is coterminous with an entity such as 'authority' or 'power' in the New Testament.
83. Green, *I believe* 87–88, who follows Caragounis, *Ephesian* 157ff.
84. Green, *I believe* 90.
85. p.212.
86. Green, *I believe* 221.
87. ibid. 229.
88. cf E. Lövestam, *Spiritual Wakefulness in the New Testament* (Lund 1963).

6

The Church in African Theology;
Description and Analysis of
Hermeneutical Presuppositions
TITE TIÉNOU

A. INTRODUCTION

1. Scope

Since the expression 'African theology' can be all-inclusive and
meaningless, it may be of value to begin this study by defining
the boundaries of the present investigation. The scope of this
paper is limited to theological statements concerning the church
in sub-Saharan Africa, but not including South Africa. The
reason for this is that the North African nations and South Africa
represent very different situations requiring separate studies. For
instance, in the South African situation, as I understand it, there
are theological emphases more akin to Black and Liberation
theologies than to what is generally known as African theology.
We shall, however, have occasion to refer to South African
authors when they deal with themes shared by the rest of
sub-Saharan Africa.

Our scope is further limited by the fact that we are examining
here only published documents on the topic of our investigation.
In the case of Africa, this is rather unfortunate because much of
our theological creativity is in oral form—in songs, sermons, and
rituals. This presentation would have been strengthened with
studies of some of these non-written theologies. Alas, I did not
have the possibility of conducting field research while preparing
this paper. Nevertheless, I will be satisfied if this study contributes, in any way, to the understanding of the issues raised.

2. The Problem

African theologians have devoted comparatively little time and effort to ecclesiology. This may be due in part to the fact that most of them think the major problem of African Christianity lies elsewhere: the need for selfhood and identity. This is reflected across the theological spectrum in some publications of the last fifteen to twenty years. In his 1965 book, *Towards an Indigenous Church*, Bolaji Idowu pinpointed the basic problem of the church in Nigeria as that of foreign domination. He even suggested that true selfhood is the *sine qua non* for the beginning of Nigerian theology:

> A theology which bears the stamp of Nigerian thinking and meditation . . . cannot be produced by a Church which is imprisoned within a foreign structure: such is forever impossible with a Church whose spiritual and intellectual nourishment is a theology supplied ready-made from abroad.[1]

The quest for independence and the need for selfhood are again reiterated in Meinard Hebga's *Emancipation d'Eglises sous tutelle* (1976) and Pius Wakatama's *Independence for the Third World Church* (1976). Moreover, some inter-African and international gatherings have recently echoed the demands for selfhood and self-reliance. The call for a *moratorium* on overseas funds and personnel issued at Lusaka in 1974[2] is one such instance. Kofi Appiah-Kubi's statements in the preface to the compendium of papers presented at the Pan-African Conference of the Third World Theologians (Accra, Ghana, December 1977) is another. He says, 'We demand to serve the Lord in our own terms and without being turned into Euro-American or Semitic bastards before we do so.'[3]

But the multiplicity of publications on the topic or the militancy of language should not make us think that the desire and the quest for selfhood on the part of African church leaders are of recent origin. E. A. Ayandele has shown that, in the case of Nigeria, they can be traced back almost to the beginnings of missionary work. He notes:

> Although the imperativeness for the Church in Africa to perceive and resolve these problems is pressing now more than ever before, it is instructive to note that *as far back as the second half of*

the nineteenth century a few uniquely clairvoyant and dedicated Christian African leaders had recognized the challenge of these problems and had made some efforts to tackle it (italics added).[4]

The African churches' quest for selfhood and identity is and always has been a dimension of their missiological ecclesiology. If we leave it aside in this essay, it is not for lack of interest or importance. Rather, it is because the second problem of African ecclesiology seems to have more theological content and fewer political overtones.

This second problem, or rather another aspect of the same problem, is that of developing an ecclesiology which is relevant to the African situation. As early as 1960, Bengt Sundkler, from his study of independent churches in south Africa, suggested:

> There is a possibility . . . that the African Protestant theologian of the future will build on [the] fact of the family as one of the main pillars of his theology, particularly of his ecclesiology. He may come to regard it as his particular task to see the Church in terms of the Great Family.[5]

In his article, Harry Sawyerr[6] noted the lucidity of Sundkler's comments in the chapter from which the above quotation is taken. In 1968, taking Sundkler's suggestion seriously, he expanded on the concept of the church as 'the Great Family' in a book-length study.[7] It is this concept that we wish to analyze in detail here.

B. PRESENTATION

The aim of Sawyerr's argumentation, as well as Sundkler's, is to relate ecclesiology to African kinship structures. They think that the church as the Great Family is the best way for achieving that goal. Sawyerr begins his investigation with a look at Paul's ecclesiology. He notes that for the apostle the Christians are all 'one man' in Christ (Gal.3:28; Eph.2:11–22); that they drink of one Spirit (1 Cor.12:13) and that they share one body and blood of Christ (1 Cor.10:16).[8] This emphasis on the oneness of the Church leads him to agreement with L. Hodgson's characterization of the church 'as *Totus Christus, membra cum capite*'.[9]

1. The Church as Family in the African Context

Sawyerr further relates the concept of the church as the whole Christ to that of the church as the Great Family in the following manner:

> The Church as the whole Christ, members of the Body integrated into the Head . . . , is therefore, in our opinion, more likely to appeal to the true feelings of the African because the idea of Jesus Christ as the first-born among many brethren can readily be introduced in this context. Such an approach could be most effective in presenting the contrast between the ancestors to whom primacy in time is attributed, reservedly attribute a *primacy in essence* (italics in original).[10]

We note here that relating the concept of the church as the whole Christ to that of Christ as the first-born among many brothers for the purpose of creating the concept of the church as the Great Family already assumes that 'Christ as first-born' is comparable to, if not identical with, 'Christ as Ancestor'. We will return later to this understanding of Christ as Ancestor and its relationship to ecclesiology. For the time being, let us further elucidate Sawyerr's position.

The concept of the church as the Great Family relates kinship in Christ to ecclesiology. It is specifically related to the age-mate kinship systems of Africa evidenced in initiation.[11] Knowing that 'the African Community embraces the living, the unborn and the dead',[12] how can Sawyerr still insist that '[the] discussion of kinship in Africa provides us with a very significant concept on which African Christians could build the concept of the Church as the Great Family'?[13] Does the image of the church as family (or household) in the New Testament, or that of Christ as first-born, rest on the premise of a community composed of living, unborn and dead people? I do not know if Sawyerr finds a lack of biblical support for his position, but I see that he appeals only to church tradition when he states that 'Christians know of the church militant, the church triumphant, in heaven, and the church expectant, in a state between the first two'.[14] I further note that in any case the living, the dead, and the unborn cannot be completely identical with the church militant, triumphant and expectant. I should think that this last fact would make one cautious about accepting the thesis of the church as the Great Family in the African Context. But we will return to that later.

C. IMPLICATIONS OF UNDERSTANDING THE CHURCH AS THE GREAT FAMILY

Sawyerr, as well as writers such as Sundkler and Haselbarth,[15] knows full well that stating that the church is the Great Family raises serious questions for theology in the African setting. We must nevertheless admire them for boldly facing the issues. In a context of essential unity and continuity between a people and their ancestors, understanding the church as the Great Family can mean only one thing: ancestors are included in the church. This is precisely the conclusion drawn by Sawyerr. Let us listen carefully to the following rather important quotation.

> All of us Africans feel that our deceased parents and other ancestors are close to us. In the present context, therefore, Christian doctrinal teaching should be directed towards, first, presenting the Church as a corporate body with a unique solidarity transcending by far anything akin to it in pagan African society; and, second, discovering a means of preserving the tribe, solidarity of living and dead, as Africans understand that relationship, but in a new idiom, that of the community of the church . . . . [Ancestors] could . . . be readily embraced within the framework of the universal church and be included within the communion of saints.[16]

E. W. Fasholé-Luke is another African theologian who links ancestor veneration, the communion of saints and ecclesiology.[17] His reasoning for suggesting such a link is quite similar to Sawyerr's. He builds on anthropological findings according to which 'ancestral cults are expressions of the family and tribal solidarity and continuity'.[18] This prompts him to suggest that the attempts to incorporate these ideas 'into Christian faith and practice . . . will be abortive, unless the Churches develop a theology of the Communion of Saints that will satisfy the passionate desire of Africans, Christians and non-Christians alike, to be linked with their dead ancestors'.[19]

Fasholé-Luke knows, of course, that African ancestors cannot simply be included in the church without sufficient evidence. He seeks this evidence in 'a more profound appraisal of the situation and a deeper theological interpretation of the beliefs about the fate of the departed'.[20] The phrase *sanctorum communionem* of the Apostles' Creed seems appropriate to him for this theological exploration. He thinks that if this phrase is interpreted 'to mean fellowship with holy people of all ages and the whole company of heaven through participation in the holy sacraments',[21] this will lead to new paths in African theology and ecclesiology.

We should note that Fasholé-Luke's interpretation of *sanctorum* comes from Karl Barth's suggestion that it is intentionally ambiguous, being both masculine plural and neuter plural.[22] He follows Barth while fully recognizing the problem of interpretation of the expression *sanctorum communionem*. F. Prat, for instance, emphatically states that the word *sanctorum* is masculine and not neuter.[23] In that case, the communion is the solidarity of all the members of Christ's body, both the dead and the living.

Fasholé-Luke prefers Barth's interpretation because this allows him to include non-Christian African ancestors in the communion of saints. He sees evidence for this in the sacrament of the eucharist. This is how Fasholé-Luke expresses himself:

> At the Eucharist Christians join with the whole company of heaven, the faithful departed, the angels and archangels, to praise and glorify God. . . . It is at this service that we can and do live with our dead in a way which is profoundly true to man's nature. It is also at this service, where we show forth Christ's death, that Africans can be linked with their non-Christian ancestors.[24]

Sawyerr and Fasholé-Luke are, therefore, in essential agreement. They want somehow to relate ecclesiology to the blood line family ties which are very important to Africans. They both recognize the fact that their suggestions create important theological problems. But Sawyerr, from his Anglican background, wonders why non-Christian dead are excluded when the church prays only for the faithful departed. He then asks, 'Is there no room for including non-Christians in our prayers? We do so for the living; as for example, when we pray for the peace of the world. Is it wrong, then, to do the same for the dead?'[25]

Furthermore, Sawyerr thinks he has found New Testament precedents for his position:

> Our interpretation of the *feeling* of Christians of New Testament times leads us to the conclusion that they had real concern for their relatives and compatriots who had died either before the establishment of the Christian Church (in the case of non-Christians) or before the Parousia (in the case of Christians).[26]

He refers the reader to Matt.27:52; 1 Cor.15:29 (baptism for the dead); 1 Pet.3:18 (descent into hell); 1 Thess.4:14–18; and the roll of heroes in Heb.11. He concludes:

> We would, therefore, go on to suggest that the prayers of African Christians might, in the providence of God, lead to the salvation of their pagan ancestors. Indeed, we must justifiably add that it is highly probable that some of the dead for whom the early Christians were baptized had never heard of the promise of salvation through Jesus-Christ.[27]

We find almost identical words in Fasholé-Luke's essay:

> We believe that the death of Christ is for the whole world and no one either living or dead is outside the scope of the merits of Christ's death. Thus both Christians and non-Christians receive salvation through Christ's death and are linked with him through the sacrament which he himself instituted. This view is supported by the fact that in his roll of heroes of faith, the author of Hebrews includes non-Christians whose faith was not perfect. We would equally affirm that the African ancestors could also be included in the Communion of Saints in this way, since they had a faith which was not perfect; but the death of Christ can make perfect the feeble faith which they had and thus incorporate them into his Body the Church.[28]

We could end our presentation of the church in African theology with the exposition of these two theologians' positions were it not for the fact that we may be accused of generalizing with one or two authors. So let us look at Haselbarth's treatment of the same topic. For him christology and ecclesiology are related in the affirmation of Christ's dominion over all powers. Passages such as Phil.2:5–11 and others which deal with Christ's lordship over the universe, the powers and the church, create a new hierarchy which includes African ancestors. Such ancestors have a 'definite place in the order of salvation', and 'to be in Christ' must no longer 'be narrowed to the individual believer's participation in the life of his Lord, but should be seen here in its universal meaning. Through their being in Christ the living and the dead are united in one family.'[29] Again he calls Christ first-born and chief ancestor.

Moving into the area of ecclesiology proper, Haselbarth notes that 'in the new hierarchy of Christ, participation in the family of God is open for the living and the dead'.[30] To those who would ask how the dead enter into the family of God (= the church), Haselbarth replies that 'the relation between the beginning among the believers and the end among the heavenly saints is a relation of faith (*analogia fidei*), not of blood and nature (*analogia entis*) as in traditional religion'.[31] This reply is not entirely satisfactory, for Haselbarth does not say how the dead acquire faith.

Considering the relationship between the ancestors and the church, Haselbarth, like Sawyerr, utilizes the categories of *ecclesia militans* (on earth) and *ecclesia triumphans* (around God's throne) to conclude that the ancestors have a meaningful role to play in the church here and now: they are 'in the family of Christ and in the same order of salvation as the living'.[32] He maintains his position despite the fact of its 'far-reaching consequences for a theology in Africa' and also despite the 'fact that our biblical information at this point is scarce'.[33] Why then the insistence on holding this view?

D.   SUMMARY OF PRESENTATION

We have chosen to present essentially one attempt to reflect creatively on ecclesiology in the African context. We have found that four authors agree that the concept of the *family* is best suited to that goal. We have seen that they extensively use African kinship structures and that this has led at least three of them to incorporate ancestors into the church, ultimately granting them salvation. Let us now examine their hermeneutical presuppositions.

E. ANALYSIS OF HERMENEUTICS

I would like, first of all, to express deep gratitude to all four authors for bringing the imagery of the family to our attention and relating it so creatively to ecclesiology. Seeing the church as a family or household is indeed a New Testament way of expressing essential solidarity within the church. In passing we may add that the image of the body expresses also the same kind of solidarity. At any rate, to mention just a few, passages such as Gal.6:10; Eph.2:19; 1 Tim.3:15; Heb.3:5,6; 1 Pet.2:5 refer to the church as the house or household of God or of the faith. The basic hermeneutical question we must ask is: In what way is the New Testament imagery of the church as household similar to and distinct from the African concept of the Great Family?

Specifically, what does family mean when one seeks to understand it is a metaphor applied to the Church? Clearly one must begin with scriptural antecedents before jumping to one's current context. F. Prat reminds us that when Paul defines the church as the household of God, he does so with the Old Testament idea of family in mind.[34] Unless it can be demonstrated that the Old Testament, New Testament, and African ideas of family are identical, it seems rather hazardous to select this model as the one suitable for Africa. If we do not let the biblical paradigm control our interpretation, then the danger of distortion of the biblical message is great. The authors whose thoughts have been examined here seem to emphasize the African context more than the biblical paradigm. In so doing they have engaged themselves in mnemic hermeneutics.

1. Danger of Mnemic Hermeneutics

It is a common practice among those interested in African theology to affirm similarities between the Bible (particularly the Old Testament) and African cultures and religions. Commenting on the place of the Old Testament in the African context, Sundkler writes:

> The Old Testament in the African setting is not just a book of reference. It becomes a source of remembrance. The African preacher feels that Genesis belongs to him and his Church or

rather vice-versa—that he and his African Church belong to those things which were in the beginning.[38]

In 1963, Harry Sawyerr took Sundkler to task on this issue with the following statement:

> When Dr. Sundkler asserts that the Old Testament becomes to the African a 'source of remembrance,' we must ask, Remembrance of what? . . . This 'mnemic theology' is in our judgment fraught with great dangers.[36]

Sawyerr's concern is justified. The question we ask is, Has he not applied mnemic hermeneutics in his understanding of the church as the Great Family? Are the dangers not the same? Our contention is that had Sawyerr heeded his own criticism of Sundkler, he would have orientated his thinking on the church as Family in a different way. For his mnemic hermeneutics really distort the New Testament emphasis here.

Mnemic hermeneutics is allowing one's own natural analogy to become the crucial key in understanding Scripture. In this case, the African understanding of family as composed of the living, the dead and the unborn is read back into Scripture without prior questioning. This in turn makes the biblical message go beyond its intended meaning.

2.   Ancestors and the Church

The basic presupposition on social structure among many ethnic groups of Africa is the essential solidarity and unity among the Ancestors, the living and the unborn. Therefore when many Africans speak of the Great Family, it is this reality they have in mind. The family includes not only the immediate and extended families presently living but also the dead as well as the children to come. Ancestors continue to play major roles in the daily lives of their relatives who are still on earth. It is in this light that Sawyerr's reference to Christ as our elder brother, once dead and now alive,[37] must be understood. How warranted is this approach from a New Testament perspective?

If it is possible to see some similarities between Christ and Ancestors (as understood by Africans), there are nevertheless major differences which should prevent us from making hasty extrapolations. Anselme Sanon has summarized the similarities and differences between Ancestors (in Bobo society) and Christ in this manner:

ANCESTORS	CHRIST
Founders of a village	Founder of his community
Inspire customs	Inspires tradition
Mediators for families	Mediator for all
Renew themselves by their descendants	Renews the life of his community
Humans living in the hereafter	God-Man

Aside from Sanon's Catholic distinctive showing itself in making Christ the one who inspires the tradition of the church, the above chart points out major areas of differences. Sawyerr himself recognizes the contrast between ancestors and Christ,[39] and yet he insists on presenting Jesus Christ as the first-born among many brethren because this 'appeals to the true feelings of the African'. He cannot fail to realize that is so because Christ would be understood as an ancestor in African *categories*. This is precisely mnemic hermeneutics. It does not concern itself with discovering the meaning of the imagery in its original context but rather it focuses attention on the feelings or hermeneutical reflexes of the audience.

It is, of course, correct to note that human commonality makes parallels inevitable between the Bible and other religious traditions. Christ can be legitimately called our elder brother and our ancestor. Also the merits of Christ's death and resurrection extend far beyond his own generation; they reach back into the past as well as into the future. Nevertheless the differences should not be overlooked. Proper hermeneutics must wrestle with *both* parallels *and* differences. This will allow the Word of God to have a corrective function as well as being grafted onto sound points of contact.

3. Family of God and Natural Family

Understanding the church as the Great Family in the African context can lead only to incorporating the Ancestors into the church, thereby granting them salvation. This is so because the Africans' Great Family includes the Ancestors. Indeed most

African people conceive 'heaven' to be a place where one is reunited with one's Ancestors. Predictably, Sawyerr and Haselbarth have drawn the above conclusion from their understanding of the African situation and the Bible. But is such an inference really valid? Can the church as God's household be identical with the natural family?

We have already noted Haselbarth's uneasiness about including the Ancestors in the church here and now, because he recognizes the slimness of biblical evidence for such a viewpoint. I think that their hermeneutics (which I have called mnemic) has caused Haselbarth, Sawyerr, and Fasholé-Luke to emphasize the natural all-inclusive African family at the expense of the New Testament emphasis. When Paul and the writer to the Hebrews use the term 'household' for the church, they almost always qualify it with 'faith' or 'God'. So the church is 'God's household' (Eph.2:19; 1 Tim.3:15); it is the 'household of the faith' (Gal.6:10). We become members of the household of God through trust in and obedience to Christ.

It is quite clear that apart from faith in Christ no one (regardless of our feelings toward that person) can legitimately be a member of God's household. To our knowledge most African Ancestors have not evidenced faith in Christ, and appeal to the efficacy of our prayers on their behalf is mere conjecture. Jesus himself provides us with the understanding of the relationship between God's family and the natural family. During an intense ministry, when informed that his mother and brothers wanted to see him, he had this stunning reply: 'Whosoever does the will of God, he is my brother and sister and mother' (Mk.3:35). So the church is *like* a family because the solidarity that binds it together can be better expressed in terms of kinship; but the family of God can never be indentical with any natural family!

The solidarity which binds all the members of the church together, though it is not because of blood relations, is nonetheless very deep and very real. This is the point of Jesus calling his disciples 'my mother and my brothers' (Matt.12:49). Indeed Christian brotherhood is such that Paul can write to Philemon to welcome Onesimus back as 'a beloved brother . . . both in the flesh and in the Lord' (v.16). So the Christian's membership in the body of Christ should supersede his ties to his natural family.

I would mention, before concluding, that Sawyerr's mnemic hermeneutics depends more on *feeling* than hard evidence. So it is feeling which causes him to conclude that Christians in New Testament times were concerned about their dead relatives even to the point of baptism for the dead. We cannot go into an analysis of the passages Sawyerr presents to defend his position as this would take us a little farther than intended here. We recognize that people everywhere and throughout history are concerned about their dead relatives. We note that the passages referred to by Sawyerr are among the most controversial of New Testament interpretation[40] and we further note that the testimony of Scripture as a *whole* requires us to recognize our ignorance about the place of unbelieving dead in the church (particularly those who had no witness of the Gospel). We do know, however, that faith in Christ is the condition for the living to be members of the family of God. As for our departed relatives, God is the only competent judge of their final relationship to him. We dare not, through hermeneutical acrobacy, say more than his revealed word!

F. CONCLUSION

For Christ and the New Testament writers, the reality of the church is one of living solidarity, where everyone is his brother's keeper. This interdependence can be diversely expressed in images such as that of the body or the family, and others. Whatever image we use to represent the church as a caring community, one thing is certain: the local church is where it all begins.

One of the basic problems I have with the description of the church as the Great Family is the emphasis the authors put on general ideas such as the place of Ancestors. In fact, African theology suffers from over-generalization. In the words of Droogers:

In the quest for Africanization of the Church, main emphasis is put on the elaboration of a typically African theology and church life rather than on the introduction of these ideas into the life of the local congregations. . . . [African theology is] characterized by a singular lack of interest in the situation of the local churches. The main work, it is thought, must be done at the continental level instead of at the grass roots.[41]

The church as family means that in local churches trust, mutual sharing of burdens, concerns and joys are developed in a spirit of kinship. So the household of God is always a visible reality. It is in this light that the 1981 General Assembly of the Association of Evangelicals of Africa and Madagascar is especially meaningful. Its theme of the local church put the emphasis on one of the most important elements of the Christian ministry.

I am aware of the fact that the hermeneutics of remembrance is practised by many interpreters of the Bible, consciously or unconsciously. It is not peculiar to the African continent. J. S. Croatto, for instance, boldly states that 'exegesis is eisegesis, and anybody who claims to be doing only the former is, wittingly or unwittingly, engaged in ideological subterfuge'.[42] For him 'a hermeneutic reading of the biblical message occurs only when the reading *supersedes the first contextual meaning. . . .* This happens *through the unfolding of a surplus-of-meaning disclosed by a new question addressed to the text.*'[43] One cannot easily expect to change those convinced that this is the correct approach to hermeneutics. My only contention is that 'the first contextual meaning' is *the only* proper way to understand the message given in any document, however complex the application may be. The Bible is no exception!

NOTES

1. E. B. Idowu, *Towards an Indigenous Church* (London 1965) 26.
2. A.A.C.C./C.E.T.A., *La lutte continue: Rapport Officiel de la Troisième Assemblée* (Lusake, Zambia 1974) 55 (Report of Working Group III).
3. K. Appiah-kubi and S. Torres, eds., *African Theology en Route* (Maryknoll 1979) viii.
4. E. A. Ayendele, *A Visionary of the African Church* (Nairobi 1971) 4.
5. B. Sundkler, *The Christian Ministry in Africa* (London 1960) 289.
6. Harry Sawyerr, 'The Basis of a Theology for Africa', *IRM* 52 (1963).
7. idem, *Creative Evangelism* (London 1968).
8. Sawyerr, *Creative Evangelism* 79.
9. L. Hodgson, *Survey of the Training of the Ministry in Africa* (London 1934) 38.
10. Sawyerr, *Creative Evangelism* 83.
11. ibid. 85.
12. ibid. 93.
13. ibid. 91.
14. ibid. 93.

15. Sundkler, *Christian Ministry*; H. Haselbarth, 'The Place of the Ancestors in a Christian Theology of Africa', *Ministry* 7/4 (1974).
16. Sawyerr, *Creative Evangelism* 94.
17. E. W. Fasholé-Luke, 'Ancestor Veneration and the Communion of Saints', *New Testament Christianity for Africa and the World*, ed. M. E. Glasswell and E. W. Fasholé-Luke (London 1974) 209–221.
18. ibid. 209.
19. ibid. 210.
20. ibid. 216.
21. ibid.
22. ibid. 214–215.
23. F. Prat, *La théologie de Saint Paul* (Paris 1961) 355a.
24. Fasholé-Luke, 'Ancestor Veneration', 217.
25. Sawyerr, *Creative Evangelism* 94–95.
26. ibid. 95.
27. ibid. 95.
28. Fasholé-Luke, 'Ancestor Veneration', 217.
29. Haselbarth, 'Place of the Ancestors', 174.
30. ibid. 175.
31. ibid.
32. ibid.
33. ibid.
34. Prat, *Théologie* 332.
35. Sundkler, *Christian Ministry* 285.
36. Sawyerr, 'Basis', 268.
37. idem, *Creative Evangelism* 93.
38. A. T. Sanon, *Tierce Eglise, ma mère* (Bobo-Dionlasso 1977) 170.
39. Sawyerr, *Creative Evangelism* 83.
40. Sawyerr's confidence about the interpretation of 'baptism for the dead' in 1 Cor.15:29 is rather surprising in view of the difficulties of interpretation surrounding that expression. Bernard M. Foschini wrote a five–part article on 1 Cor. 15:29 in *CBQ* in 1950–1951 (12 [1950] 379–388; 13 [1951] 46–75, 172–198, 276–283). He notes that this expression has always been obscure and is a 'crux interpretum'. He has found more than forty opinions among scholars! So the least that one can say is that Sawyerr's evidence for praying for the salvation of unbelieving ancestors is rather shaky!
41. A. Droogers, 'The Africanization of Christianity: An Anthropologist's View', *Missiology* 5 (1977) 451.
42. J. S. Croatto, *Exodus: A Hermeneutics of Freedom* (Maryknoll 1981) 2.
43. ibid. 3 (italics in original).

7

The Church in the Liberation Theology of Gustavo Gutiérrez
Description and Hermeneutical Analysis

EMILIO A. NUÑEZ

A. INTRODUCTION

At the present time there are several liberation theologies in Latin America, but the best known of them is the one articulated by Gustavo Gutiérrez, a Peruvian priest, in his book entitled *A Theology of Liberation*.[1] The following ecclesiological reflection will be based especially on this book. There are other liberation theologians who are known in the English speaking world—for instance, Juan Luis Segundo and José Miranda. Nevertheless, because of the limitations of this paper the discussion will be reduced to the ecclesiology of Gustavo Gutiérrez. In order to have a better understanding of his ecclesiological approach, it will be necessary first of all to provide at least a general description of the methodology he employs in his work. Then I will present a general description and evaluation of his concept of the nature and mission of the church.

B. A NEW WAY OF DOING THEOLOGY

1. Theology as Reflection on Praxis

Gutiérrez points out that during the first centuries of the church the theological emphasis was on the spiritual aspects of the

166

Christian life. It was theology as wisdom. The theologians were more concerned about a metaphysical world than about the realities of earthly life. Platonism and Neo-platonism were dominant in the theological reflection of the early church.

Then a change took place in the twelfth century, Gutiérrez says, when theology began to establish itself as a science. Thomas Aquinas used Aristotelian categories in his theological system. According to Gutiérrez, Aquinas kept the balance between theology as wisdom and theology as rational knowledge. But this was not the case in scholastic theology, especially after the Protestant Reformation, when the tendency was to reduce theology to dogmatic definitions, apologetics, the condemnation of doctrinal errors, and the authoritarian teaching of the institutional and hierarchical church.[2]

In contrast to theology as spiritual wisdom and theology as rational knowledge, Gutiérrez indicates that liberation theology is 'a critical reflection on praxis'.

> Theological reflection would then necessarily be a criticism of society and the Church insofar as they are called and addressed by the Word of God; it would be a critical theory, worked out in the light of the Word accepted in faith and inspired by a practical purpose—and therefore indisolubly linked to historical praxis.[3]

Gutiérrez understands this reflection not as a denial but as a complement to the other permanent tasks of theology. In other words, he sees a place for both theology as wisdom and theology as rational knowledge; and he claims not to be proposing a new theological subject, but 'a new way of doing theology'.[4] Nevertheless, it is evident that his theological method is not merely complementary but dominant. Liberation theology is to a large extent a reaction against the traditional methods of doing theology.

The word *praxis* means, in this context, much more than the practice of some Christian virtues. Xosé Miguélez concludes that in a sense Gutiérrez is using this word as the Marxists do.[5] To them praxis has a strong political connotation. It has to do with the effort on the part of the proletariat to change the structures of society, having in view a new project for the future, viz. the new man in a classless society.

It is not difficult to find this meaning in the 'historical praxis' and 'social praxis' advocated by Gutiérrez. He admits that there is a Marxist influence on his concept of praxis.[6] But of course he does not have a totally materialistic view of history.[7]

2. *The Point of Departure*

If in some traditional hermeneutical methods the context of the biblical writer was prominent, there are now theologians who give priority to their own social context in the effort of building a theological system that attempts to be relevant to the contemporary world. The point of departure in the hermeneutics of liberation theology is the Latin American context. This is actually one of the fundamental distinctives of Gutiérrez's work. As Dennis McCann indicates:

> Indeed, perhaps the most significant claim to be made for liberation theology is that it summons the reader to recognize the importance of its broader context. This way of doing theology is a deliberate attempt to respond to the challenge of historical consciousness.[8]

In the opinion of Segundo Galilea, a Roman Catholic theologian, Gutiérrez's method is not 'new' in an absolute way because it is closely related to 'pastoral theology', or to a 'theology of the realities' in which Christians live. According to Galilea, liberation theology is also a traditional way of doing theology in America, where some of the outstanding theologians and priests from Spain were concerned, during colonial times, about 'theologizing' in response to the new reality in which they were spreading the message of Christianity. Examples of these forerunners of liberation theology in Latin America are Vitoria and las Casas, who became the defenders of the American aborigines in the name of the Christian faith.[9]

But Gutiérrez's way of doing theology is new, Galilea says, in contrast to the dominant theology of recent times, a theology which is too abstract and too weak from the pastoral standpoint. It is also new because it is produced within the Latin American context. Other theological systems have as their point of departure the affluent society of Europe and North America.[10] Liberation theology emerges from a context of economic dependence and underdevelopment, from a situation of extreme poverty and social injustice. A different context has produced a different approach to the theological task.

That liberation theology is not totally original is obvious. What theology could be entirely original after nearly twenty centuries of Christian thought? Liberation theologians are indebted to their colleagues in Europe. Antonio Matabosch, a Roman Catholic writer, says:

> Liberation theologians depend on the progress made by European theology in the last decades, especially on the theologies on earthly realities (Thils), work (Chenu), history (Daniélou and Vol Balthasar), progress (Alfaro), hope (Moltmann and Alfaro), and politics (Metz). . . . Without the contribution of these theologies, it would have been impossible to write a theology of liberation.[11]

It is undeniable that liberation theologians use European categories in their theological reflection, but they insist their special concern over the Latin American context has brought them beyond the avant-garde European theologians in the effort to meet the challenges of modern society. For instance, J. Moltmann is, according to Gutiérrez, too futuristic in his *Theology of Hope*.[12] Hugo Assmann, another liberation theologian, is also critical of both Moltmann and Metz because of the ambiguity of their socio-analytic content.[13] Liberation theologians would like to see a more profound analysis of modern capitalism in the work of their European colleagues. Gutiérrez affirms that the political theology of Metz would be much improved by some Marxist contributions which are not sufficiently represented in his work.[14]

The Marxist influence on liberation theology is evident. The Marxist use of praxis in Gutiérrez's theology has already been mentioned in this paper. Gutiérrez seems to be in agreement with the idea, expressed by Sartre, that 'the Marxist system as a framework for all contemporary philosophical thinking cannot be superseded'.[15] Gutiérrez thinks that Ernst Bloch, an 'esoteric Marxist', gives a more adequate concept of human hope than Moltmann.[16] All through his work Gutiérrez follows, to some extent, Marxist presuppositions in his analysis of society, and in his answer to the social problems in Latin America. On his part, Hugo Assmann explains that the concept of liberation, as opposed to economic and political dependence, does not come from post-Conciliar reformism in the Roman Catholic Church. This concept, says Assman, has been rather under the influence of the vocabulary used by the movements of national liberation, by leftist revolutionaries, and by Latin American 'neo-Marxists'.[17]

Galilea speaks of four tendencies he sees in liberation theology at the present time. The first tendency emphasizes the biblical notion of liberation and the application of this concept to our society. The second tendency focuses on Latin American history and culture as a point of departure, and on the liberating potential possessed by the people in these countries. The emphasis of the third tendency is economics and class struggle, and the various ideologies confronted by the Christian faith. In this aspect of liberation theology there are points of contact with the Marxist analysis of society. But this analysis is used only insofar as it is valid for the social sciences today. The fourth tendency is, according to Galilea, more an ideology than a theology, and it is definitely under the influence of Marxism. 'In this case', Galilea says, 'we are no longer on theological grounds, and there is no reason to speak of a *theology* of liberation.'[18]

In practice, it may be quite difficult to distinguish one aspect of liberation theology from another; but it is possible to say that the first three tendencies are represented in the type of liberation theology that is becoming widely known today.

Liberation theology is under the influence of Marxist thought, and Karl Marx was a European, as are Moltmann, Metz, and the other theologians mentioned above. Strictly speaking, the fountainhead of liberation theology is Europe; but its representatives are not merely an echo of what has been said on that continent. They have taken some steps forward in the direction of a radical interpretation of the Christian faith, in response to the social conflict in Latin America. And they are taking this context as their point of departure.

What liberation theologians propose is not an analysis of the social scene in the light of the Scriptures in order to formulate an eminently biblical theology. Rather than a movement from theology to society, liberation theology is a movement from society to theology. Assmann declares, '[The] contextual starting point for a "theology of liberation" is the historical situation of dependence and domination in which the peoples of the third world find themselves.'[19] He adds, 'The usual perspectives of the exegetes who "work from the sacred text" no longer satisfy us, since we want to "work from the reality of today".'[20]

Contemporary evangelical theologians in Latin America recognize the importance of the social context for biblical hermeneutics, but they also believe in the final authority of God's written revelation, and in the importance of sound exegesis to formulate an authentic biblical theology.

If the point of departure is the social context, and this context determines the meaning of the biblical text, then this meaning is subjected to the changes of the social context. Such is basically the 'hermeneutical circle' proposed by Juan Luis Segundo, who says that the church needs 'a continual change in [its] interpretation of the Bible in the light of the continual changes in our present society, both individual and social'.[21]

3. *The Hermeneutical Norm*

Without denying the importance of the social context for a meaningful and relevant interpretation of the Christian faith in modern society, evangelical theologians may ask immediately what is the ultimate criterion in Gutiérrez's methodology. He states that his theology is an attempt at reflection which takes as its point of departure 'the gospel and the experiences of men and women committed to the process of liberation in Latin America'.[22] Theologians should let the Word of the Lord judge them in the struggle for liberation.[23] The critical reflection on praxis has to be carried out in the light of faith, taking into account 'the sources of revelation'.[24]

Gutiérrez realizes that a theology enlightened by revelation may put the process of liberation in a wider context, helping at the same time to avoid the pitfall that Christian involvement in that process may become mere activism or a sacralization of a particular ideology.[25]

In regard to the traditional teaching of the church, Gutiérrez says that 'a theology which has as its point of reference only "truths" which have been established once and for all, and not the Truth which is also the Way, can only be static, and, in the long run, sterile'.[26] At the same time he does not reject the doctrinal contribution of the universal church,[27] expecting that from now on theology as wisdom and theology as rational knowledge will have the historical praxis as its point of departure and context.[28]

Apparently, Gutiérrez is trying to keep in tension the teaching of the church and his own approach to theology; but he does not completely succeed in his effort. Although he uses expressions like 'revelation', 'the Word of God', 'the gospel', and 'the Scriptures', his emphasis is on the social context and the revolutionary praxis to change social structures. There are very few references to the Scriptures in his section dealing with methodology. And even when he expresses his allegiance to revelation, we cannot avoid asking what he means by 'the Word of God'. McCann, a Roman Catholic theologian, concludes:

> . . . like some Catholic progressives, liberation theologians recognize that the Church's reading of Scripture is subject to the vicissitudes of history. The Word of the Lord is not a cognitive absolute infallibly apprehended and faithfully taught by the Church. Like any other word in history, it must be interpreted. Its meaning is always relative to the context.[29]

The norm or hermeneutical principle determining the meaning of liberation theology is not the biblical text but the social context and the social praxis of the church. Evangelical theologians, committed to the principle of *sola Scriptura*, cannot avoid holding strong reservations concerning the relativizing of the Word of God in liberation theology.

The evangelical church in Latin America has to contextualize the Scriptures in order to be relevant to contemporary society; but to interpret God's written revelation in response to individual and social needs it is not necessary to subject the *meaning* of the biblical text to the ever changing social context. Latin American evangelicals oppose without hesitation any hermeneutical system that attempts to undermine the authority of the written Word of God.

4.   Theology and Praxis

The social context, which is the point of departure for liberation theology, has to be changed by the praxis of the people; and out of this revolutionary action new theological perceptions will continually emerge. In other words, praxis is also a point of departure for this system of thought. Gutiérrez explains:

> The theology of liberation differs from such theologies as those of development, revolution, and violence, not only in a different analysis of reality based on more universal and radical political options, but above all, in the very concept of the task of theology. The theology of liberation does not intend to provide Christian justification for positions already taken and does not aim to be a revolutionary Christian ideology. It is a reflection which makes a start with the historical praxis of the people.[30]

Liberation theologians do not limit themselves to analyzing and describing the social context. Their theology is much more than a mere denunciation of social injustice in Latin America. Gutiérrez indicates that 'a critical reflection on praxis' is also a theory of a given practice.[31] Following the Marxist dictum, liberation theologians believe that the objective is not just to explain society, but to change it. Consequently, the first step in doing theology has to be a personal commitment to the liberation of those who are oppressed and exploited by an unjust society.

In this sense, liberation theology is not the cause but the effect of praxis. In the drama of social and political liberation, theology is always 'a second act'. Praxis is followed, not preceded, by theory. There are chapters of liberation theology that cannot be written at the present time, because they have to be the result of a given practice. The theology of liberation is based on the experience of faith derived from the actual involvement of the church in the liberating process. It is a theology in the making, and it will continue to be open to new developments, as long as the creation of the new society is only a hope for the Latin American people.

Gutiérrez cannot be satisfied with a theology which has become fossilized in medieval, dogmatic affirmations of a hierarchical church. Having opted for the poor, he is interested only in a theology forged on the struggle for freedom, justice and peace. In the conclusion of his book, he says: '[We] will not have an authentic theology of liberation until the oppressed are able to express themselves freely and creatively in society as the people of God.'[32] It is not going to be a theology produced by the experts, but by the poor of Yahweh. Gutiérrez would be in agreement with James H. Cone, who in his *Black Theology* writes that 'theology ceases to be a theology of the Gospel when it fails to arise out of the community of the oppressed'.[33]

In conclusion to this general description of Gutiérrez's new way of doing theology, it may be said that in the opinion of most evangelical theologians Gutiérrez's method is objectionable most of all for its relativizing of the Word of God on behalf of political hermeneutics. It is in the area of biblical interpretation that the conflict between evangelical theology and the theology of liberation becomes sharper. Simultaneously there is a profound disagreement with liberation thelogians over their low view of biblical authority. Of course, Gutiérrez is a Roman Catholic, and Roman Catholicism does not officially adopt the high view of Scriptures adhered to by evangelicals.

Inevitably, the theology of liberation leads to disturbing questions in ecclesiological matters. Gutiérrez declares that a radical revision of what the church has been and what it now is has become necessary.[34]

C.   THE NATURE OF THE CHURCH

From the standpoint of its major concern, liberation theology does not ask what the church *is*, but what it means *to be* the church in a context of extreme poverty, social injustice and revolution. The emphasis is on praxis, not on abstract ecclesiological definitions. In the context of liberation theology the mission of the church seems to be more important than its nature. There is, nevertheless, a general description of the nature of the church in Gutiérrez's work.

1.   The Church: The Universal Sacrament of Salvation in History

One of the most remarkable declarations of Vatican II is the one related to the church as the sacrament of salvation—a visible sign of saving grace—for the entire world.[35] In traditional Roman Catholic theology, a sacrament is defined as 'a thing perceptible to the senses, which on the ground of Divine institution posseses the power both of effecting and signifying sanctity and righteousness'.[36] According to Miguel Nicolau, 'the sacrament is an efficacious sign to produce that which is signified'.[37] In other words, the sacrament is much more than a visible sign of sanctifying grace; it also confers this grace on man.

In the *Dogmatic Constitution on the Church* (Vatican II) there is no definition of sacrament and no explanation as to exactly how the term is to be applied to the church. There is in Roman Catholic theology both a narrow meaning of the word 'sacrament', with reference to the seven sacraments, and a wider sense presupposed by the *Constitution* and applied to the church.

Commenting on Vatican II, Aloys Grillmeier says that 'the notion of the Church as the sacrament of salvation forms a close link with patristic and modern ecclesiology'.[38] He explains the sacramental character of the church on the basis of the biblical word μυστήριον, which the Latin translations of the Scriptures rendered by *sacramentum*. In regard to the use of μυστήριον in the Constitution on the Church, Grillmeier says that this word signifies 'the whole economy of salvation, the eternal plan and decree of God to bring the world into the fellowship of salvation with himself in Christ'.[39] Then he adds that the intention of the Council was to ascribe to the church the value of 'sacramental symbolism' and 'instrumentality' in relation to God's purpose of salvation for all mankind.[40]

In the Documents of Vatican II, especially in both the *Dogmatic Constitution on the Church* and the *Declaration on Non-Christian Religions*, the door seems to be open to a universalistic concept of salvation. In the view of the Council the faith of an adherent of a non-Christian religion is salvific if it is based on the desire to please God and expressed by good works which follow the dictates of conscience.[41]

The speculations of Catholic theologians like Karl Rahner are behind the Council's doctrine of salvation. Rahner came to the conclusion that nature is not actually separated from grace; nature is infused by grace, and all men are already endowed with sufficient grace to impel them towards God.[42]

In his essay on *Christianity and the Non-Christian Religions*, Rahner affirms that a non-Christian religion may contain 'some supernatural moments given by grace'. This grace is granted to man because of Christ. Consequently, it is possible to say that such a non-Christian religion is 'legitimate', without denying its errors and depravation.[43]

Rahner declares that because each man is under the influence of supernatural and saving grace, there are 'anonymous Christians' in non-Christian religions.[44] The proclamation of the Gospel is necessary to give the 'anonymous Christian' the opportunity to make explicit his faith and to grow as a Christian in the fellowship of the church.[45]

In the post-Conciliar period the danger of universalism continues to be present in the Roman Catholic Church. In his book *On Being a Christian*, Hans Küng opposes the 'stupid particularism' that completely condemns other religions. What he proposes for Christianity is not 'exclusiveness' but 'particularness' in the search for truth alongside other religions. The goal is to find 'a new critical and inclusive synthesis, without false antithetic exclusivisms'.[46]

Gutiérrez interprets the teaching of the Council on the sacramental nature of the Church as a decentralization of the church—a rejection of the ecclesiocentric attitude by which medieval Roman Catholicism proclaimed that outside the institutional church there was no salvation. In alliance with the state the church considered itself as the only depositary of saving truth for mankind. There were no elements of this truth beyond the boundaries of the Roman Catholic Church, and consequently religious freedom was opposed by the papal hierarchy. In the documents of Vatican II this ecclesiological perspective has been changed, although Gutiérrez's opinion is that the Council did not go far enough in its reversal of the ecclesiocentric tendencies of traditional Roman Catholicism.[47]

Gutiérrez emphasizes that the church is a 'sacrament of universal salvation'. In his chapter on 'Liberation and Salvation', he says that man is saved if he opens himself to God and to other human beings, even if he is not clearly aware that he is doing so. This is valid for Christians and non-Christians alike, for all people.[48] Divine grace—whether accepted or rejected—is in all men,[49] especially in the poor, who are in a unique way God's people on earth. One of the distinctives of liberation theology is its emphasis on 'God's preference for the poor'. But the whole world, Gutiérrez believes, is under the saving grace of God.

According to Gutiérrez, it is not possible to speak any more of 'a profane world'. There is no distinction between a sacred world and a profane world. Salvation is also found outside the church. There is a 'universalization' of the presence of God. Every man, without exception, is a temple of God. That which is outside the temple does not exist any more.[50] Consequently, we can meet God in our encounter with men, especially in the poor, in the historical development of mankind.[51] Christ is in our neighbour.[52] All men are in Christ, 'efficaciously called to fellowship with God'.[53] To be an anonymous Christian is not an impossibility.[54]

Nor is there in Gutiérrez's theology a distinction between sacred history and secular history. There is only one history in which God carries out his saving work.[55] And in the final analysis there is no distinction between the church and the world. The church is not only present in the world; it is part of the world. The church is not 'a non-world', it is 'humanity itself attentive to the Word. It is the people of God which lives in history and is oriented toward the future promised by the Lord.'[56]

In a paper presented to the International Theological Commission in Rome, 1976, Karl Lehmann, a Catholic theologian, said that in liberation theology 'the frontiers between the Church and the world are blurry, or they disappear in a total way'.[57]

Gutiérrez attempts to avoid all dualism. He rejects the temporal/spiritual and profane/sacred antitheses, which 'are based on the natural-supernatural distinction'.[58] He recognizes, of course, that there are people who accept the Word in an explicit way; but at the same time he affirms that the church has to be evangelized by the world and to be converted to the world. A theology of the Word must be complemented by 'a theology of the world in the church'.[59]

Gutiérrez seems to ask for a dialectical relationship between the church and the world; but the dividing line between both entities tends to be obliterated in liberation theology. And the emphasis is not on the world becoming the church, but on the church becoming the world.

Conservative evangelical theologians in Latin America are in agreement with Vatican II and Gutiérrez in the rejection of the idea that outside the institutional church there is no salvation. Nevertheless, repudiating any universalistic tendency, they insist that salvation is found only in Christ, as he is revealed in the Scriptures, under the inspiration of the Holy Spirit. To be saved the sinner has to come personally, in faith and repentance, to the Son of the living God.

The gospel traces a dividing line between those who receive Christ and those who reject him (Jn.3:36; 14:6; Acts 4:12; 2 Thess.1; 1 Tim.2:5). In evangelical theology the church is both a sign of saving grace and a sign of divine judgment, because the Christian message includes the offer of perfect salvation and a warning of eternal condemnation to the world.

The New Testament teaches that the church does not belong to the world, but is in the world, and it has been sent to the world to be salt and light to the world (John 17; Matt.5:13–16). The church is called to maintain its own identity as the people of God on earth (Titus 2:11–14; 1 Peter 2:9–10).

2. *The Church as the Christian Brotherhood in the World*

As the sacrament of universal salvation, the church is related in liberation theology to the creation of human brotherhood.[60] Gutiérrez says that there is a rediscovery of 'the communitarian dimension of the Christian faith as well as new ways of living it'.[61] The church is the community of those who confess Christ as their Lord; but it is also the sign of unity among men. According to Gutiérrez, the unity of the church will not be achieved apart from the unity of the world. 'Christian unity is a gift of God and a historical conquest of man. It is a process, the result of overcoming all that divides men.'[62]

Gutiérrez explains that what makes separation between man and man is social injustice. Class struggle is a problem that cannot be denied. The Christian community itself is split by this social conflict. 'It is not possible to speak of the unity of the Church without taking into account its concrete situation in the world.'[63] Therefore the church has to become involved in the struggle for the establishment of a classless society.

In the opinion of Gutiérrez, this perspective 'is changing the focus of the concerns of ecumenism'.[64] The ecumenical goal is not just Christian unity, or religious unity, but the unification of the whole world. It is *secular ecumenism*, which argues, as Gutiérrez does, that church unity would be furthered by over-coming social evils in close cooperation with those who are dedicated to the cause of changing social structures in Latin America and in other parts of the world. That many of these revolutionaries do not profess the Christian faith is not an obstacle for such a cooperation, in the light of Vatican II, and the social encyclicals of John XXIII and Paul VI.

The church has to be involved in the effort towards world unity because the kingdom of God is already here, and is active in the movements designed to unify mankind. It does not matter if the church loses its own identity in the ecumenical process. After all, in the ecclesiological perspective of liberation theology the church is not an end in itself; it finds its meaning in its capacity to signify the reality of the kingdom of God, which has already begun in history. 'Outside of this reality the Church is nothing; because of it the Church is always provisional; and it is toward the fulfillment of this reality that the Church is oriented.'[65]

To accomplish its mission of signifying the kingdom, the church has to search for new ecclesial structures, which 'can barely be discerned on the basis of our present experience'.[66] But the church is not supposed to be anxious about its structural changes. This would mean it was concerned about its own survival. And 'the point is not to survive, but to serve. The rest will be given.'[67] In other words, the church has to be open to its own renewal, to the extreme of experiencing radical structural changes on behalf of the kingdom.

The analysis of the kingdom concept in liberation theology is beyond the purpose of this paper. Suffice it to say at this point that for liberation theologians the kingdom is the gift of God and the work of man, with special emphasis on human action to build progressively the βασιλεία τοῦ θεοῦ on earth. Gutiérrez says that this emphasis fosters an expectation of a new era, of man's 'epiphany' or 'anthropophany',[68] the glorious manifestation of man.

By contrast, the testimony of the Scriptures and the experience of mankind throughout history indicate that it is impossible for man to achieve all this by himself, much less by violent means which generate nothing else but violence. By themselves men cannot usher in the new world promised by God and inaugurated by the second coming of Christ.

In conclusion to this general evaluation of the nature of the church in Gutiérrez's theology, it is necessary to say again that his major emphasis is not on the nature of the church but on its mission. Nevertheless, he has said enough to reveal his own thinking about what the church is in the history of salvation. His emphasis is of course more sociological than theological. His references to what the church is in itself are mainly based on Vatican II, but partly on the reflections of other contemporary theologians, and partly on his own thinking.

There is a deplorable lack of biblical exegesis in Gutiérrez's ecclesiology. He does not make any effort to expound the nature of the church on the basis of the Scriptures. The clear ecclesiological teaching of the New Testament is missing. If Gutiérrez had let the Scriptures speak by themselves on this important matter, his ecclesiology would have been different.

D.   THE MISSION OF THE CHURCH

If the social praxis in the process of liberation and the participation of the Christian community in that process constitute the point of departure and the basis on which to verify all theological thinking,[69] then the mission of the church has a political dimension.

Guitérrez does not apologise for the political emphasis of his theology. It is his conviction that there are three levels of meaning in the concept of liberation: 'political liberation; the liberation of man through history; liberation from sin and admission to communion with God'.[70] He describes his hermeneutical method as political, and affirms that in the final analysis the real meaning revealed by theology is found in historical praxis.[71]

The emphasis is on social context and history. By 'history' he understands not only the record of past events, but also that which is happening now, the events which are taking place in society, the concrete experiences of men and women in their own social milieu, the cultural, social and political development of mankind, the exercise of God's sovereignty over individuals and nations, the struggle of his people to establish a just society on earth.

Gutiérrez declares that the purpose of the church is not to save, in the sense of 'guaranteeing heaven'.[72] The work of salvation is a reality which occurs in history.

Salvation embraces all men and the whole man; the liberating action of Christ . . . is at the heart of the historical current of humanity. The struggle for a just society is in its right very much a part of salvation history.[73]

According to these words, salvation is never ahistorical; it cannot be simply spiritual, or otherworldly. It includes political liberation here and now. In consequence the mission of the church cannot be defined in the abstract. But how is the church supposed to respond to the challenges of society? How is the church going to proclaim and implement the political dimension of the gospel? What is, after all, the mission of the church today? Gutiérrez answers these crucial questions from the standpoint of liberation theology.

1. Identification with the Oppressed

In Latin America to be Church today means to take a clear position regarding both the present state of social injustice and the revolutionary process which is attempting to abolish that injustice and build a more human order.[74]

In support of this option, Gutiérrez and other liberation theologians point out that in the Old Testament the Lord Yahweh has a preference for the poor, defending them against their oppressors. They add that in the New Testament the Son of God identifies himself with mankind, especially with the poor when he becomes incarnate. He was born in poverty, he lived and died as a poor man, and in his life and ministry he took the side of the oppressed. 'In terms of righteousness, God is partisan: he does take sides . . . one cannot be *for* the poor and oppressed if one is not *against* all that gives rise to man's exploitation by man.'[75]

Commenting on the documents of the Third Episcopal Conference, held in Puebla, Mexico, in 1979, Gutiérrez says that the bishops were right in declaring that the preference for the poor does not exclude other people from the gospel message; it is a preference, not an exclusion. But God's bias is still there, in God's liberating purpose.[76]

In view of God's own attitude toward the poor, Gutiérrez indicates that the church has to convert itself to the oppressed, and become poor, in order to speak out in solidarity with those who suffer social injustice. 'Only by participating in their struggle can we understand the implications of the Gospel message and make it have an impact on history.'[77] Any claim to non-involvement 'is nothing but a subterfuge to keep things as they are'.[78]

Evangelical Christians may question the idea that the love of God is prejudiced on behalf of a social class. It cannot be denied that in the Bible God is revealed as the defender of the oppressed and the One who is going to judge the oppressors. But the Scriptures teach also that all human beings are 'under sin', and that 'there is no one righteous, not even one . . . ; for all have sinned and fall short of the glory of God' (Rom.3:9–10,23). At the same time the New Testament reveals that God loves the world, the totality of mankind, and is willing to save whoever believes in him. This is true in regard to both the oppressed and the oppressors. A God who takes sides with a social class, in the way proposed by liberation theology, does not fit the biblical presentation of the character of God and his saving action in history.

On the other hand it is also undeniable that Christians are not called by the gospel to identify themselves with the oppressors in their evil-doings against the oppressed, nor to be indifferent to social injustice. Christians must exercise a ministry of reconciliation in the world—reconciliation of man with God (vertical dimension), and reconciliation of man with his fellow human beings (horizontal dimension).

2.   *Prophetic Denunciation*

The option of deciding for the poor has to be made visible in the life and ministry of the church. As declared by Gutiérrez, one way in which the church can make clear its position in regard to social issues is by means of its prophetic ministry. This ministry includes the denunciation of that which is wrong in society, and in the church itself. Gutiérrez says:

> The Latin American Church must make the prophetic *denunciation* of every dehumanizing situation, which is contrary to brotherhood, justice, and liberty. At the same time it must criticize every sacralization of oppressive structures to which the Church itself might have contributed. Its denunciation must be

public, for its position in Latin America society is public. . . . The Church must go to the very causes of the situation and not to be content with pointing out and attending to certain of its consequences.[79]

Gutiérrez does not make a distinction between the ministry of the church as church and the political actions of individual Christians in society. The Latin American experience shows that it is not always possible for the church as church to exercise a ministry of public denunciation of social and political evils. This is true in the case of both rightist and leftist governments which do not allow any public criticism of a political nature on the part of the people.

It is not easy to fulfil the prophetic ministry of denunciation when the lives of many Christians are at stake. And there are situations in which the church has to be concerned about its own survival for the benefit of the entire nation. Each church in its own particular context has to discover what is best for the kingdom of God.[80]

Evangelical theologians insist that in the Scriptures the prophetic ministry of denunciation of social evil is also a demand of repentance, a call back to God and his commandments. Commenting on this subject, Klaus Bockmuehl, a European evangelical theologian, concludes:

> The prophetic office of the church is the public 'accusation on the basis of law and Gospel' (even for Stephen, Acts 7); it consists of a directly addressed accusation and call to repentance.
>
> To 'denounce' to the public may be fashionable, but it is not biblical. The other, really prophetic way, has been little travelled in recent times. There can only be a denunciation of the sin to the sinner himself.[81]

Furthermore, evangelical Christians in Latin America must realize that the Word of the Lord, not a political ideology, has to be the criterion by which to judge and the basis on which to denounce the sins of the individual and of society.

3. Annunciation of the Kingdom

Gutiérrez affirms that the prophetic ministry consists also in the announcement of 'the love of the Father who calls all men to union among themselves and communion with Him'.[82] It is the proclamation that the kingdom of God is coming. But this announcement is not supposed to be only spiritual or futuristic. A situation of injustice and exploitation is incompatible, Gutiérrez says, with the kingdom. The Word of the Lord ought to point out this incompatibility, in order to make the people aware of their own oppression and stimulate them to seek their own freedom.

Even the proclamation of the Gospel becomes in this way a denunciation of social evils and a means to promote a radical change in society. Gutiérrez states that the church should politicize by evangelizing.[83] In his evaluation of liberation theology, Edward Norman interprets politicization as the 'transforming of the faith itself, so that it comes to be defined in terms of political values'.[84] On his part Gutiérrez explains that he is making reference to the political dimensions of the gospel only.[85] However, in liberation theology there exists the danger of reducing Christian proclamation to socio-political address.

4. Political Action

In Gutiérrez's way of thinking, the mission of the church is much more than identification with the poor, denunciation of social injustices, and proclamation of the kingdom of God; it is most of all a political involvement. Gutiérrez says that the critical function of the church runs the risk of remaining on a purely verbal and external level, apart from any action and commitment in the political arena. 'Prophetic denunciation can be made validly and truly only from within the heart of the struggle for a more human world.'[86] The denunciation has to be an action, 'not only a word, or a text'.[87] Edward Norman comments:

> Christianity today is, in this sense, being reinterpreted as a scheme of social and political action, dependent, it is true, upon supernatural authority for its ultimate claims to attention, but rendered in categories that are derived from the political theories and practices of contemporary societies.[88]

In response to the challenge which comes from liberation theology to the Latin American Church, it may be asked what particular form of political involvement the church should take in this particular context. Gutiérrez anticipates this question, and for a moment he is so cautious in dealing with it he seems not to be committed to any political ideology.

He suggests that 'the concrete measures for effecting the denunciation and the annunciation will be discerned little by little', and that 'it is difficult to establish ahead of time . . . the specific guidelines which ought to determine the behavior of the church, taken as a whole, in these questions'.[89] Positions taken at every step are not valid for all eternity. He prefers to recognize the incomplete and provisional character of any and every human achievement, and to look at the eschatological promise, which is always open to new possibilities in the expanding horizon of the future.[90] In other words, the church is not supposed to sacralize any ideology or political accomplishment. There will not be finality until history achieves its eschatological end.

When will the eschatological end come? Liberation theologians prefer not to have a rigid eschatological scheme. The kingdom of God is viewed as a reality that finds itself in the eschatological tension between the 'now' and the 'not yet'. This kingdom does not belong only to the future, nor is it simply other-worldly. God's kingdom is here and now as 'a process which becomes closely related to the constant dynamic of the historical process',[91] and is moving toward its consummation.

As has already been pointed out in this paper, to Gutiérrez the kingdom of God is a gift of God and a work of man; socio-political liberation is a human achievement and a manifestation of the kingdom. Without the liberation that man attains by himself there is no growth of the kingdom. Assmann says that the kingdom is always open to what is ahead, in 'constant futurization, even in its conquests'.[92]

Both Gutiérrez and Assmann want to avoid fully identifying the kingdom with a particular political system. Nevertheless, the total panorama of liberationist theology is that of a commitment to a particular socio-political system. Gutiérrez has taken a political position. His own theology forces him to take an option of a political nature.

John P. Gunnemann has said that when alternative power structures that might give shape to the experience of marginal peoples are not offered, the peoples 'may turn to other paradigms for organizing their experience, whether dualistic, marxist, or rationalistic'.[93] In Gutiérrez's case there is no absence of a political alternative. His inclination to socialism is evident.[94] It may be the 'Latin American socialism' of the Argentinian 'Priests for the Third World', or the 'democratic socialism' of Bishop Sergio Méndez Arceo, from México, or other type of socialism.[95] The question to be asked of Gutiérrez is whether the new revolutionary movements in Latin America will create a 'Christian socialism' or will simply follow the Cuban example.

Because he is disenchanted with the concept of development, Gutiérrez turns to the thesis that 'Latin America will never get out of its plight except by a profound transformation, a social revolution that will radically change the conditions it lives at present'.[96] Gutiérrez is thus committed to class struggle: 'Neutrality is impossible . . . it is a question of which side we are on. . . . When the Church rejects the class struggle, it is operating as a part of the prevailing system.'[97] The purpose of participating in this struggle is 'to eliminate the appropriation by a few of the wealth created by the many . . . it is a will to build a socialist society'.[98] He advocates social ownership of the means of production.[99]

But there are, of course, some questions with regard to the participation of the church in class struggle. For instance, what about the universal character of Christian love and the unity of the Church? The Scriptures teach that God loves all and that Christians must love as he loves. Gutiérrez tries to solve this problem by saying that Christian love does not mean avoiding confrontation. 'One loves the oppressors by liberating them from their inhuman condition as oppressors, by liberating them from themselves.'[100] How does this liberation come into effect? The church should liberate the oppressors by combating them: 'In the context of class struggle today, to love one's enemies presupposes recognizing and accepting that one has class enemies and that it is necessary to combat them.'[101]

If this love is taken to its ultimate consequences, it may mean what James H. Cone describes in the following words:

> The power to love oneself precisely because one is black and a readiness to die if white people try to make one behave otherwise. . . . The black experience is the feeling one has when he strikes against the enemy of black humanity by throwing a live Molotov

cocktail into a white building and watching it go up in flames. We know, of course, that there is more to getting rid of evil than burning buildings, but one must start somewhere.[102]

To Gutiérrez, the commitment to class solidarity and social conflict is the necessary and inescapable means to express love in a practical way. This participation is also justified because it leads—he says—to a classless society, without owners and dispossessed.[103] The end justifies the means.

But Gutiérrez should know better. There is a great difference between teaching and writing in a peaceful environment and living in a country where hate and violence are every day destroying human lives, even the lives of children, women and elderly people. It is a fact that institutional violence—the violence of the oppressors—is also responsible for the psychological, moral and physical destruction of large numbers of human beings; but not all Christians, including many who oppose social injustice and take sides with the oppressed, are willing to accept terrorism as the way out of an inhuman situation.[104]

At this point we must ask what the Bible has to say about the problem of violence, and the political involvement of the church. The answer to this question would require far more space than that allowed to this paper. Besides, as far as the church and its mission are concerned, the main concern of Gutiérrez is not biblical exegesis. Nevertheless we should observe how he uses the Scriptures primarily in a paradigmatic way.

The emphasis of liberation theologians on Israel's liberation from slavery in Egypt as the chief biblical paradigm for total liberation is well known. But other theologians have pointed to some elements in the narrative of the Book of Exodus that are overlooked or deemphasized by liberation theology: the covenant of Yahweh with Israel, the supreme religious purpose of the liberation, the conflict between Satanic power—represented by the magicians—and the power of the Lord, the ethnic exclusiveness of Israel, the fact that the people did not participate directly in their own deliverance. They did not fight against the Egyptians. It was God who liberated them by supernatural means (Exod. 3:8,20; 14:14). In this sense Israel's liberation cannot be a paradigm for a revolutionary movement in which the oppressed fight the oppressors.

There are, of course, valuable principles for the instruction and praxis of the church today in that meaningful event of Israel's history. For instance, the people were aware of their own degrading situation; they decided not to remain in slavery for ever, and did not give up their hope of deliverance. They cried to the Lord, and he listened to them.

Liberation theologians also use as a paradigm of revolution the Old Testament prophets, whose ministry was not limited to revealing the future by means of apocalyptic utterances. They were also social reformers. But their message was a call to repentance on the basis of God's Word.

In the New Testament the greatest prophet of them all is revealed: Jesus of Nazareth, who is for the church the highest example to follow, in his character, words and actions. What was his attitude regarding the political situation of his time? Theologians are divided on this matter. Some of them simply say that he was not interested in reforming social structures, and that his only concern was the conversion of the individual. J. G. Davies admits that in effect 'Jesus was apolitical and it is vain, on the evidence available, to seek to argue otherwise.'[105] But he adds that in Jesus' time 'there was no rigid separation of religion and politics, and that the public ministry of Jesus had political consequences'.[106] This is basically Gutiérrez's point of view:

> If we wished to discover in Jesus the least characteristic of a contemporary political militant we would not only misrepresent his life and witness and demonstrate a lack of understanding on our part of politics in the present world; we would also deprive ourselves of what his life and witness have that is deep and universal and, therefore, valid and concrete for today's man.[107]

Gutiérrez concludes that the political attitude of Jesus is found in the universality of his purpose and work:

> For Jesus, the liberation of the Jewish people was only one aspect of a universal, permanent revolution. Far from showing no interest in this liberation, Jesus placed it on a deeper level, with far reaching consequences.[108]

After pointing out that Jesus had a liberating mission, which touched 'every aspect of man's existence in the world', Andrew

Kirk affirms: 'What Jesus never offered, however, was a complete liberation in this present age from the complex of ambiguous political power. Such liberation belongs only to the time of the new creation of all things.'[109]

Certainly there is no way to prove that Jesus was directly involved in changing social structures as a political activist would do it, much less that he encouraged his disciples to organize in his name a violent revolution. The same can be said of the apostolic ministry. That in different epochs Christians have participated in violent revolutions is a historical fact; but the question is whether such examples should be taken as the basis on which to argue that involvement in a violent revolution is the mission of the church as church. The discussion in this issue is not yet closed, and it may be open for long years ahead. Conservative evangelicals in Latin America prefer to maintain the distinction between the political involvement of individual Christians and the mission of the church as church.

There is in Gutiérrez's theology an overemphasis on what he calls the political dimension of the gospel, to such an extent that the mission of the church becomes political action, and its message may be reduced to a political denunciation of social evil.

The idea that the church has a political function is not foreign to Roman Catholicism in Latin America. Through the centuries the Roman Catholic Church in this part of the globe has been deeply involved in politics, largely on behalf of the dominant class. What is different in liberation theology is the denunciation of this alliance of the church with the 'oppressive structures of society', and the demand for a change of allegiance on the part of the church, for the benefit of the oppressed. In other words, the direct political involvement of the church has to continue, but now on the opposite side.

Without denying the social implications of the gospel,[110] the most important question is whether Gutiérrez's ecclesiology conforms to the doctrine of the church in the New Testament. The answer to this question is that as in the case of his discussion on the nature of the church, Gutiérrez overlooks fundamental biblical passages when he comes to deal with the mission of God's people on earth. Once again the lack of biblical exegesis at the foundation of Gutiérrez's ecclesiology is noteworthy.

E. CONCLUSION

Liberation theology is not totally original; it has been produced under the direct influence of European systems of thought. Dennis McCann has rightly observed:

> In a situation of ideological conflict, liberation theologians there-fore are urged to take up the weapons of criticism. Ironically, these weapons also come from Europe. Liberation theologians either adopt the methods by which European progressives have already criticized Catholic tradition and give them a radical political content, or they adopt those Latin American social theorists, themselves inspired by European philosophy.[111]

At the same time liberation theology is an indigenous theological system, because it is rooted in Latin American reality. Gutiérrez's 'new way of doing theology' consists of taking the Latin American context as the point of departure, to 'theologize' from within the revolutionary praxis of those who are trying to change radically the structures of society.

But liberation theologians do not have a high view of the Scriptures. In the final analysis their criterion to determine the validity of their theological reflection is not the biblical text, but the social context and the revolutionary praxis of the oppressed. This 'new way of doing theology' inevitably leads to radical questions and disturbing conclusions on ecclesiological matters.

Although Gutiérrez makes reference to the Word of the Lord as an important factor in the theological task, he does not seem to be interested in expounding key New Testament passages, such as Matt.16:16–18; Eph.1–3; Col.1; 1 Cor.12–14, to explain the nature of the church and its mission.

The sacramental view of the church may open the door to universalism, because it blurs or obliterates the distinction between the world and the body of Christ. The concept of church unity in Gutiérrez's ecclesiology is inclined to 'secular ecumen-ism'. He sees the mission of the church as a commitment to the cause of the oppressed, as an active involvement in class struggle, and as a direct participation in the revolutionary effort to establish a classless society in which there will be neither owners nor dispossessed.

Gutiérrez never adopts a critical attitude toward leftist ideologies, overlooking the fact that there is also oppression and a notorious violation of human rights in countries which are under leftist systems of government.

Conservative evangelicals in Latin America are interested in discovering and preserving the meaning conveyed by the biblical writers in their own cultural context. They are equally concerned with the relevant communication of the biblical meaning in perpetual dialogue with the social context. The ideal is to take into account in the hermeneutical endeavour both the biblical meaning—as far as this may be known—and the social context, having as the norm what God has said in his written revelation, not speculations of modern man.

Evangelical theologians see positive elements in liberation theology—for example, the rejection of the traditional Roman Catholic principle that outside the institutional church there is no salvation; the recognition that the church is not just the hierarchy but the totality of God's people (a step that reduces clerical arrogance); the strong emphasis on the communitarian dimension of the church, and on the fact that salvation is for the whole man; the criticism against a church which in the past has taken sides with the oppressors, and become wealthy and powerful in the midst of poverty; the profound concern for the oppressed; the plea for church renewal on behalf of the poor; the impassioned call to the church for a Christian life of service in love; and the challenge to theologians to do their theology not in the comfort of an office, but in solidarity with the people in their sufferings, longings and hope.

It cannot be denied that liberation theology has directly or indirectly challenged conservative evangelical theologians in Latin America to reevaluate their own thinking and to recuperate in their teaching some biblical elements which they have left out, or deemphasized, under the influence of North Atlantic theology. But the basic ecclesiological questions asked in this paper, and other questions related to liberation theology as a whole, are still valid and should not be underestimated in a fair evaluation of this system of thought.

Latin American theologians must answer the challenge of liberation theology and produce an ecclesiology based on the Scriptures, in response to the particular needs of the Latin American context.

NOTES

1. Gustavo Gutiérrez, *A Theology of Liberation* (New York 1973).
2. ibid. 6.
3. ibid. 11.
4. ibid. 15.
5. Xosé Miguélez, *La Teología de Liberación Y su Método* (Barcelona 1976) 48–49.
6. Gutiérrez, *Theology* 31–32.
7. Miguélez, *Teología* 48–49.
8. Dennis McCann, *Christian Realism and Liberation Theology: Practical Theologies in Creative Conflict* (New York 1981) 132.
9. Segundo Galilea, *Teología de la Liberación. Ensayo de Síntesis* (Bogotá, Colombia 1976) 16–17.
10. ibid.
11. Miguélez, *Teología* 11.
12. Gutiérrez, *Theology* 279–288.
13. Hugo Assmann, *Teología desde la Praxis de la Liberación* (Barcelona 1973) 44.
14. Gutiérrez, *Theology* 224.
15. ibid. 9.
16. ibid. 215–220, 240.
17. Assmann, *Teología* 33.
18. Galilea, *Teología* 27–28.
19. Hugo Assmann, *Opresión-Liberación: Desafío a los Cristianos* (Montevideo, Uruguay 1971) 50.
20. Assmann, *Opresión-Liberación* 141.
21. Juan Luis Segundo, *Liberación de la Teología* (Buenos Aires 1975) 12.
22. Gutiérrez, *Theology* ix.
23. ibid.
24. ibid. 11.
25. ibid. 11.
26. ibid. 13.
27. ibid. x.
28. ibid. 14.
29. McCann, *Christian Realism* 159.
30. Gustavo Gutiérrez, *Liberation and Change* (Atlanta, GA 1977) 83.
31. Gutiérrez, *Theology* 11.
32. ibid. 307.
33. James H. Cone, *A Black Theology of Liberation* (Philadelphia 1970) 17–18.
34. Gutiérrez, *Theology* 251.
35. 'Dogmatic Constitution on the Church', *The Documents of Vatican II* (New York 1966) 1,48.
36. Ludwig Ott, *Fundamentals of Catholic Dogma* (St. Louis, Missouri 1958) 326.
37. Miguel Nicolau *et al.*, *La Iglesia del Concilio* (Bilbao, Spain 1966) 48.
38. Aloys Grillmeier, 'The Mystery of the Church', *Commentary on the Documents of Vatican II* (New York 1967) vol. 1, p.139.

39. ibid. 140.
40. ibid. 140.
41. 'Dogmatic Constitution on the Church', 16; 'Declaration on Non-Christian Religions', 1.
42. Karl Rahner, *Theological Investigations* (London 1961–67) vol.1, pp.297–318; J. P. Kenny, 'Supernatural Existential', *New Catholic Encyclopedia* vol.13, pp.816–817. In his book on *The Search for Salvation* (Downers Grove, Illinois 1978), David F. Wells comments on Rahner's 'supernatural existential' (pp.141–146).
43. Karl Rahner, *Escritos de Teología* (Madrid 1964) vol.5, pp.135–156.
44. ibid. 152–154.
45. ibid. 153–155.
46. Hans Küng, *Ser Cristiano* (Madrid 1977) 105–141.
47. Gutiérrez, *Theology* 259.
48. ibid. 151.
49. ibid. 151.
50. ibid. 151, 193.
51. ibid. 196–203.
52. ibid. 196.
53. ibid. 71.
54. ibid. 71.
55. ibid. 153.
56. ibid. 261.
57. Karl Lehmann, 'Problemas Metodológicos y Hermenéutics de la Teolgia de la Liberación', *Teología de la Liberación* (Madrid 1978) 13.
58. Gutiérrez, *Theology* 69–72.
59. ibid. 260–261.
60. ibid. 262.
61. ibid. 252.
62. ibid. 277–278.
63. ibid. 277.
64. ibid. 278.
65. ibid. 261.
66. ibid. 261.
67. ibid. 262.
68. ibid. 213
69. ibid. 11–13, 143.
70. ibid. 176.
71. ibid. 13.
72. ibid. 255.
73. ibid. 168.
74. ibid. 265.
75. Gustavo Gutiérrez, 'Liberation, Theology, and Proclamation', *Concilium* 6 (1974), as quoted by J. G. Davies in *Christians, Politics, and Violent Revolution* (New York 1976) 100.
76. Gutiérrez, *La Fuerza Histórica de los Pobres* (Lima, Peru 1979) 242–248.
77. Gutiérrez, *Theology* 269.
78. ibid. 266.

79. ibid. 267.
80. *The Grand Rapids Report on Evangelism and Social Responsibility* (Exeter, 1982).
81. Klaus Bockmuehl, *Evangelicals and Social Ethics* (Exeter 1979) 31.
82. Gutiérrez, *Theology* 268.
83. ibid. 269.
84. Edward Norman, *Christianity and the World Order* (Oxford 1979) 2.
85. Gutiérrez, *Theology* 270.
86. ibid. 268.
87. ibid.
88. Norman, *Christianity* 2.
89. Gutiérrez, *Theology* 272.
90. ibid.
91. Hugo Assmann, *Opresión-Liberación* 163–164.
92. ibid. 164.
93. John P. Gunnemann, *The Moral Meaning of Revolution* (London 1979) 220.
94. Gutiérrez, *Theology* 27–33.
95. ibid. 111.
96. Gustavo Gutiérrez, 'Notes for a Theology of Liberation', *TD* 19 (1971) 141–147; quoted by Robert McAfee Brown, *Religion and Violence* (Philadelphia 1973) 95.
97. Gutiérrez, *Theology* 275.
98. ibid. 274.
99. ibid. 112.
100. ibid. 276.
101. ibid.
102. Cone, *Black Theology* 56–57.
103. Gutiérrez, *Theology* 276.
104. It is impossible to overlook in this connection the very well known examples given by Martin Luther King and Helder Camara. See John Perkins, *With Justice for All* (Ventura, CA 1982).
105. J. G. Davies, *Christians, Politics, and Violent Revolution* (New York 1976) 23–26.
106. ibid.
107. Gutiérrez, *Theology* 226.
108. ibid. 231.
109. J. Andrew Kirk, *Theology Encounters Revolution* (Leicester, England 1980) 173–174.
110. *The Lausanne Covenant*, Clause 5.
111. McCann, *Christian Realism* 157.

8

Social Justice
Underlying Hermeneutical Issues
RUSSELL P. SHEDD

A. INTRODUCTION

Karl Barth said that the function of evangelical theology is to formulate a question regarding the truth, meaning thereby that the task of the theologian is to ask if the church is understanding and communicating (with word and life) the gospel correctly.[1] It is possible to believe the Bible from cover to cover yet fail to discover the fundamental truth it contains.[2] A life-changing surrender to the Author and Lord of the Bible as well as a continuing submission to the regenerating Holy Spirit, the Bible's divine interpreter, are the essential preconditions to the challenges of Scripture being heard and heeded. Nevertheless, we must be aware of the danger of culture obscuring our recognition of God's will in his revealed Word. The concerns of social justice present precisely this challenge. Those who have held most tenaciously to the high view of biblical inspiration have frequently suffocated the divine demands for his people to exemplify his deep concern for justice. This is true despite justice being:

> . . . one of the most highly respected notions in our spiritual universe. All men, religious believers and non-believers, traditionalists and revolutionaries invoke justice and none dare disavow it. Search for justice inspires the objurgations of the Hebrew prophets and the reflections of the Greek philosophers. It is invoked to protect the established order as well as to justify its overthrow . . . a universal value.[3]

195

The perceived neglect of concern for social justice on the part of evangelicals must then be attributed in large measure to the way they understand the Bible.[4] To believe the Bible is not sufficient if it is not understood. The aim of serious Bible interpretation seeks first of all to determine the 'plain meaning of the text',[5] the *sensus literalis*. But Christians 'interpret the meaning of Scripture for matters of faith in quite different ways. The hermeneutic problems that arise in interpreting the Bible as an authority for faith do not evaporate when the Bible is consulted with regard to moral practice. . . .'[6] Both the meaning of the text and the emphasis placed on some passages in detriment to others have been transmitted to us by our evangelical traditions which in turn mold our convictions in regard to right and wrong in theology and practice. 'Ideally the art of interpretation, hermeneutics, attempts to reconstruct the culture-historical context of the materials under study before proceeding to their application.'[7] This is the expectation and purpose of all communication. God's word is not a new word (novel though our situation be), but the same original word the prophets wrote and the apostles inscripturated. It needs comprehension and relevant application to the complexity of individual and world situations. When our cultural and traditional understanding are perceived to be opposed to the clear biblical norms, the hermeneutical problem becomes acute.[8]

Evangelicals in the past were no more blind to the theological lapses and social sins of the world than are sensitive, observing people anywhere. After all, the evangelicals' contribution in by-gone generations to alleviating social injustice through concerted opposition to child-labour, slavery, and totalitarianism are common knowledge. Positive examples of social betterment such as orphanages, hospitals, asylums, relief of hunger and numerous evils, material and social, have not ceased today.[9] During the last decade or two, the temporarily silent voice of evangelical concern for justice[10] has been raised again in some quarters, both to the north and to the south of the equator. Ronald J. Sider's timely contribution urging affluent Christians to live more simply has gained a wide hearing in the English-speaking world. René Padilla, Samuel Escobar, Orlando Costas and lesser known colleagues in the Latin American Fraternity of Theologians have sought to make their position known, arguing that the truncated gospel that missionaries have proclaimed in the Third World produced churches alienated from the fundamental concern of God's kingdom for righteousness. However, the majority of the younger growing evangelical churches are unconvinced, if indeed they have ever been challenged to consider the arguments favouring involvement in socio-political or economic issues at a structural level. The majority of the evangelical churches of Brazil have studiously avoided direct political involvement. Nor have they taken a united stand in favour of the opposition to the right wing government. But they do present many shining examples of Christ's love to the homeless, the hungry, the sick and the needy. Three predominating factors partially explain this lack of interest: (a) a traditional preunderstanding of the Bible created by the bitter fundamentalist/modernist controversy which encouraged evangelicals to react against the 'social gospel' and cling tenaciously to salvation promises of a perfect life beyond the grave;[11] (b) the negative impact of the socialist alliance with atheism exemplified in the Marxist challenge to all religion and freedom; and (c) the conviction that winning the world must precede any serious attempt to improve it. These, among other reasons, moved evangelicals to blacklist the denunciation of oppression and social injustice and erase the issues from the agenda.

But widespread world travel, the mass media and inner city ghettos cannot fail to have an impact on our evangelical sensibilities. Sooner or later we must all face the question whether all of us are not in some measure responsible for the obvious inequity in the world about us. Despite activism and shrill voices from the political left, social justice appears to be as much a mirage today as it did almost two hundred years ago, when radical humanism made its presence felt in the French revolution.[12] Later Marx and Nietzsche developed and disseminated the seeds of the communist and fascist ideologies. The consequent conflagrations of the 20th century's wars and massacres are familiar enough. The impact of humanism and evolutionary thought has left serious scars and a critical division in world opinion opposing socialism to capitalism.

Evangelicals sometimes hesitate to debate the issues of social injustice because of their conviction that God is sovereign.[13] Admitting that God is involved, yet reluctant to dogmatise concerning how the holy, omnipotent Creator orchestrates the events of the world, evangelicals keep silent and their views remain shrouded in mystery. Does God demonstrate his concern for the inhuman evil and suffering experienced in history, and if so, how?[14] Does the fractured and despairing reality of our times confirm the biblical affirmation that the whole world lies in the lap of the evil one (1 Jn.5:19)? Is it proper to read the Bible and look at society's running sores and console ourselves on the incontrovertible evidence of total depravity? Although this doctrine has gained credibility from current headlines of newspapers and TV news, are we guilty? The evangelical response to such questions suggests that no better behaviour can be expected of man until he is converted, not *en masse* but individually. The sole hope of mankind is repentance, regeneration and restoration to his biblical responsibility before God and to love for neighbour.[15] Yet frequently the consequences of conversion have not noticeably affected the church's perception or practice of ethics and justice.

Compassionate Christians do recognize the existence of a biblical mandate to perform 'good works'[16] such as relieving the sufferings of men and protesting the deprivation of religious freedom or persecution by communist regimes. But their list of good works would scarcely include active subversion of predominantly unjust governments such as Idi Amin's regime in Uganda. Violent revolution is anathema to the majority of evangelicals,[17] who by and large endorse as a matter of principle Paul's declaration that governments are ordained by God to punish offenders against justice.[18] Where corruption and oppression reach intolerable levels, Christians have long held that patience will be rewarded by God's judgment on guilty nations and rulers (even as the O.T. prophets announced to Israel). Man's violation of God's righteous demands will result in the cataclysmic obliteration of existing wicked structures in the glorious return of the King, whose absolute right alone is to reign over the earth in righteousness.

Christians who seek to follow the Bible give priority to missionary proclamation of the gospel rather than relief of the needs of the deprived. Financial and human resources, being as limited as they are, have discouraged concerted efforts to affect the fate of hundreds of millions of benighted dregs of humanity.[19] More deprived than the physically hungry are the billions that live in the interminable night of the soul, ignorant of the limitless power of the gospel to spark hope and create genuine brotherhood (Rom.1:6). Thus the dichotomy has been resolved by most evangelicals in favour of saving words rather than good deeds. To sustain this posture further, responsibilities once regarded as the church's have been relinquished to government agencies engaged in promoting human betterment and relieving suffering.

Ambivalence concerning government social programmes has characterized evangelicals since social protection against the ravages of life became a state concern. Many welcome the improvement in the living conditions that state programmes have effected. Nevertheless, there is a rising chorus lifted against 'godless humanism'. Moral majority evangelicalism, convinced that there is a conspiracy created by humanists to extinguish our freedom to worship God and obey the Scriptures, has begun to unite and fight back. Tim LaHaye, a well-known moral majority spokesman, defines humanism as '. . . a man-centered philosophy that attempts to solve the problems of man and the world independently of God'.[20] The humanists are powerless to reduce crime, violence, promiscuity, drug abuse and divorce; therefore the evangelical right has the divine mandate to take firm control of the reins of government. Otherwise, Western civilization is threatened by anarchy and destruction.[21] Since humanism is predicated on relativism and evolution, Francis Schaeffer has warned that its ultimate end will be chaos.[22] Moral absolutes rooted in God's revealed will are being replaced by 'situation ethics', which is equivalent to moral permissiveness, and poses a threat to our traditional Christian values on a massive scale. In this movement to unite the evangelical right we may find a counterpart to the polarization of the left in which Roman Catholic liberation theology and the World Council of Churches have united to extirpate social evils on a global scale.[23]

Various issues have been raised for hermeneutics by the opposition between the left and the right. While evangelicals denounce the sins that undermine traditional cultural values committed primarily by individuals,[24] the left focuses on evil in society as a whole. Social justice raises the question of the righteousness of a given class or group, a government or a

nation,[25] calling to the bar of justice the political power structures and international business, challenging economic and racial
expressions of evil. Does the Bible guide us in matters of
equitable trade relations with the so-called third world? Is it
sinful for a government to allow unemployment above a mini-
mum level or to bar free access to equal opportunity for health
care and education? Are Christians vocally and actively to oppose
any legally supported racial discrimination? Are they comman-
ded by God to pressure their governments to break relations with
any government that imprisons and tortures political (and Christian) minorities within its borders? Such a list could be prolonged
almost endlessly.

Still more basic to the hermeneutical issue than the collective
versus individual sins is the church's involvement in the world.
Because Christians have been rescued 'from this present evil age'
(ἐκ τοῦ αἰῶνος τοῦ ἐνεστῶτος πονηροῦ (Gal.1:4) are they
therefore to eschew militancy and become non-combatants on
the societal stage of life?[26] Now that Adam's transgression visited
upon all succeeding generations has been deleted from the
believer's account (Rom.5:12–29), graciously settled by the last
Adam, are evangelicals to limit their hostility to opposing the
devil and his forces (cf Eph.6:10–18)? Does C. I. Scofield's
message to the prophetic conference in Philadelphia in 1918
display the Bible's attitude toward social issues?

> I pray that God may guide all your proceedings, especially in the
> putting forth of a fearless warning that we are in the awful end of
> the times of the Gentiles with no hope for humanity except in the
> personal return of the Lord in Glory.[25]

Comforting as such a position is, it may not express the whole
of God's will if the Bible is rightly understood.

B.   REASONS FOR CHRISTIAN INVOLVEMENT IN ISSUES OF SOCIAL JUSTICE

The biblical rationale for seeking to eliminate social inequity lies
in man's origin and potential destiny as well as in God's universal
love for the world (Jn.3:16; Matt.5:43–48). Western civiliza-

tion's roots are deeply imbedded in the Bible's revelation of the origin of man descended from a single father and mother and created in God's image.[26] The common sharing of all men in the *imago dei* means that all men are heirs to inalienable rights to dignity and purposeful meaning.[27] To agree with Lincoln on the axiom that all men are created equal, but deny the participation in the *imago* means that in the final analysis there is no reason for common responsibility among men.[28] Because socialistic humanism has gained power, while denying the creation of man in the divine image, human dignity and equality have evaporated into mere slogans highly useful for propaganda purposes. George Orwell satirized the consequences of socialism, rejecting the foundation of equality in his *Animal Farm*.[39] Djilas and more recently A. Solzhenitsyn have described the historical consequences of the ideal society which lacks a foundation in divine creation.[30] The far-reaching significance of the truth about human origins is summed up in the Bible's command to love one's neighbour as one's self (Lev.19:18; Matt.22:39). However, the failure of men to live as brothers, although creation has made them such, is due to the inherent selfishness that sin has made universal. Replacing unjust structures with more equitable ones will finally be crowned with failure unless a far more profound transformation is wrought in the men who establish them and wield their power. For this reason evangelicals must ever contend that the first responsibility of the church is the proclamation of the gospel and depend on the consequent spiritual change wrought by the Holy Spirit to create a community in which the unconverted may see a model of the kingdom of God. The concerns of social justice must therefore be always kept in a subordinate relationship to evangelism, which is God's means of restoring the image of God through the indwelling Christ (Col.3:10). We may properly affirm that the goal of mankind is the 'perfection of community'[31] of those who have become a body through the incorporating action of the Holy Spirit (1 Cor.12:13). The God who has given sinners his most precious gift, his Son, cannot commend indifference to the squalour in which countless millions eke out their tortured existence waiting hopelessly for the kingdom to be offered to them. For this reason Jesus Christ commands his followers to go into all the world and make disciples of all nations teaching them to obey all of the commands he gave to them (Matt.28:19f.). While socialist liberals categorize the inequalities of the world as criminal, an insult to man and God,[32] evangelicals incongruously appear to accept with too much tranquility that much of that same world has not yet heard the saving message. On the other hand, where the gospel has been proclaimed and accepted, new joy and hope have replaced the prevailing despair.[33] The traces of the image of God have begun to appear (cf Rom.8:28f. and 2 Cor.3:2,18).

C.   THE NATURE OF SOCIAL JUSTICE IN THE OLD TESTAMENT

To many secular humanists, social justice may not mean much more than the replacement of capitalism by state socialism, thereby facilitating the equitable burden of production and guaranteeing the fair distribution of the world's riches to all men 'according to their needs'. Others would add to this base the dimension of international peace so that all threats to individuals would be eliminated, above all nuclear destruction. Still others prudently recognize that failure to provide meaning for man's life misses the mark. Why pursue peace, prosperity and security if boredom and *ennui* propel men to contemplate suicide? In the Bible, social justice has its *raison d'être* in man's relationship to God and the revelation transmitted to man recorded in the Scriptures. God is the guarantor of the weak, protecting them against the insatiable 'will to power' in the strong. The structures which God ordained for Israel through Moses had as one of their prime objectives this impartiality of God reflected in the institutions governing the lives of his covenant people.

God is the original and absolute land-owner (Ps.24:1; cf Ps.50:12 and Deut.10:14). Therefore title to any proportion of it does not concede total rights of possession to human owners. Since the Hebrews belonged to an agrarian society, the restoration of alienated lands to the original owners was an important provision in the divine legislation. 'The land shall not be sold permanently, for the land is mine . . .' (Lev.25:23). The natural human tendency to seek to acquire more and more land and create a monopoly was not to be permitted. Rather than the weak and the poor being forced into slavery by depressed times, whether of famine or personal tragedy (as in the case of Naomi,

Ruth.1:1; 4:1–11), they could make a new beginning. Similarly, Israelite slaves (reduced to bondage by hard times and incapacity to repay a debt) were to be granted freedom at pre-set seven year intervals (Deut.5:12).[34] Women's rights too were to some extent protected by law. Those who committed unintentional manslaughter could find permanent protection against the blood avenger by moving to one of the cities of refuge conveniently located throughout the land.

Unmistakably, Israel's laws were instituted by God to create and sustain a just society for all of its citizens regardless of class or status. The nation thereby would reflect God's own passion for justice and his impartiality. God ordered the affluent not to neglect or despise the poor (Deut.15:7ff.). Indeed, one of the purposes of the sabbatical rest of the land was to provide food for the destitute (Exod.23:11). God's legislation permitted no racial discrimination. Foreigners, widows and orphans were to be extended humane treatment (Deut.10:18ff.; 24:17). Court trials were to be fair regardless of the social status of the accused (Exod.23:1,6,7; Lev.19:15f.) and bribery of officials was to be avoided (Exod.23:8). Because it is unjust, economic oppression is declared to be contrary to God's law (Deut.24:17). Usury and loans must benefit the needy rather than the capitalist loan shark (Exod.22:25f.). Innocent men were not to suffer for the crimes of the guilty (Deut.24:16).[35]

Since God hates oppression, he broke Israel's slave shackles (cf Exod.23:10; Deut.15:15). Since he is the giver of prosperity and distributor of wealth, God demands acknowledgment of his generosity with thankful worship (Deut.8:11–20), accompanied by a commitment to justice. God is a God of justice and mercy; hence he required the cancellation of debts and loans at set times (Deut.15:1–6), and thus he shows the desired pattern for a state that acknowledges him. But his justice threatens wrath and heavy penalties to be visited on leaders who disregard his merciful and just laws.[36] In his concern for the destitute, he ordered that every third year the tithes were to provide sustenance for the landless Levites, aliens and widows and orphans (Deut.26:12–15). Social legislation and rules for worship are juxtaposed in the Pentateuch to underscore the principle that God commands not only that people maintain a proper vertical relationship with himself, but also give due importance to their

relationship with the creation and especially with their neighbours. Duty toward God and responsibility toward man inextric-
ably mesh, in that they are fundamentally inter-related. Jethro
correctly assessed the importance of a government in which
leaders are capable, fear God, hate dishonest gain and love the
truth (Exod.18:21).

But divine institutions and revealed laws do not guarantee that
men will execute the will of God in government. The history of
Israel reveals at best erratic attempts to apply the divine norms.
The times of the judges were years of weak government in which
every man did 'what was right in his own eyes', despite the
nominally theocratic government. The pressure of the surrounding nations was not resisted with vigour, resulting in the
adoption by Israel of the nature religions in the interest of
protecting against the incursions of marauding armies from those
same neighbours. Neither priests nor judges had the ability to
establish a government in which God's just laws were obeyed and
the consequent blessings reaped.[37]

The centuries of ineffective government which followed motivated Israel to seek in a monarchy a stronger central authority.
The elders transmitted the will of the majority to Samuel who in
turn requested of God the installation of a king who would
maintain a higher level of social justice (1 Sam.8:4–5,20). God's
response (1 Sam.8:11–18) clearly shows that the high hopes that
the nation held for a human king were never to be realized, for
injustice would increase (1 Sam.8:11–18). Subsequent centuries
proved this prediction to be correct.

Although God relinquished his nominal role of theocratic
sovereign over Israel in deference to the nation's wish to be like
her neighbours, he did not abdicate his responsibility for the
king's moral behaviour. Saul was soon deposed by God for failing
to obey orders. David, although a favourite with God, heard
Nathan, the prophet, rebuke him sharply for a particularly crass
instance of monarchical injustice (2 Sam.11,12). No contemporary near-eastern monarch would have imagined that such moral
restrictions would apply to the king.[38]

Solomon's oppressive forced labour levies, along with his
idolatry, rent the kingdom in two under his son Rehoboam (1
Ki.11:33; 12:4), undeterred from a policy that continued his
father's iron-fisted rule (1 Ki.12:1–15). The vicissitudes of

national fortune rose and fell with a dreary succession of kings who occasionally obeyed the just rule that God had legislated for his people. In time, ever more blatant disobedience forced God to decree the demise of both Israel and Judah as self-governing states by sending them into exile under Assyria and Babylonia. Despite the reiterated message of prophets who denounced unjust oppression and announced the threatening consequences of failure with divine punishment, the nation rarely honoured God with the humble repentance necessary to avoid his judgment.

Even the revival led by Josiah in Jeremiah's day which drew throngs of worshippers to the temple, brought no profound change or return to the ancient paths (Jer.6:16–16:21). John Bright observes:

> So men have always reformed, cutting out the grosser immoralities and participating more actively in the work of the church. The social sins which are society's sickness continue (Jer.5:23–29), and the clergy have come to terms with them to everyone's satisfaction.[39]

Not only idolatry and false religion but oppression (the worship of one's own power and welfare at the expense of the weak) was the cause for the nation's exile (Jer.34:3–17). The history of Israel's exploitation of the needy called for prophetic denunciation, but also elicited the promise of a coming king who would change the nature of man so that he could produce actions and attitudes characteristic of repentance.[40]

The O.T. presents both the demand for social justice and the history of human failure in practising righteousness. God totally rejects any split between religion and justice (both being undergirded by divine law fixed in the nature of God himself). Not only individuals alone but unjust social institutions controlled by merciless retainers of power are the objects of the divine ire. Such institutions embrace the whole society in a web of social wickedness, such as unjust and oppressive taxes, high rents, cheating customers with false weights, enslavement of the poor (cf Isa.10:1–4; Amos.4:14; 5:10–15; 6:4–7; 8:4–6;9:8; Ps.94:20–23). Rooy has demonstrated convincingly that righteousness and justice are not different levels of holiness which the people may choose to pursue at their own discretion, but synonyms.[41] When men flout justice, God will not accept their worship, however costly and sacrificial, since injustice and idolatry are equivalent in his sight (Amos.5:25f).

D.   SOME IMPLICATIONS OF THE OLD TESTAMENT VIEW OF JUSTICE FOR THE NEW TESTAMENT

What implications can be drawn from the teaching on social justice expressed in the O.T.? This complex question will receive different answers depending on one's hermeneutics and not merely on whether the interpreter holds to a high or low view of the O.T. Can a key be discovered that will aid us in perceiving the obligations incumbent on the church of the N.T. and of our day?[42]

We may begin with the reminder that there is one obvious discontinuity between the people of God in the O.T. and the church in the N.T., despite the titles that they share in common. Peter calls the church a 'holy nation' (1 Pet.2:9, ἔθνος), meaning not a state or country nor subjects under a government, but a people united by social, racial and cultural ties;[43] and Paul calls it the 'Israel of God' (Gal.6:16). This however does not mean that the apostles thought of Christians as a state. The N.T. church has no sovereign territory not politically recognized boundaries, nor even particularity of race[44] (cf Rev.5:9; Matt.28:19; Acts 1:8). Structures that characterize a government such as a police force, a court system, political parties, an army, as well as complete control over the national economy are totally alien to the N.T. description of the church.[45] The church is far more like a brotherhood than a state, for she does not extend membership on the grounds of birth, but is a voluntary association. The people of God have no means of coercion more powerful than exhortation, admonition, public reproof and eventual exclusion, to maintain the integrity of its membership (cf Matt.18:15ff; 1 Cor.5:1–13). Because of the voluntary nature of the association of the members of the church, its employees do not protest against hiring practices, low pay scale, or unfair working conditions, even though they may exist. No one attempts to unionize church workers even if by comparison with colleagues doing the same work in the secular world they are being exploited. While the church as the new covenant people rightly exercises spiritual sanctions, the secular state has divine authorization to enact and impose laws by the sword (Rom.13:1–7).

Now we may freely grant that the most significant contribution hermeneutics can offer is not the correct relationship between systematic theology and historical theology, but between theology and practice, i.e. between the gospel and action.[46] It was just such a necessary relation between his words and practice that Jesus endorsed in the sermon on the mount (Matt.7:15–27). The theology of the New Testament is not unrelated to life. Christians are obligated to practise righteousness. Their relationship to the structures of society and government is subordinate to their subjection to the Lord of the church; therefore Christian employers, officials or authorities of any kind are obliged to hear the Word of God and obey it. If those structures are exploitative believers must raise their voice against injustice and treat their employees or subordinates with justice. Only thus can they demonstrate faithfulness to God and the veracity of their profession as Christians and members of the church whose head is Christ.[47] This linkage has always been truly applicable among Christians. The claim that the 'older hermeneutics is strangely silent regarding the oppressive/repressive *status quo* and remarkably impotent in changing it'[48] can be true only with respect to the *status quo* of the secular state, not the local church or some denomination. A prophetic exposition of the divine will to the secular state is not incumbent on the preacher of the Word *in the same way* as it was in Israel. Otherwise, to be consistent, the state would have to be misconstrued as Christian and under the immediate aegis of Christ, the righteous king. Similarly, for men of God to expose indignantly the evils of collectivities, economic or political, assumes that they will listen, as indeed the true Christian must.

On the other hand we must not close our eyes to the typological significance of God's law revealed under the old covenant for his people of the new. God's concern for righteousness in all the earth is not diminished by the cross, the resurrection and inauguration of the new age. Christians continue to live in the world though they are citizens of heaven (Phil.1:27). As constituent members of society and a political state, they must exercise their rights and responsibilities in such a way that both will be improved. They will do well to proclaim as widely and emphatically as they can that 'righteousness exalts a nation but sin is a reproach to any people' (Prov.14:34).

The first and primary message that the church must announce to the state and the dominators of the evil structures of the world is God's demand for repentance (cf Acts 17:30). When leaders submit to the lordship of Jesus Christ, whom God has enthroned as Messiah and Lord of the world (Acts 2:36), the question of injustice can be settled. For injustice is primarily a symptom of a broken relationship between man and God. 'There is no authority except from God' (Rom.13:1 NASB) can mean only legitimate authority. Countless examples throughout history of a misused right to rule make it plain that blind following of a state's or tyrant's commands may mean denying Christ's lordship.

In this light, it becomes clearer why Jesus directed his criticism against the lawyers and Pharisees for their unjust oppression of the common people (see Matthew 23). Both John the Baptist and Jesus confronted the nation's leadership in the role of O.T. prophets, for the people gave allegiance to them as divinely appointed representatives from God and interpreters of his will. Before the Roman governors neither the Baptist, Jesus nor Paul (e.g. Matt.27:11ff, and parallels Jn.18:28–19:6; Acts 24:1–26:32) had a word to say about the evils of Roman domination over the Jews or the rest of the world, even though more than half the population of the empire were exploited slaves taken by force from conquered lands. Stephen addressed the Sanhedrin in these terms: 'You stiff-necked people, with uncircumcised hearts and ears! You always resist the Holy Spirit!' (Acts 7:51–53). He would have been out of place repeating this condemnation before the Roman Senate, or the Emperor Tiberius. The leadership of the Jewish people claimed to interpret the will of God, but the Emperor and his lackeys made no pretence of doing so.

Although God hated injustice in Rome as much as he did in Israel, his strategy for dealing with such structural evil was distinct. All wickedness must be exposed if it is practised in the church, whether by true or false Christian leaders (cf Gal.2:1–21; 2 Pet.2; Jude and the seven letters in Revelation 2–3). But suffering for the right at the hands of the secular power is blessed, as Peter said:

> Always be prepared to give an answer to everyone who ask you to give the reason for the hope you have. But do this with gentleness and respect, keeping a clear conscience so that those who speak maliciously against your good behaviour in Christ may be ashamed of their slander. It is better, if it is God's will, to suffer for doing good than for doing evil' (1 Pet.3:15–17).

Such statements are not exceptional in the N.T. Surely they find their inspiration in the attitude Jesus displayed when activists sought to enlist his commitment to their cause.[49] Should God's people pay taxes and thereby condone and support the injustice of the Roman oppression? Or should Christians practise civil disobedience, whether actively or passively, and thereby proclaim to the world how God has identified himself with the men who are willing to risk their lives to fight political and economic structural evil? The exhortations of the N.T. favour paying taxes and submitting to the authority of the rulers, though the state be largely unjust (Matt.22:15–22 and parallels).

A parallel situation may be observed in the prophets' excoriation of Israel and Judah in distinction to their condemnation of the pagan nations and their unjust treatment of the helpless people of God. The oppressed of the world are outside the purview of the prophets' message. Millions of victims of inhumanity occupied the Near East; their plight was fully known to God, yet there are few divine mandates to warn pagan rulers against oppressing their own citizens, and these of the most general sort (e.g. Prov.14:34).[50] The sufferers that can count on God as their vindicator are limited primarily to those that have him as their God, united to him through his electing mercy and sealed in the covenant. Touch them and one touches the 'apple' of God's eye.

We find no divergence here between the O.T. and the N.T. Persecution of Christians (a blatant form of injustice) will bring upon its perpetrators the certain wrath of God (Phil.1:28; 1 Thess.1:5,6; Rev. *passim*). It is vain to search in the N.T. for some hope that the church will grow sufficiently large to become a majority in the state, seize power and install a government that can impose justice on society. With the passing of the centuries the Constantinian church did achieve dominance; but history has scarcely given her 'Christian' rule high marks for the practice of justice.[51]

Whether dominion over the state has been relegated to high priest, Sanhedrin or Roman governor, the 'authorities' (οἱ ἄρχοντες) are blind to the long term implications of their decisions (1 Cor.2:8). Paul declares that the authorities are servants of God (cf 1 Thess.2:1ff; Tit.3:1; 1 Pet.2:13ff; Rom.13:4), authorised by him to maintain justice by punishing the guilty, exonerating the innocent and rewarding the deserving. When the same state, Rome, at least partially, became identified with the persecuting Beast in the Apocalypse, however, John prophesies divine retribution (also on the future satanic Antichrist) in similar terms to those of the prophets announcing the destruction of Babylon or any other state that dares to oppress the people of God. Nero ended three decades of benevolent co-existence with Christians, protected under the provisions of the *religio licita* umbrella enjoyed by Judaism, and clasped fire into Rome's bosom. The same holds true today when persecuting, oppressing governments, whether of the right or the left, oppress the church.

All injustice will be avenged by God in the course of history and beyond, not only the injustice perpetrated against God's people. His wrath is revealed from heaven against 'all unrighteousness of men', both private and institutional (Rom.1:18). It may be safe to assert that this wrath is poured out historically in diverse parts of the world when governments topple, heads roll, rulers are deposed and powerless men momentarily become strong (Lk.1:52), only to fall in turn if they do not practise righteousness. Still, to limit to the see-saw of rising and falling power the entire visitation of God's wrath can scarcely be correct. There remains a future day, the Bible declares, in which every injustice will be avenged and every wrong righted. Then Jesus Christ, the righteous judge, will pass sentence upon all men (Heb.9:27; Jas.4:12; Rev.18:11–13, where slavery is indicated as a prime cause for the destruction of the Harlot; 19:5,20f; 20:13f).[52]

It is not uncommon to hear it said that the history of the church and the world is so unitary that the church is the living example of the one meaning of history.[53] Be that as it may, their destinies are totally distinct.[54] The true sons of the kingdom may be spoil for the ruthless (Heb.10:32–34), exploited labourers oppressed by land-owners (Jas.5:4), or innocent martyrs murdered by those who live in luxury and wanton pleasure (Jas.6:6), but their tormentors will face a fearsome day of reckoning. Those who like Lazarus suffer in Christ during this life will be comforted in the next, while those who like the rich man live self-centred, hedonistic lives, unheeding the cries of the downtrodden, will experience only agony in the second death in the age to come (cf Lk.16:23f,25 NIV).

Paul's epistles demonstrate the same understanding when they address the Christian slave. The slave is under obligation to give his master obedient, respectful service 'with fear and trembling', as if he were serving Christ himself (Eph.6:5f). Slaves are encouraged neither to rebel nor to escape, but to submit humbly to their masters because Christ is their real Master. It is he who will restore to them all that is their rightful due (Eph.6:8). Free men will receive their righteous reward in cases where they have been defrauded (Eph.6:8). Paul does not condemn slave masters for possessing bondmen, but he warns them that they will be held accountable for the manner in which they treat their slaves (Eph.6:9; Phlm.14–16).

Christian wives are urged to submit to their unbelieving husbands (1 Pet.3:1; note that 'likewise' refers to the manner in which slaves are to submit). The connection with the unbelieving husband belongs to the 'old age'; therefore it is considered to be 'interim' and significant mainly in its offering opportunity to win him to faith in Christ (1 Pet.3:1–6).

Paul consistently fails to encourage Christians to form a pressure group and thereby win needed respect to improve their lot. Rather, the apostle gives the churches an example in his welcome of suffering, thereby filling up 'what is lacking in the sufferings of Christ' (Col.1:24). Afflictions in this life are not in any way comparable to the future 'weight of glory' (2 Cor.4:17; cf 5:10). Evaluating the injustice in the world as an unmitigated evil means that the interpreter has missed the fundamental biblical significance of faith as opposed to sight. The central viewpoint of the N.T. is the two-aeon structure.[55] To cause men to suffer, whether by persecution or maintaining the unjust structures of society, is invariably evil and worthy of condemnation. But Christians are not to pay back evil with anything but good (Rom.12:17,21; Matt.7:12).[56]

Jesus practised just such a form of 'politics' during his earthly life. He expressed no interest in leading an army to conquer Rome and establish justice in the Empire, nor did he try to replace the Jewish authorities. He urged men to repent and escape the wrath to come (Lk.21:34–36). It is difficult to substantiate Jon Sobrino's declaration that 'Jesus adopts a stance that is rooted in the poor and is meant to benefit them. In that sense the first principle for concretizing moral values is nothing else but the first principle of Christology itself: i.e. incarnation.'[57] No, the poor also were called to repentance. The marginalized were not considered 'saved' by their sufferings in distinction from the dominating oppressors. Jesus' words were, 'Whoever does the will of God, he is my brother and sister and mother' (Mk.3:35). The direction of Jesus' thought seems to be that the poor are blessed (Lk.6:20), as well as the hungry (v. 21), not because misery and deprivation are idealized,[58] but because the people Jesus has in mind are subjects of the king ('yours is the kingdom of God', Lk.6:20). God is opposed to human pride and self-esteem which produce rivalry, hatred, envy and violence.

Jesus did not institute a permanent communal society in which all the members were required to give up their possessions. Perhaps John Yoder is right in ascribing the demands of Jesus to a special Jubilee celebration.[59] He did not require his followers to make vows of poverty or become slaves. The 'good news' he preached was directed to the poor (Lk.4:18f; 7:22), because the weak and the humble have less difficulty entering the narrow gate of the kingdom (Matt.7:13f). Most men choose the wide road and the broad gate not because they are wealthy exploiters or oppressive rulers, but because they are egocentric, self-reliant and proud (cf 1 Tim.6:17).[60] Inclusion within the kingdom does not depend on class distinctions; but it does demand receiving the rule of God over one's life as a 'little child' (Mk.10:15; Matt.18:3). Conversion is just such an experience granted by God to those that are willing to become child-like. Nicodemus had to be born again and become humble enough to relearn the 'wisdom' of God. (Jn.3:3,5).

Jesus repelled the rich and the powerful from the kingdom, not from some exclusive partiality to the poor, but because of its total demands. All men are invited to share in the messianic banquet, but at the crucial moment the prosperous were too busy reviewing their newly acquired property to accept the invitation (Lk.14:18; Matt.22:5); another had to test his yoke of oxen essential to his farm-expansion programme (Lk.14:19). As long as the wealthy are assured of the places of honour at the wedding feast (Lk.14:7,8) they will condescend to come. The extraordinary sacrifices demanded of candidates, such as selling all of one's posessions, make it 'impossible' for such men to enter the kingdom (Lk.14:33; Mk.10:27). But the poor must pay a price too: 'hate' one's father and mother, wife and children and carry the cross of Christ (Lk.14:26f). A disciple can serve only one master, not both lord Mammon and lord Christ (Matt.6:24).[61] Even a camel can pass through the eye of a needle more readily than the wealthy can enter the kingdom (Mk.10:25). But it is not only the greedy person who is denied entrance (being 'choked with worries and riches and pleasures of this life', Lk.8:14), but the ambitious religionist as well.[62] Because he seeks glory from his fellow churchmen, he fails to seek the glory that is from God (Jn.5:44), making it impossible to believe (i.e. be saved). Zacchaeus was rich and powerful; yet owing to a deep heart change, he heard Jesus make the joyful announcement that salvation had come to his house. The chief priests and lawyers were barred (Lk.19:9,10), the repentant publican 'justified' (Lk.18:14).

Paul states clearly that the covetous and swindlers will not inherit the kingdom (1 Cor.6:10), not merely because they pervert justice, but because their values are limited to this age. The kingdom must be sought as one's primary concern (Matt.6:33). An example of such pursuit is the heart that out of love for God stores wealth in heaven (Matt.6:20,21). Jesus explains in the parable of the 'Unjust Steward' what he means. By making friends through generous giving to the needy ('by means of the mammon of unrighteousness'), unselfish Christians are assured of being welcomed by those friends into the 'eternal dwellings'.[63] But Christians can be trapped, as a bird in a snare, by the desire for riches which conduct them on to lusts that plunge men into ruin (1 Tim.6:9). Love of money is a root of all kinds of evil, the worst being 'to wander away from the faith' (v.10).

Summing up, we may make the following observations. First, the key to the interpretation of the Bible lies in God's moral nature, the creation of man in his image, the selfish individualism of fallen man. Second, God has graciously inaugurated the new age through the life, death and exaltation of his Son, Jesus Christ, so that the new and the old age exist concurrently. Third, God did not enjoin his new covenant people to form a state nor to seek political power or economic might by which they might change the world. Rather, they must voluntarily choose weakness and poverty to reflect the wisdom of God demonstrated in the death of Jesus on the cross. Fourth, the church must reflect God's concern for justice by recognizing and opposing it, not by violence (the state alone has divine authorization to wield the sword), but by living it, above all in its own ranks. The concerns of the kingdom are paramount over all temporal ambitions; hence wealth and possessions must be held lightly and shared with the needy, above all with the family of God (Rom.12:13). Fifth, the Christian has double citizenship, heavenly and earthly. While the heavenly has priority, the believer is obligated to fulfil his earthly duties toward the state, choosing the course open to him that best favours justice and morality.

E.   THE HERMENEUTICS OF LIBERATION THEOLOGY

Since God condemns social sins plainly and frequently as private sins,[64] it is inconsistent for evangelicals to hold a high level of commitment to the veracity of the Bible but give short shrift to the concerns of social justice. The proponents of liberation theology, the majority being Latin Americans, have thrown down the gauntlet to both conservative Roman Catholics and Protestants alike, challenging them to 'praxis' in the struggle to eliminate injustice. We are told that apathy and non-involvement in the struggle against injustice in the face of the intolerable oppression practised in much of the third world will not suffice, nor will excuses diminish the responsibility of the church for the evils of society.

Liberationists take their cue from existential theology and its emphasis on the present situation; but they have veered far to the left. Rather than individual salvation and santification, social reality presents the valid starting point for theological reflection.[65] Deep roots reach down to Feuerbach's radical transformation of Hegel's 'spirit' into anthropology. He believed that philosophy must become religion and politics by providing something ultimate to hope for. From Feuerbach to Marx required only a small step, but an important one: Marx moved from theory to the formulation and practice and from observation to galvanizing action. Karl Marx's contribution was to call the oppressed proletariat to unite and overthrow the unjust exploiting capitalist system and create the New Man, a universal brotherhood.[66] Marx's success cannot be explained by his inadequate explanation of the causes of inequality and injustice, but in its emotional appeal.Blame is attributed invariably to others and not to any failure of the lower classes nor to the judgment of God.[67]

Liberation theology, although a Latin American invention of the early 1960s, leans heavily on liberal German thinkers such as E. Bloch, J. B. Metz and J. Moltmann. Traditionally, Roman Catholic members of the elite in Latin America, including the hierarchy, supported the wealthy landowners and industrialists; and thus stratified society into social classes at opposite extremes of the economic scale. Prior to the 'Marxist analysis' made by such men as G. Gutiérrez of Peru, H. Assmann of Brazil and J. Miranda of Mexico among numerous others,[68] hope for a more just society was based on economic development. Scarcely two decades following World War II were needed to shatter the dream of industrialization improving the lot of the poor. The needy were exploited in the cities as they had been on the land, thus making authentic liberation urgent.[69] Since God is a God who liberates and the Bible is the account of man's struggle against oppression, we are told that a theology of liberation must undergird the impetus for transforming the world into a just society.

Hermeneutics has been turned upside down by this new way of 'doing theology'. Holy Scripture is no longer the source. It offers little ground for promoting the class revolution.[70] But the suffering of the nameless masses, with whom Jesus identified and whom God especially loves, provides the ideal point of departure. Thus it is called 'theology' rather than ideology. Hugo Assmann says, 'The Bible, I know of only one Bible; the sociological Bible of facts and events here and now as a Christian.'[71]

There is a hermeneutical circle, claims Juan Segundo, and the majority of the liberationists agree.[72] First the Christian conscience must be aroused to the point of profound dissatisfaction with the *status quo*.[73] No Christian must be allowed to accept irresponsibly the injustice solidified in the structures of government, economics and society as divinely authorised or predetermined (cf Isa.10:1–4; Deut.26:5–9). This 'suspicion' must then be applied to the ideological superstructure in general and to theology in particular, proceeding to question even biblical interpretation which omits the important data. It is useless to answer the new questions with the old answers in a vain attempt to break the hermeneutical circle. But equally one must not simply interpret the 'source of our faith, which is scripture, with the new elements at our disposal'.[74] This way the importance of the method increases at the expense of the meaning and content of the text.

When the interpreter adds to this the strident emphasis laid on 'praxis' and struggle, it becomes possible to detect echoes of Galatianism, no longer restricted to individual salvation, but now expanded to include the redemption of society through man's efforts. Since for most Latin Americans the church offers salvation as the mediator of God's grace through the sacraments to individuals, why not turn attention to society, too long neglected, and take the lead in saving the world? As ancient judaizing revolutionaries sought to arouse the nation of Israel to her God-given responsibility of liberating the oppressed, modern 'messiahs' hope to kindle fervour strong enough to change the course of history. No longer is the nation of Israel to be liberated from the heel of Rome, but the whole world is to be liberated from the oppression of multinationals and colonialists. Nationalistic figures, such as Bar Kochba, 'did theology' in the past, convinced that God was on the side of those who would sacrifice to bring in God's perfect kingdom. 'Like the Judaizing in early Christianity, this understanding of the Old Testament also fails to observe the proper distinctions between the acts and ordinances of God in the Old Covenant and those in the New.'[75]

Many and diverse have been the optimistic proposals made to solve the social and political ills of the world. The so-called 'social gospel' permeated the liberalism of the last generation, confident that the divine spark shared in common by all the sons of the one God could be coaxed into a demonstration of unselfish social amiability.[76] But once the obstinacy of the entrenched forces of evil (mainly capitalism)[77] became evident, the call for a more violent deposition of the dominating class was heard. Arnold Toynbee sees in Marx's analysis, now adopted uncritically by liberationists, 'the distinctively Jewish . . . element in the traditional religious inspiration of Marxism, the apocalyptic vision of a violent revolution. . . . (Marx's) Messianic Kingdom is conceived as a dictatorship of the Proletariat. But the salient features of the traditional Jewish apocalypse protrude through this threadbare disguise, and it is actually the pre-Rabbinical Maccabaean Judaism that our philosopher-impressario is presenting in modern Western costume. . . .'[78] If Toynbee is right in this assessment, it is not surprising that this political hermeneutic has inspired commitment in those who believe that Marx is more biblical than are evangelicals or traditional Roman Catholics.[79]

José Comblin, consistent with this pre-understanding, explains the underlying hermeneutic endorsed by Vatican II which views the church, the 'people of God', as a continuation of Israel. 'There has never been a break between Israel and God's people, between the Old and the New Testaments; the same people march on.'[80] Thus the church did not cease being a historical people nor become by the events of the passion of Jesus Christ and the Pentecostal outpouring of the Spirit a suprahistorical fellowship. Paul's choice of the term ἐκκλησία (purely a political term for Comblin) has significance for us. Both Paul and the Septuagint use ἐκκλησία to maintain 'the political meaning of the people of Israel'.[81] Although the church and Israel are a single continuum, there has been one important change which, according to Comblin, has made this continuum into an ecumenical people, 'open to all peoples, nations, tribes and languages'.[82] But this openness is conditioned by commitment to the cause of liberation. The rejection of the traditional interpretation of the Christian message 'refuses to leave the gospel in the hands of the powerful . . . and insists that a proper interpretation of Scripture is freeing rather than oppressive.'[83]

But such a reading of the N.T. smacks of misreading it by interpreting it with a 'horizontal' bias which minimizes God's intervention and overemphasizes man's capability to bring in the kingdom of God with righteousness. Such a reading is triumphalistic[84] and utopian. Ellis perceptively remarks that liberation theology's concern for subjugated people is to be commended.

> But in terms of its biblical hermeneutic it must be classified as a reactionary, philosophical manifestation of an ancient error of salvation by works. For that the words of Augustine are not inappropriate. 'It is because the philosophers will not believe in this beatitude (of eternal life) which they cannot see that they go on trying to fabricate here below an utterly fraudulent felicity built on virtue filled with pride and bound to fail them in the end.'[85]

When one endorses Gutiérrez's position and admits to only one history, not two (one spiritual and the other profane and temporal), it means that all Christians, to be Christians, must engage in the struggle to transform this world into that ideal state of peace or 'shalom'.[86] The enemies of this new world must be subdued, silenced, maybe imprisoned. Thus that new theology contrasts directly with Jesus' command that his followers love their enemies (Matt.5:43–48).[87] H. O. J. Brown is accurate in recognizing that 'Christianity does not seek a solution to evil in human society by eliminating its evil members, whether they be thought of as a race, as by the Nazis, or as a class, as by the Communists.'[88]

Since liberation theology does not approach Scripture from a neutral point of view but from the commitment to change the world, then any other reading of the Bible, according to its proponents, is to misunderstand it. So the importance of the Bible does not lie in its presentation of absolute truth, but in its capacity to motivate. Severino Croatto uncovers this methodology:

> A theology of liberation is not worked out with books, not even with the deep knowledge of Biblical exegesis. The Biblical message springs out of the event . . . before being 'dried out' into a nationalistic system. . . . For theology of liberation . . . there is

no other primary source than Latin American facts-of-liberation. Again facts 'uncover' the meaning.[89]

Under the guise of applying an authoritative view of the paradigmatic events of the exodus, some events are accepted as history, but this new higher criticism permits only a modicum of biblical 'facts' to inform present reality. But even that use of the exodus becomes highly suspect. Croatto claims the right to reinterpret when one undertakes to produce a genuine hermeneutic of this O.T. 'event'. 'It possesses other connotations, which remain hidden until the "situation" brings them to light. For example: the exodus was a political (social) happening, but it is also evident that it is an event which inspires every economic and cultural liberation.'[90] It is assumed, says J. A. Kirk, that it is possible to recover a nucleus of history with all supernatural elements removed.[91] But so high-handed a method does not find favour even with another theologian of liberation, J. L. Segundo, who criticizes this 'naive explanation' which 'maintains that the exodus event is the key to the interpretation of Scripture as the whole, including the Gospels and the rest of the New Testament.'[92] For the results of the enquiry are already contained in the initial premise and the biblical message has no power to correct the presuppositions of the interpreter.[93]

Like R. Bultmann's compulsion to demythologize, this hermeneutic may be practised only with a corresponding remythologization, the proclamation of a groundless hope in man's control of his future once he begins with the right question or 'analysis' suppled by Marx. If the exodus has anything to teach us, is it not that man is totally incapable of freeing himself or bringing his behaviour into conformity with God's justice?

Gerhard Sauter correctly notes that Christianity knows nothing of a 'theology of conquest' unless it be in the sense of the final home of God's people, into which they can enter and in which they can 'find rest' and 'dwell' (Heb.3:11,18; 4:1ff; 12:22; 13:14).[94] Whether it is the original exodus or that proclaimed by the prophets, 'The Exodus is determined by the goal lying at the end of the way and thus *not* by what it had left behind.'[95] God will reveal himself as the living God who gives the dead new life. The exodus metaphor cannot be defined by means of the dialectic between freedom and slavery.[96] Liberation theologians have used an allegorical hermeneutic drawing analogies between the situation of Israel and the modern proletariat. 'In this reduction, the unsolved problems of the present are reflected back into the past, in order to resolve them in this way . . . so that "interpretation" and "praxis" appear to stand in striking accord.'[97] The concrete and literal features of the text are lost to the timeless and symbolic content, all of which is arbitrary and imaginative. Sauter's conclusion is worth quoting: 'Ethical statements cannot be reached at all by way of such correspondences which establish a principle of analogy between God's being and our world, between God's actions and ours.'[98] For God ordered Israel to conquer the Canaanites in the conquest of the land, but there is no ground for concluding that Christians or Jews have a divine mandate to take the land from the Palestinians in the same manner.

In this new way of reading the Bible we have a hermeneutical door wide enough for more than the proverbial nose of the camel to penetrate. Roman Catholicism has long held that it is legitimate to seek the *sensus plenior* beyond the literal, intended meaning of the text. But with Vernon Grounds we are forced to ask, 'Are there, in fact, levels and layers of meaning to be uncovered progressively with the emergence of new challenges and crises in the ongoing pilgrimage of the church?'[99] There may be new applications of old truth, or new discoveries of meaning demonstrably in the text; but are there new meanings in the text discovered less by exegesis than by fallacies of question-framing? Only the already convinced will fail to recognize in such a hermeneutic an invitation to discover 'arbitrary inventions'.[100] Thus we are asked to refute the findings of grammatico-historical exegesis as one option among many. Such a conclusion takes us back to A. Schweitzer's *The Quest of the Historical Jesus*,[101] where he demonstrates that each successive epoch found its own thoughts in Jesus. Bonino highlights this danger as well as anyone when he points to 'the text of Scripture and tradition forced into the Procrustean bed of ideology and the theologian who has fallen prey to this procedure is forever condemned to listen to the echo of his own ideology. . . . [it] has muzzled the Word of God in its transcendence and freedom.'[102]

But distortion of the intended meaning of the text is not limited to Roman Catholic endorsement of the less than literal meaning of the Bible. Canaan Banana, addressing the World Council of Churches, claims that the common understanding of Jesus and his message errs on the side of spirituality. Interpreters wish to keep clear of temporal connotations 'to preserve Jesus from becoming a political leader'.[103] Adopting Gutiérrez's strong opposition to spiritualization because the only way to the spiritual is God's material creation, Banana warns us that to refuse to enter into the spiritual realm through the only available gate—historical temporal encounter—is to risk remaining outside forever in an imaginary spirituality.[104] Thus (to take a key passage, Lk.4:18ff.), one must see that Jesus interprets Isaiah in political and economic terms. The reality of the historical Jesus in the world must be accepted so that one may discover in him the plenitude promised to the poor, 'the hungry he has filled with good things' (Lk.1:53).[105]

But such an interpretation stumbles on the hard rock of Jesus' own explanation of his mission and his actions. Jesus said, 'Today this scripture is fulfilled in your hearing' (Lk.4:21). He did not join the guerrillas of his day, nor seek some means to release political prisoners from the jails of Palestine.[106] He did perform miracles in the material realm; he did feed the hungry on two occasions, thereby revealing his compassion for the needy; but his core purpose was to instill faith in himself as the Son of God who came to save the lost by giving his life a ransom for many (Lk.19:10; Mk.10:45). He taught that all men must repent (Lk.13:5) and be re-born (Jn.3:3,5), so that they could count on their heavenly Father supplying all of their needs (Matt.6:25–34). Jesus invites all the downtrodden to come to him for relief and rest, not surely in the sense that they would no more have to work physically, but in the spiritual sense of salvation from sin and guilt and the assurance of life in the new age (Matt.11:28ff.; Jn.6:27). He gave sight to the blind, a genuinely physical healing; but through it he called attention to the spiritual darkness of the 'blind' who refuse to repent (John 9).

Jesus did not play down the physical reality of human existence. Man is a spiritual/physical being. Nor is the salvation Jesus came to being limited to the afterlife. Rather, it radically restructures human life in the world because Christians are already experiencing the realities of the new age (cf 1 Cor.7:29–

31). Jesus did not intend his new command to become a pious slogan, but to describe concretely the new fellowship he came to create (Jn.13:34). The restructuring that liberation theology hopes to effect in society by means of the committed struggle against domineering power has already been demonstrated in the primitive church and repeatedly throughout history. Christians have practised a spontaneous generosity which incarnated the words of Jesus, 'It is more blessed to give than to receive' (Acts 20:35; 2 Cor.8:1–5). Luke describes the earliest history of Christianity in which the practical outworking of the economic teaching of Jesus became reality (Acts 2:44f.; 4:32–5:11). Without coercion or struggle, Christians relinquished their possessions for the benefit of the poor and needy. The explanation for such unusual expressions of self-less love can be found only in the pouring out of the Spirit of God according to the promise made long before by Joel (2:28–32) and Ezekiel (36:26–28), as well as by other prophets. It cannot be lost on the careful reader that the reality of the Holy Spirit and his power is scarcely to be found in the writings of liberation theologians or among the pronouncements of the WCC.[107]

The N.T. denies to any self-proclaimed Christian the right to claim the name if he is indifferent to the needs suffered by the family of God. If he closes his heart to the known need of a brother he denies the existence of God's love within (1 Jn.3:17). The brother's need and the supply are obviously material, but the motivation to give to a destitute member of the church is spiritual, the love of God abiding in the Christian's heart. Future judgment will be based on the demonstration of believers' concern (Matt.25:31–46).

To fulfil the royal law by loving one's neighbour as oneself, James writes, eliminates partiality, racism or dishonouring the poor in the church (2:6–9). The motivation to treat respectfully the down-trodden man will not primarily arise from a better structuring of society, but by the change wrought in the hearts of individuals who have genuine 'faith in our glorious Lord Jesus Christ' (Jas.2:1 NASB). Faith expressed only by words is roundly condemned as worthless. The unclothed and hungry brother cannot be fed and warmed with mere words but physical sustenance (Jas.2:15,16).

Banana wonders if the spiritual dimension can be omitted from Christ's death and it still be redemptive.[108] Is the 'universal or absolute meaning of the life and death of Christ to be found in His assuring the poor and only the poor of the certainty of fulfilment when they are engaged in their struggle against the oppressor'?[109] Surely such an understanding must be read into the N.T., not derived from it. Struggle there is in the Christian life, but not against the retainers of the world's money and power, but against the principalities and powers, the expressions of spiritual wickedness in heavenly places under the tutelage of the spirit who now works in the sons of disobedience (Eph.2:2). Paul is very clear too, that there is a battle to be waged against the 'flesh', man's selfish independence from God (Gal.5:17,18) and temptation to enthrone some temporal good in the place of God. Will not a struggle for material and political betterment not include also the temptation Jesus had to face when Satan offered him all the kingdoms of this world and their splendour if he would but worship him (Matt.4:8)?

Although Christians must avoid epistemological reductionism ('there is no truth outside or beyond the concrete historical events in which men are involved as agents—there is . . . no knowledge except in action itself'[110]), we must nevertheless face tough questions—e.g., on which side of the struggle between the solidarity trade union and the socialist state of Poland did God range himself? Jesus gave his disciples a hermeneutical key to solve such conundra. He gave them the model of the servant-leader, the submissive master (Lk.22:25–27). J. Gonzalez asks, '[How] can we know that those who interpret from the perspective of the powerless will be less biased than the current [interpretation]?'[111] His answer is that the Bible was written from the perspective of the powerless and oppressed. But it is too often forgotten that this stance (in Paul, for instance) was chosen voluntarily, not forced on the biblical authors other than by God's Spirit. It becomes apparent in the apostle's argument against his Corinthian opponents: they had become kings, as it were, while Paul and his fellow-apostles were voluntarily 'last of all' (1 Cor.4:8f.).

The 'mind' (φρόνημα, 'attitude', 'outlook' or 'way of think-ing') of Jesus Christ is the one secure hermeneutical clue to the understanding of the Christian's responsibility to the world. Paul succinctly describes his 'mind' as involving Jesus' voluntary self-emptying (in contrast to Adam's grasping for the honour and power of being like God), becoming incarnate in human flesh, choosing the role of a servant and obeying the Father even to the point of choosing the most humiliating death of all on the cross (Phil.2:5–8). Any adequate hermeneutic must unmask the self-seeking desire for power and human recognition. Jesus' way, which Paul imitates and bids his readers emulate, is the way of the cross, a life lived for others, sacrificing oneself for a world perishing through ignorance of the saving truth and for the church committed to the relief of destitute members of the 'family'. Moreover, such material expressions of compassion are not to be limited to the redeemed. God has made his people salt and light (Matt.5:14–16), meaning that like the Good Samaritan, Christians are under the Master's orders to extend compassionate mercy to all 'neighbours' in need (Lk.10:36f.).

F.   CONCLUSION

As we conclude it might be profitable to compare evangelicals and the neo-liberals (or new left)[112] to the rich young ruler who came to Jesus for an evaluation of his interpretation of God's requirements as revealed in Scripture. He must have expected the Master would affirm his commendable life-style with a possible adjustment or two (cf Mk.10:17–22). Affluent evangelicals would doubtless be saddened by Jesus' unrestricted condemnation of the inclination to think that knowledge is virtue and that awareness of evils is identical with the will to uproot them.[113] Certainly they would be shocked and saddened if Jesus made plain that he meant what he said, viz. 'No one of you can be my disciple who does not give up all his own possessions' (Lk.14:33).

On the other hand the liberationists would be dismayed at Jesus' coolness toward their activism grounded in optimistic humanism. Would not Jesus be likely to agree with Charles Malik, former president of the United Nations General Assembly?

They tell you, solve the social and economic problems and paradise will supervene on earth; they tell you everything is a function of economics, politics, and social relations. This is all false. You could have the most just society, economically, socially and politically and people's hearts would still be rotten to the core.[114]

No war on either class or structures, nor the spread of political religion which imagines some proximate benefit or some conditioned good as man's final goal, can ever satisfy a man in search of God and reality.

The account of the rich young man tells us that his 'face fell' (Mk.10:22 NASB) and he turned away. Should we conclude from this that any hermeneutic that does not shake the foundations and unmask hypocrisy is false? On the other hand, interpretations that provoke repentance and cries for mercy have the ring of truth. The credibility and attractiveness of liberation theology arises from the complacency and selfish otherworldliness so characteristic of first world evangelicalism. What other hope for the world is there than repentance and spiritual renewal? God's word through Micah is not at all unclear; 'He has showed you, O man, what is good. And what does the Lord require of you? To act justly and to love mercy and to walk humbly with your God' (Mic.6:8 NIV).

NOTES

1. Karl Barth, *Evangelical Theology, an Introduction* (New York 1963) cited by Noé S. Gonçalves, 'Base Biblica para Um Estilo de Vida Simples no Antigo Testamento' (Mogi das Cruzes SP, Brazil 1981) 1.
2. John A. Mackay, *A Preface to Christian Theology* (New York 1941) 67.
3. Chaim Perelman, *Justice* (New York 1967) 3.
4. Liberals reject the idea that Christian morality and ethics are primarily concerned with the relationship between men and God. See *Religion in Sociological Perspectives*, ed. Ch. Y. Glock (Belmont, CA 1973) 175.
5. Gordon D. Fee, *Pulpit Helps*, vol.7, no.3 (Dec. 1981) 1.
6. Edward L. Long, Jr., 'The Use of the Bible in Christian Ethics', *Int* 19 (1965) 149, cited in B. C. Birch and Larry L. Rasmussen, *Bible and Ethics in the Christian Life* (Minneapolis 1976) 54.
7. Donald R. Curry, 'A Collection of Essays on Community', *Missiology* 3 (1975) 369.

8. cf René Padilla, 'Hermeneutics and Culture', *Down to Earth*, ed. J. R. W. Stott and R. Coote (Grand Rapids 1980) 67.

9. cf Sherwood Wirt, *The Social Conscience of the Evangelical* (New York 1968) 48ff. See also Emilio Antonio Nuñez, 'La Influencia de Protestantismo en el Desarollo Histórico de Guatemala', *Boletin Teológico* 2 (1978) passim; and Samuel Escobar, 'Beyond Liberation Theology: Evangelical Missiology in Latin America', *IBMR* 6 (1982) 110.

10. Brazilian Lutherans, Methodists and Episcopalians have espoused liberation theology in their theological colleges. Some Pentecostal groups have occasionally endorsed a political candidate. The vast majority of Brazilian evangelicals (and there are millions) support the right-wing government, or the democratic process. Because of wide-spread corruption, little hope remains for government imposed justice via legislative fiat. In the US, as early as 1947 Carl F. H. Henry called attention to the 'narrowing of the evangelical message to the changing of individuals and the consequent failure to oppose social evils' in *The Uneasy Conscience of Modern Fundamentalism* (Grand Rapids 1947) 23, 26, cited in Wirt, *Social Conscience* 48. Cf Richard F. Lovelace, *Dynamics of Spirital Life* (Downers Grove, IL 1979) 355–358.

11. Ch. Y. Glock affirms that as far as social issues are concerned, ministers are likely to maintain silence in direct proportion to the conservativeness of their theology.

12. See James Billington's monumental *Fire in the Minds of Men: Origins of the Revolutionary Faith* (New York 1980) *passim*.

13. David R. Griffin, 'Values, Evil and Liberation Theology', *Encounter* 40 (1979) 6ff.

14. Herbert Butterfield's opinion is convincingly argued in his *Christianity and History* (New York 1949 1950). According to this Christian historian, man's pride gorged on power leads to a divine 'thus far and no farther', so that the evil rulers of the world and their kingdoms fall by divine intervention—but not, however, in a wooden, predictable fashion.

15. Charles Colson's *Born Again* (Old Tappan, NJ 1976) and his more recent *Life Sentence* (Lincoln, VA 1979) support the evangelical contention that regenerate Christians can challenge the evil structures and improve them. On the whole, J. C. Ryle spoke the evangelical's general convictions when he wrote: 'So long as the Devil is the prince of the world and the hearts of many are unconverted, so long there will be strife and fighting. . . . Let us cease to expect that missionaries and ministers will convert the world and teach all mankind to love another. They will do nothing of the kind. They were not intended to. They will call out a witness and people who shall serve Christ in every land; they will do no more' (*Expository Thoughts on the Gospel: St. Luke* [New York n.d.] vol.2, pp.361–362, cited by Vernon Grounds, 'Premillennialism and Social Pessimism', unpublished paper). Norris Magnuson, *Salvation in the Slums: Evangelical Social Work, 1865–1920* (Metchen, NJ 1977) claims that a virile social conscience marked evangelicalism from 1865 to 1920. Although conversion was their aim, evangelicals nevertheless gave aid freely and opposed societal and individual sinfulness. Lovelace, *Dynamics* 47, points to still earlier

evangelicals who spearheaded the transformation of the social conscience of the state and society both in England and America.

16. Evangelical pulpits do not stress 'good works' in their ministry, therefore Bible-believing Christians do not generally think they are important (cf Matt.5:16; Eph.2:10 and many other passages in the New Testament). R. E. Frykenberg, 'World Hunger: Food is not the Answer', in *Christianity Today* vol.25, no.21 (Dec. 11, 1981) 36–39 points out that much of the practical effort expended on attempts to aid the neediest of the world is inept due to the barriers governments and bureaucrats raise against such aid. On the other side, see Russell T. Hitt, 'The Latin American Experiment', *Eternity* (Nov. 1957) 14–17. The Grand Rapids Consultation on the relation between evangelism and Christian social responsibility, 1982, made plain that Christians must not separate love for 'souls' from love for people. See the Declaration IV, C.

17. Not very successful attempts to facilitate the coming of the kingdom of God by political revolutionaries were promoted by Christians during the Münster Rebellion (1535) and by the Fifth Monarchy Men of Oliver Cromwell in the 1600s. Of course the opinion that God favoured the America Revolution in the 1700s is held by many American evangelicals and liberals alike. Cf Michael Novak, *A Theology for Radical Politics* (New York 1969) 74ff.

18. Rom.13:1–7; 1 Pet.2:13ff. Cf J. H. Yoder, *The Politics of Jesus* (Grand Rapids 1972) 195ff.

19. Cf R.E. Frykenberg, *World Hunger*, passim.

20. Tim LaHaye, *The Battle of the Mind* (Old Tappan, NJ 1980) 27.

21. ibid.26. Popular writers and preachers such as Tim LaHaye, Jerry Falwell and Francis Schaeffer show that their pre-understanding of at least American culture is that it is basically Christian. Consequently, 'humanism' threatens it as an invading alien atheistic philosophy. But are not consumerism, materialism and white supremacy also characteristic of the American way of life?

22. Francis Schaeffer, *How Should We Then Live?* (Old Tappan, NJ 1976) 51f.

23. For information and analysis of the World Council's support of left-wing 'liberation', see Edward Norman, *Christianity and World Order* (Oxford 1979); Harvey Hoekstra, *The WCC and the Demise of Evangelism* (Carol Stream, IL 1979); and Ernest Lefever, *Amsterdam to Nairobi—WCC and the Third World* (Washington DC 1972).

24. Russell P. Shedd, 'Pecado e Salvaçao na Americana Latina', in *O Presente, O Fututo e a Esperança Crista* CLADE II (1979) 87ff. Cf Lovelace, *Dynamics* 235.

25. In O. T. Allis, *Prophecy and the Church* (Philadelphia 1945) 253 cited in Grounds, 'Premillennialism'. This not untypical detachment of evangelicals can be detected in Allan MacRae ('Bible Prophecy', *American Mercury* [Oct. 1958] 34, cited in W. Dyrness in 'The Age of Aquarius', *Handbook of Christian Prophecy*, ed. C. E. Armerding and W. W. Gasque [Grand Rapids 1977] 23): 'The study of prophecy is difficult but rewarding. God has revealed to us many facets of His plan. How exciting it is to follow the

events as they transpire and observe the operation of His mighty hand.' José Miranda, *Marx and the Bible: A Critique of the Philosophy of Oppression* (Maryknoll, NY 1974) 36, decries the 'conservatives'' manner of interpreting the Bible by adopting whatever meanings move them. He insists that 'such belief has been promulgated in order to prevent the Bible from revealing its own subversive message'.

26. cf e.g. Mortimer Arias, 'Evangelization from the Inside: Reflections From a Prison Cell', *IBMR* 5 (1981) 101. Arias quotes a fellow political prisoner coming back from a Bolivian interrogation session after the July 1980 coup: 'I am ashamed of being a human, not even animals treat other animals as we treat human beings.' Many other examples of social injustice can be found in E. and M. Arias, *The Cry of My People* (New York 1980) *passim*.

27. James M. Childs, Jr., *Christian Anthropology and Ethics* (Philadelphia 1978) 13,18–31.

28. Classic evolutionary theory explains man's rise by chance survival of the strong and fit. It is wholly impossible to argue for inherent human social justice if this theory is accepted. The concept of man propounded by Marx, who denied any essence in Man, has been carefully weighed by J. Andrew Kirk in 'The Meaning of Man in the Debate Between Christianity and Marx,' *TFB* no.2 (1974) 4: 'If Marx had used Biblical categories to express himself, he would have denied that man is created in the image of a personal and infinite God. . . . Man belongs exclusively to matter.' According to Marx, Man is the aggregate of his social relationships (ibid. 5) capable of reflection and self-realization through work and making history. So man is truly man when he is transforming the natural world (ibid.) Reinhold Niebuhr interpreted the 'myth' of creation of man in God's image as the fundamental paradox of finitude and freedom. See Dennis P. McCann, *Christian Realism and Liberation Theology* (Maryknoll 1981) 56.

29. *Animal Farm* (New York 1954).

30. M. Djilas, *The New Class* (New York 1957, 1972) 26. This book and more recent releases such as A. Solzhenitzen's books show that an idealistic system is not sufficient incentive to guarantee justice in a society. It has now been verified historically that the leaders of Marxist societies have committed unimaginable atrocities in their pursuit of their high ideal. See further, Kirk, 'Meaning of Man', 9.

31. Emil Brunner, *Justice and the Social Order* (New York 1945) 45. Brunner helpfully points out that community can exist only where there is difference. Without difference there may be unity but not community which presupposes reciprocal giving and taking.

32. See Gustavo Gutiérrez, *A Theology of Liberation* (Maryknoll 1973) 291ff.

33. The secular press in Brazil has reported this phenomen with regard to the Pentecostals in leading articles in *Manchete* and *Revista Veja*.

34. cf Sherwood Wirt, *Social Conscience* 10.

35. See further, Ronald J. Sider, *Rich Christians in an Age of Hunger* (Downers Grove, IL 1980) 87–95.

36. Noé S. Gonçalves, 'Base Biblica', 3.

37. C. S. Lewis, *The Weight of Glory* (London 1949) 36–38.
38. cf Blaise Pascal, *Pensées*, where he acutely observes that power creates opinion and consequently rules the world (nos. 235–242). See also Michael Novak, *Theology* 77, who claims that the social order rests upon a base of violence covert or overt. Politics is power.
39. John Bright, *The Kingdom of God* (Nashville 1953) 107.
40. J. Andrew Kirk, *Liberation Theology* (Atlanta 1979) 173 calls it ontological alienation.
41. Sidney Rooy, 'Righteousness and Justice', *TFB* no.4 (1978) *passim*. Rooy reminds us that 'justification, righteousness and justice, all come from one root word in the language of the New Testament, therefore the meaning of each term should be sought in the life of the passage and not in pre-formed traditions' (p.3).
42. A much broader problem is discussed in Daniel P. Fuller's *Gospel and Law* (Grand Rapids 1980) 105, questioning the dispensational and covenant theology understanding of salvation by faith, apart from the law. Fuller argues that there are not two sets of promises in the Bible, conditional and unconditional. There is only one kind, and receiving the promise depends on keeping the conditions, called by Paul 'the obedience of faith'.
43. BAG 217.
44. cf Richard Foulks, 'La Singularidade del Pueblo de Dios', position paper presented at the Consulta Internacional of the Fraternidade Teologica Latino americano in S. Paulo, 1977, p.3. Neither Israel in the Old Testament nor the church in the New can claim purity of race.
45. Vatican City may be a *bona fide* state but the more like a state the church becomes, the less like the church of the N.T. it is.
46. The Grand Rapids Consultation on Evangelism and Social Justice (1982) has clearly stated the church's mandate to 'infiltrate' society as 'salt', 'light' and 'leaven' (see the Declaration, V. D.). The practical problems and tension that arise from the church wielding temporal power are made amply clear in Malachi Martin, *Final Conclave* (Briar Cliff Manor, NY 1979).
47. See Charles R. Taber's provocative editorial suggestion, in *Gospel in Context* 2/3 (1979) 3, that the church in China has rightly opted for institutional death, but continues in the lives of its members, as over against the compromising position of the state churches in Nazi Germany.
48. V. Grounds, 'The Hermeneutics of Liberation Theology', unpublished paper, Conservative Baptist Theological Seminary, p.17.
49. Oscar Cullmann, *Jesus and the Revolutionaries* (New York 1970) 30.
50. Jonah did warn Nineveh of impending judgment, but he made no mention of the guilt of the dominating class as opposed to the poor masses. The entire city must repent and all the city will be spared if it does.
51. It is instructive to read Fyodor Dostoyevsky's incomparable presentation of the Grand Inquisitor's thoughts concerning justice and freedom in *The Brothers Karamazov*, trans. Constance Garnett (New York n.d.). Cf Vasily Rozanov, *Dostoyevsky and the Legend of the Grand Inquisitor* (Ithica 1972).

52. One of the most notable changes in Roman Catholic hermeneutics has transpired between the Middle Ages and the present. In the past, judgment of sin, whether in purgatory or hell, was a central theme of Roman Catholic teaching. Recent church pronouncements are strangely silent regarding the doctrine of future punishment. As one instance, note the Puebla document #1141-1165 that decribes the 'tumultuous and impressive cry going up to heaven with increasing power. This is the cry of a people suffering and demanding justice, freedom and respect for the most elementary rights of persons and peoples.' But where is the note of divine judgment pronounced by John the Baptist or Jesus? Is Paul's reference to the accumulating divine wrath a mere figure of speech? (Rom.2:5-9).

53. Hugo Assmann, *Theology for a Nomad Church* (Maryknoll, 1976) 36.

54. The primitive church made the distinction between the Christian and the world quite clear. Note the outlook of the Epistle to Diognetus: 'It is neither in country, nor language, nor customs, for they do not dwell in cities in some place of their own, nor do they use any strange variety of dialect, nor practice an extraordinary kind of life. . . . Yet while living in Greek and barbarian cities according as each obtained his lot and following the local customs . . . they show forth the wonderful and confessedly strange character of their own citizenship. They dwell in their own fatherland but as if sojourners in them; they share all things as citizens and suffer all things as strangers . . . to put it shortly, what the soul is in the body, the Christians are in the world.' Cited in S. B. Babbage, *The Vacuum of Unbelief* (Grand Rapids 1969) 94-95.

55. cf Russell P. Shedd, *Man in Community* (London 1958) 111-112, 127ff; G. E. Ladd, *A Theology of the New Testament* (Grand Rapids 1974) 396ff., 541.

56. cf John H. Yoder, *The Politics of Jesus* (Grand Rapids 1972) 199. Oswald Chambers's comments on Matt.5:39ff. are helpful: 'These verses reveal the humiliation of being a Christian. Naturally, if a man does not hit back it is a manifestation of the Son of God in him. . . . The teaching of the Sermon on the Mount is not—Do your duty, but—Do what is not your duty. It is not your duty to go the second mile, to turn the other cheek, but Jesus says if we are his disciples we shall always do these things. . . . Never look for right in the other man, but never cease to be right yourself. We are always looking for justice; the teaching of the Sermon . . . is—Never look for justice, but never cease to give it' (*My Utmost For His Highest* [New York 1935] 196).

57. Jon Sobrino, *Chistology at the Crossroads: A Latin American Approach* (Maryknoll 1976) 124. Liberationists show favour or disapproval of Jesus' behaviour as a model or 'literal guide for our actions in the 20th century' (J. Segundo, *Liberation of Theology* [Maryknoll 1976] 31) just as they do with the Bible itself.

58. cf Gutiérrez, *Theology* 289-291. Jacques Dupont, 'Os Pobres e a Pobreza segundo o Ensinamento do Evangélio e de Atos dos Apóstolos', *A Pobreza Evangélica* (S. Paulo, 1976) 49, argues that Jesus' concern is that the poor will show God's justice and love in his Kingdom.

59. *Politics* 74–75.
60. cf Reinhold Niebuhr *Christian Realism and Political Problems* (New York 1953) 8ff. J. Sobrino, *Christology* 52, identifies man's sin as rooted in his desire for security.
61. cf Yoder, *Politics* 45.
62. Sobrino, *Christology* 53.
63. For a contextualized interpretation of this parable, see Kenneth E. Bailey, *Poet and Peasant* (Grand Rapids 1976).
64. cf Justo Gonzalez, *Liberation Preaching* (Nashville 1980) *passim*.
65. cf Robert M. Brown, *Theology in a New Key* (Philadelphia 1978) 60. Gutiérrez (*Theology* 255) says, 'It seems clear today that the purpose of the Church is not to save in the sense of guaranteeing heaven. The work of salvation is a reality which acts in history.'
66. Donald R. Curry well says, 'The perennial fascination of men of every nation for the meditations of Karl Marx, as well as for religion itself, is predicated on the folk notions that they have in common: *holism*, or the belief that the universe is more than the sum of its parts; *emergence* . . . the idea that the universe's future is contained within the seeds of its past; and *materialism* (Engels 1888) 360–402 or the German version of the Greek concept of *Hylozoism*, the idea matter and life are but differing aspects of each other, and convertible the one into the other', in a letter to Cyril Belshaw, 1980. The *Communist Manifesto* opens with: 'There is a spectre (spirit: ghost) haunting Europe—the spectre of Communism.' Marx has adapted Genesis concentrating on the idea of labour as the transforming possibility, the synthesis uniting the thesis of birth and the antithesis of death. Cf also Kirk, *Liberation Theology* 160–166.
67. See Reinhold Niebuhr, *The Irony of American History* (New York 1952) 117–118, cited in McCann, *Christian Realism* 113.
68. See further, Russell P. Shedd, 'An Evangelical Looks at Liberation Theology', *TWF* 17/2 (Winter 1982).
69. cf J. L. Segundo, *Theology for Artisans of a New Humanity* (Maryknoll 1973) 2; and Paulo Freire, 'Educatión, Liberación y la Iglesia' in 'La Educación y la America Latina', in *Boletin Teológico* 10 (1974).
70. cf Segundo, *Liberation* 111.
71. cf Hugo Assmann, *Theology* 61; Alfredo Fierro, *The Militant Gospel* (Maryknoll 1977) (1975 in Spain) 353–354. V. Grounds, 'The Hermeneutic', 13.
72. Segundo, *Liberation* 7. Paulo Freire, a Brazilian educator, is best known for his proposed solution to the poverty of northeast Brazil through conscience raising (*concientização*) so that pressure applied to the government by concerted action of these newly educated might gain their rights. See *Pedagogy of the Oppressed* (New York 1970).
73. cf Wirt, *Social Conscience* 131–132.
74. cf Kirk, *Liberation Theology* 159.
75. E. E. Ellis, 'Foreword' to L. Goppelt, *Typos* (ET Grand Rapids 1982) xii.
76. cf Walter Rauschenbusch, *Christianity and the Social Crisis* (New York 1964) 67. Severino Croatto affirms that the Christian has the 'grace' (received through baptism) to discover God in his (human) history, not

only *individual* history, but also communal and universal (*Liberacion y Libertad* [Buenos Aires 1973] 20, cited in S. Escobar, 'Beyond Liberation', 112).

77. David R. Griffin points out, after attending a conference in Mexico under the title 'Encounter with Theologies': 'Capitalism is seen by the Latin American theologians as the source of oppression and hence as the evil that must be overcome. . . . Many of them have come to accept a more or less Leninist revolutionary strategy' (private communication, July 15, 1979).

78. A. J. Toynbee, *A Study of History* (Oxford 1935–39) vol.5, pp.178–179, cited in Ellis, 'Forward', xii.

79. It can be convincingly argued that those who attempt to synthesize Christianity and Marxism inevitably champion heretical versions of both. Cf C. F. H. Henry in 'Footnotes', *Christianity Today* 21/22 (Aug. 12, 1977) 28.

80. J. Combin, *The Church and the National Security State* (Maryknoll 1979) 185, cited in Stanley M. Key, 'The Doctrine of the Church in Liberation Theology', a paper presented to the author at the Trinity Evangelical Divinity School (Dec. 7, 1981) 8.

81. ibid. 186.

82. ibid. 187.

83. Gonzalez, *Liberation* 13.

84. Kirk, *Liberation Theology* 152.

85. E. E. Ellis, 'Forward', xiv, citing Augustine, *City of God* 19.4.

86. cf Gutiérrez, *Theology* 166ff., and Kirk, *Liberation Theology* 158.

87. This injunction to love one's enemies is one of the most quoted by the Fathers according to E. Massaux, *Influence de l'Evangile de S. Matt. sur la littérature chrétienne avant S. Irenée* (Louvain 1950): see index to Matt.5:43–48. The New Testament shows that, despite the spiritual opposition between the church and the world, there is surprisingly little condemnation of the world *qua* people.

88. Harold O. J. Brown, *Christianity and the Class Struggle* (New Rochelle, NY 1970) 30. One could be tempted to see a modern counter-reformation in the identification of the enemies of Christianity as those who oppose the theology of liberation, while the true church is made up of those who 'struggle for a just world in which there is no oppression, servitude or alienated work which will signify the coming of the Kingdom' (Gutiérrez, *Theology* 168). Thus eschatology has become what K. Popper calls 'historicism' in which there are specific laws which can be discovered, and upon which prediction regarding the future of mankind can be based (*The Open Society and Its Enemies* [London 1980] vol.1, 8–9.).

89. S. Croatto, *Liberación Libertad* (Buenos Aires 1973), introduction. J. Miguez-Bonino writes: 'There is scarcely any doubt that God's Word is not understood in the Old Testament as a conceptual communication but as a creative event, a history-making pronouncement' (*Doing Theology in a Revolutionary Situation* [Philadelphia 1975] 89).

90. Kirk, *Liberation* 101.

91. ibid. 149.

92. Cited in V. Grounds, Hermeneutic', 34.
93. Kirk, *Liberation* 149.
94. Gerhard Sauter, '"Exodus" and "Liberation" as Theological Metaphors: a Critical Case-study of the Use of Allegory and Misunderstood Analogies in Ethics', *SJT* 34 (1981) 482.
95. ibid. 486.
96. ibid. 489.
97. ibid. 495.
98. ibid. 505.
99. V. Grounds, 'Hermeneutic', 26.
100. cf J. Miguez-Bonino, *Doing Theology* 102.
101. A. Schweitzer, *The Quest of the Historical Jesus* (ET London 1954³).
102. J. Miguez-Bonino, *Doing Theology* 87.
103. C. Banana, 'Good News to the Poor' in *Your Kingdom Come* (World Council of Churches, Geneva 1980) 109.
104. ibid. 109. Cf Gutiérrez, *Theology* 166.
105. ibid.
106. See the *non sequitur* in Sergio Arce's reasoning in 'Cristo y la Liberación Social' in *Cristo Vivo en Cuba* (DEI, 1978) 79, pointed out by Escobar, 'Beyond Liberation', 113.
107. See Abraham J. Malherbe, *Social Aspects of Early Christianity* (St. Louis 1977) 23, where he points out that Christians were criticized for social not political reasons. Pagans were offended by the intimacy of Christians who used emotionally tinged terms such as 'dear', 'precious' and especially the term 'brother' (p.26).
108. C. Banana, 'Good News', 118.
109. ibid.
110. cf Bonino, *Doing Theology* 88. G. MacEoin and Nivita Riley, *Puebla, a Church Being Born* (New York 1980) 34–35, show the consternation of the progressives at the retrenchment of the CELAM positions as compared to that of Medellin.
111. Gonzalez, *Liberation* 16.
112. cf David J. Hesselgrave, 'The Contextualization Continuum', *Gospel in Context* vol.2, no.3 (1979) 9.
113. cf McCann, *Christian Realism* 7.
114. Charles Malik, 'Fallacies of the Age', *In Form, Bulletin of Wheaton College* (July 1981) 1.

Index of Names

Index of Scripture References